sweet tooth

sweet tooth

a memoir

TIM ANDERSON

LAKE UNION
PUBLISHING

Published by Lake Union Publishing, Seattle

www.apub.com

ISBN-13: 9781477818077
ISBN-10: 1477818073

Cover design by Sam Dawson

Library of Congress Control Number: 2013919514

Printed in the United States of America

*To Charmaine Nation (1949–2004), who was
a second mother to so many, be they stroppy teenagers,
abandoned dogs with personality disorders, or cats
rescued from dumpsters.*

*To my dearly departed Dad, who would have only been
slightly embarrassed.*

TABLE OF CONTENTS

"Let Tim eat cake."
—Marie Antoinette
Versailles
(Later beheaded)

SOME CANDY TALKING

To a boy whose ideal snack was Little Debbie Zebra Cakes, the existence of a disease like diabetes seemed like the dark work of a mean God.

It sounded horrifying on its face. For one thing, it actually included the word "die" in its very first syllable. And, I mean, *really*. A disease where you not only can't eat sugar but also have to take multiple injections a day AND prick your finger morning, noon, and night to do a blood test? What kind of life is that? What are you supposed to eat on your birthday? On Halloween? On Saturday mornings while watching *The Smurfs* and *The Bugs Bunny/Road Runner Hour*? The answer to all of these questions—in a world without the scourge of diabetes—is obvious: Mississippi mud cake, ice cream, Snickers, 3 Musketeers, candy corn, Mars, FireBalls, Cookie Crisp, Gobstoppers, Cap'n Crunch, Count Chocula, Franken Berry, Trix, Cocoa Puffs, Whoppers, Fruity Pebbles, Hershey's Kisses, Key lime pie, and/or Lucky Charms.

This was in 1980, long before type 2 diabetes—historically an affliction of the old, the fat, the unhealthy, and the hereditarily unlucky, and also known as "adult onset diabetes"—was becoming shockingly common among young people who can't sit comfortably in front of a television without a cheeseburger in both fists. Diabetes was not terribly common among America's youth back then. But it did happen. The first diabetic kid I ever knew was David, a guy in my second grade class at Effie Green Elementary in Raleigh, North Carolina. His older sister was friends with my older sister, and he was originally one grade ahead of me, but he had been held back a year. Why this was so was a mystery to everyone in Mrs. Fleming's class, but it was a mystery pretty satisfactorily (if not actually) solved by one classmate's estimation that it probably had something to do with the disease he had. That disease, of course, was diabetes.

But the interesting thing was that David, unlike the categorically unhealthy young diabetics of today, was the most athletic kid in class. He had type 1—"juvenile"—diabetes, which made up and continues to make up about ten percent of total diabetics in the country. He had done nothing to bring on the disease; it had just happened because it was in his family, and for some reason it chose him.

David was a star soccer player, swimmer, and runner—and was probably also a master on the uneven bars in his downtime. The kid effortlessly excelled at every sporting activity he tried. So obviously he and I weren't friends. A scrawny, skinny kid with no apparent talent for anything besides memorizing television show theme songs, I admired him from afar for his prowess on any field and for his handsome athletic socks and cleats. *Why can't I be more like him?* I wondered. Look at that golden blond hair. Those cute little freckles. The perfectly proportioned young boy's physique. The ability to know what to do with a soccer ball when it came to him. I wanted all of that for myself. The only thing of his that I didn't want—the only thing that, in fact, made me feel luckier than him—was his disease. Sadly, it was the only thing of his I would ultimately get.

So, to sum up: a disease that prevents you from picking through a Whitman's Sampler to make yourself feel better for not having any male friends; that prohibits you from accepting with a smile that lollipop offered by the bank teller at the drive-thru; that completely upends your tradition of day-after-Halloween discount candy shopping; that forces you to jab yourself day in and day out with syringes and finger prickers; and that can just happen randomly without any warning—*yeah*, I thought. *That'll probably happen to me one day.*

The type 1 diabetes gene is a mysterious beast—it appears out of the blue and gives few if any indications that it is indeed living in your body and getting set to ruin your young life. It lived in three of my mother's uncles and then leapfrogged completely over her generation and avoided every single other sibling and cousin before landing squarely on me. In the summer of 1988, seven years after meeting David, my pessimistic prognostication would come true. In July of that year, I would be taken to a hospital in Baltimore, Maryland, with the highest blood sugar level they had ever recorded and would, after a lengthy midnight stay in the emergency room lobby, ultimately be diagnosed with type 1 diabetes and blasted with a boatload of insulin. I would be taken to a room in the middle of the night and, as I lay scared to death in the tightly made bed, given a Diet Shasta.

<hr />

I have always had a sweet tooth. The biggest one in my family. My skinny frame absolutely belied the number of sweets I knew I could put away if ever given the chance. Luckily, I was never given too many chances, thanks to my vigilant mother, who didn't allow sodas in the house, didn't buy candy or sweets, and only occasionally made pies and cakes. Once a month, she would offer to buy each of us kids a box of sweet cereal. We called it our "monthly cereal," and I for one took this agreement between mother and child very seriously indeed. But I was the only one. My two older brothers and my sister enjoyed their boxes of Peanut Butter Crunch and Boo Berry and Honey Smacks, sure. But they didn't *desire* them like I did. They didn't hop out of bed on Saturday mornings with visions of Crunch Berries dancing in their heads. They really could take it or leave it.

As a child, I looked forward with great pleasure to a time far in the future when I would reach full manhood and could live my own life, free of the constraints of a sensible mother's imposed dietary restrictions; a life full of MoonPies, Little Debbies, Kit Kats, Fig Newtons, Cadbury Easter eggs, Hershey Bar pies, Twinkies, and Girl Scout cookies, all washed down with a giant-assed Yoo-hoo. This is the life I saw for myself as I sat at my desk in Mrs. Fleming's class, lazily gazing over at David as he reached into his desk to retrieve his blood glucose monitor and took out his horrible medieval instruments of death. He would momentarily use this mysterious equipment to prick himself, obtain a blood sample, and test his blood sugar level before enjoying his afternoon snack, a small collection of saltine-and-peanut-butter crackers wrapped in tinfoil.

Wow, I probably thought. *That is a snack simply* begging *to be dipped in chocolate.*

When accompanying my mother to the grocery store I could easily spend a half hour in the candy aisle, noting to myself all of the Hershey products I would stock my cupboards with—not to mention the punch bowls full of fun-sized malted milk balls and sugar-coated gumdrops I would have laying around and available for instant gratification in every room—once I was grown up and master of my own destiny and snacks. Of course, on those trips I would arrive home with not so much as a single solitary chunk of chocolate or piece of candy corn. But oh, the things I could convince myself I was eating (Crunch bars! Chips Ahoy! Cracker Jack!) as I sat on the floor of our living room in front of the television, peeled a banana during my evening game shows, and, in a fit of profound gustatory frustration, shoved it into my mouth.

———

The urge for sugar throughout my young life was strong, yes. I wanted it, and I wanted it bad, from the moment I was born.

But as you grow older, the world gets more complicated, and there are more important things to deal with than a silly need for Toblerones or Nutter Butters. As my fifteen-year-old body was, unbeknownst to me, rapidly depleting its reserves of insulin, it was also under siege from another equally dangerous and debilitating force: raging adolescent hormones. Hormones directing my thoughts, commandeering my innocent hands, and insisting that they do an odd, immoral, and exquisite thing in bed, in the dark, in the middle of the night, with a box of Kleenex handy. Worse, the hormonal urges behind this thing I was doing could best be described as "pretty damn gay."

Now, I'd done some experimenting a few years before with Derrick, a boy on my Little League team. "Experimenting," like a scientist would do—testing out what it was like to kiss a boy, to explore a naked male body with my hungry hands, to put a stiff dong in my mouth. These types of utterly scientific things. But they were just meaningless childhood activities, things that we would only do with each other and nobody else, ever, because we were just bored, you know? I hadn't seen him since I'd gone to middle school. And yet three years later the urge to get back into the lab was still very strong, and getting harder to ignore. Derrick was back in my life on an almost nightly basis, whether he knew it or not.

My pulsating pink hormones were on fire that June and turned me into something of a small-time crook. I was visiting my aunt and grandmother in Jamestown, New York, for the month of June, something I'd done every summer since I was a toddler. And though I loved Aunt Sue and Nana dearly, their previously exquisite delightful company became less and less fulfilling to me the older I got and the further I ventured into the thorny, throbbing, slick, and sweaty swampland that was teenage sex obsession. Sure, I still liked sitting down with Nana at one p.m. every weekday to have a cup of tea and listen to Paul Harvey on her old-fashioned radio tuner. Yes, I could be convinced to play a few happy hands of gin rummy with Aunt Sue or King's Corner with their ancient neighbor Sheila. And of course, I was never not interested in going out to Friendly's for a tuna melt and a hot fudge sundae. But this particular summer, there was a battle going on between my brain, my heartbeat, my sweat glands, and my loins that could not be quelled with a few scoops of ice cream. What on earth could do the quelling? Follow me into the newsagent.

One day I went there with Aunt Sue so she could pick up a paper on her way down to the grocery store. As always, I made a beeline for the rack of music magazines that lined a shelf on the far wall. Aunt Sue paid for her newspaper and asked me if I wanted to stay and read while she shopped. I nodded silently as I flipped through the latest issue of *Billboard* and waited for her to leave. Because I'd just seen a stack of magazines on the floor behind me that had apparently just been dropped off—still bound together by a plastic strap—that looked interesting.

The magazine was called *Bolt*, and it was as glossy as the dickens. On its cover was a close-up photo of a blond surfer dude with glassy blue eyes and an overheated expression on his face, like he'd just run up a steep staircase, bench-pressed a Toyota, or eaten a spoonful of wasabi. In my naïveté, I'd assumed it was an exercise magazine, much like the hyper-homoerotic *Exercise for Men* that I'd always enjoyed flipping through at my local grocery store in Raleigh and which invariably featured on its cover stripped, ripped, and ready hunks with abs that could utterly destroy you.

I looked over at the owner of the shop, who was busy selling lottery tickets to a customer at the cash register, then bent down and pulled an issue from the top of the stack, making sure not to tear the plastic strap holding the other slippery issues together like naked oiled-up soccer players caught in a net. Turning my back to the register, I opened it. The first image I came to—of a blond surfer (named "Dylan") and another guy who appeared to be a really good friend of his ("Cody") getting all grabby with each other's crotches—made me gasp. I immediately closed the magazine and looked around to make sure I hadn't disturbed anyone over at the cash register. I was relieved to find that the line was growing with customers and that no one was paying me any mind, but I did notice that above the checkout counter a giant round convex security mirror was mounted, allowing the owner to get a clear view of the back of the store and, in particular, the shelves of porno mags against the far wall, separated from the rest of the magazines by two swinging saloon doors with the obligatory warning that if you are not eighteen you'd better just *git*. This, it turned out, was my lucky day: The new stack of *Bolt* magazines had arrived just as the store was getting busy, so the owner hadn't had a chance to spirit them away yet. I set down the issue of *Bolt*, hiding it behind an issue of *Rolling Stone*, and, breathless and desperate, began perfunctorily picking up and pretending to thumb through *Musician*, *Spin*, and *Billboard*, returning to the *Bolt* magazine as often as possible to get another look at Dylan and Cody's tea party.

After a few more minutes of surreptitiously stealing glances at *Bolt*, I decided that no force in the world—not God, not jail, and definitely not a freaking convex mirror—could keep me from taking that magazine home with me and reading it from cover to cover, all night if necessary, until I was good and sore. I looked over at the register again and saw that the owner was bagging up some two-liter bottles of soda for the last customer in line, so it was now or never. I turned away from him and faced the back of the store, where another convex security mirror on the far wall captured me on its stupid fat face. I quickly lifted up my T-shirt and stuffed the magazine in, flat against my clammy waist, half above the belt, half below. I then calmly, steadily walked out of the store, briefly locking eyes with the owner, whose vaguely menacing expression—probably my paranoid imagining—seemed to say to me, "You know, son, fags don't ever win the lottery." I didn't care, though. I had something under my shirt (and down my pants) that you couldn't put a price on: a big old hunk of sugar named Dylan.

I got that magazine home, immediately locked myself in the bathroom, sat down on the furry toilet seat, and jerked myself silly while looking at the most beautiful pictures I'd ever seen in my life. Dudes. Naked dudes. With other naked dudes. With rock-hard bodies. Chowing down on each other like chocolate. And not a limp wrist or Judy Garland album in sight. The scorching collection of glossy, rippled studs in the pages of *Bolt* notwithstanding, I still remained somewhat convinced that real gay men didn't look like these guys—that gay men in the real world just couldn't convincingly wear a football jersey or boxing shorts and found the urge to wear makeup, go to cosmetology school, visit piano bars, and snap just too hard to resist. The only gay men I'd ever met (that I knew of) were two guys who went to our church, sang in the choir, and were active in our local Little Theatre. Nice salt-of-the-earth guys, but about as butch as hot cocoa. And being the only real-world example I had of what gay men were, they were naturally what *all* gay men were. But *Bolt* magazine allowed me to imagine a world in which hot dudes, if offered enough money, could be cajoled into doing any number of things that would make the crushing loneliness of the future gay life I figured was my destiny a little less weepy and desperate.

Now, I'm not at all suggesting that my descent at age fifteen into the deep, dark dungeon of delicious, honey-dipped immorality fondue that became my gay porno mag obsession led directly to God's decision to punish me one month later with a disease that would render my future plans for that house made of Heath bars and Pillsbury cream cheese icing with the picket fence constructed of white-chocolate-covered pretzels completely unrealistic. That would be absurd. All I know is this: The week after I pilfered that gorgeous magazine and started reading it every day at least once, I started getting up in the middle of the night—sometimes two or three times—to go to the bathroom, something I'd never done before, ever. What I didn't know was that, though my young body had finally achieved a much-needed helping of sexual satisfaction, it was also in the early stages of insulin depletion. In the following weeks my blood sugar would continue to rise and I would start to experience most of the classic symptoms of the newly diabetic: incredible thirst, constant need to go to the bathroom, blurry vision, and overwhelming lethargy. One month later, on a school trip stopover in Baltimore, I found myself wandering through the Baltimore Orioles stadium so dehydrated I could barely open my mouth and with vision so blurred I could scarcely make out the collect call instructions on the pay phone I eventually found to call my mother back in Raleigh.

"Mom, there's something wrong with me," I said when I finally reached her. Well, there were *several* things wrong with me, but probably better to take them one at a time.

"'Don't worry, Tim, you'll be just fine.'
But Tim never made it to the water-ski line."

—Ruth Fulghum, "Ode to Tim," 1993

CHAPTER 1
LOSING STREAK

When I was fifteen, I had it on good authority that Jesus was the Son of God and that if you did anything like lose the key to your bicycle lock, your birth certificate, or your mom's lipstick, you could pray to him and, if you put your faith in him, asked with all due respect, and were asking for the right reasons, he would show you that you'd left it in your Members Only jacket, which was currently being slept on by your cat on the living room couch.

In other words, someone was in charge up there, and he knew what and where all your junk was. I was still a firm believer in Jesus Christ as the Son of God and my personal savior as I wound down my freshman year of high school in 1988. Around the middle of the year I'd joined Young Life, a Christian fellowship organization that met once a week at a student's house for powwows full of singing, refreshments, and friendly, wide-eyed testimonials about the power of Christ from the college-aged Young Life staffers. As a kid with few friends who barely made it through middle school alive, I was terrified of social situations, so I was drawn to Young Life because there was absolutely nothing threatening about a bunch of Christian young people singing songs, wearing baseball hats, and grinning like Shirley Temple.

TIM ANDERSON

But, though at the time I was certainly a believer, it wasn't really a love of Jesus that compelled me to visit random students' houses every week to sing along to weepy Christian rock classics like "Friends" by Michael W. Smith or "El Shaddai" by Amy Grant. It wasn't the testimonials about how the love of Jesus can help you battle the pressure from your peers to give in to sex, drugs, and alcohol. (Even at that age, I knew my can't-say-no impulses and understood very well that had any single boy on the face of the earth walked up to me and offered me any of those three things, I would have walked across glass to accept it.) Nor was I driven by a particular need to publicly declare my faith and commune with other young people who felt the same. No, I may have come to Young Life for the camaraderie and the feeling of belonging to some social group, however square. But I stayed for Brad.

Brad was one of the college counselors who, with his trusty acoustic guitar and completely and constantly lit-up face, led the singing every week at the beginning of the meetings. His songbook wasn't terribly broad; lots of Christian rock feel-good-athons and some forays into the more squeaky-clean fare from the past thirty years of the American pop charts—the Monkees' "(I'm Not Your) Steppin' Stone" and U2's "I Still Haven't Found What I'm Looking For," for example. But he made up for the blandness of his song choices with a breathtaking display of muscular forearms, snug blue jeans, and elegant guitar strumming. Honestly, most of the time I was joined with everyone else in song I had no idea what I was singing, who was sitting next to me, what day it was, or what the name of the current president of the United States might be. I just knew that Brad was at the front of the room and that his velvet voice, bushy eyebrows, and lips curled into an electric smile were making us all better Christians. And that if you squinted just so, you could snatch a glimpse of supple man-nipple through his white T-shirt.

Many Tuesdays, Brad and a few other Young Life staffers would come to my high school and meet up with folks to remind them of the meeting that night at so-and-so's house. On those days I was always sure to scramble out to the blacktop meeting point in front of the school as soon as humanly possible so I might get a chance to chat with him before all the other Young Lifers were able to cockblock me. I wasn't always successful; often I would fight my way through the hallways of slow-moving, hip-swinging, shit-talking kids, bounding through them like a pinball, only to discover upon my exit that a bunch of folks had already overtaken Brad and I would have to settle for some friendly chatter with Brad's buddy Todd, a much less alluring Young Life staffer.

Certainly, at age fifteen, I was not ready to admit to myself the real reasons for my obsession with Brad. He was just a dude I really really liked to hang out and sing songs with and who I would kill another human being to be able to see naked. And that was it. Sure, I did find myself fantasizing about how, one day, Brad and I would take our mutual love for Jesus and singing to the next level. We'd start hanging out, just the two of us: doing each other's hair, wearing each other's clothes, and going to the movies, the park, church, restaurants, bars, and, eventually, when we were drunk enough, the bedroom, or at least the couch. But all of that didn't have to happen now. I could wait. For the time being, I just wanted to see him every Tuesday so that I could think about him the rest of the week.

One Tuesday, after we had finished the jovial sing-along that always opened each Young Life meeting, Brad, Todd, and the other staffers showed us a slide show about a Young Life camp up at Saranac Lake in upstate New York near the Canada border, the location of an annual retreat that they wanted everyone to try to go to. Strapping young high schoolers were pictured, and damn, were they having a great time—splashing each other in the lake, climbing trees, cooking out, holding hands and praying, doing a rope swing, eating hot dogs, and parasailing. It looked like heaven on earth, the kind of celestial paradise where the boys never had their shirts on, where showers were possibly communal, and anything—absolutely anything—could happen. I couldn't help but look at the slide show and imagine Brad and me in every picture, rubbing suntan lotion on each other's backs, feeding each other hot dogs, reading Leviticus under the sun while sharing a big beach towel.

The trip was expensive—a few thousand dollars. And God knows my parents and I didn't have that kind of cash. Thankfully, my man Brad had ideas for broke white boys like me.

"Listen, guys," he explained in his dulcet tones after the slide show, "if you want to go but you're worried about money, let me know. We've got some programs for raising money that we can tell you about, and usually it's pretty helpful."

I talked to Brad after the meeting and let him know that I, for one, really wanted to go because it seemed like a great opportunity to commune with the Lord and learn to parasail and, you know, renew my faith and meet lifelong friends and finally finish the Book of Revelation and, I don't know, get a suntan. He nodded and smiled, and said that he would call me this week and we could talk about raising the funds. Could he get my number?

I think we all know the answer to that.

"Have you ever parasailed?" I asked my girlfriend Dawn. Did I not mention my girlfriend Dawn? Terrible omission. Dawn had curly blonde hair and loved her jean jacket more than anything else in the world. Like most girlfriends of young gay boys, Dawn went to a different high school, and I mostly just saw her on weekends. And though she was a big-hair metal fan, she was also chaste, for the most part. Sure, upstairs in her room there was French kissing, there was boob groping, there was a little bit of grinding. Yes, she ventured downward with her hand a few times to inexpertly grasp and jostle my male parts. But we would invariably get bored after a while, stop, and put on a cassette tape or something.

"Oh yeah," she answered in her deadpan way, laying back on her pillow, draping her jean jacket over herself, and putting on her aviator glasses. "It was fun, I guess. If you like getting soaked and being knocked around on a big raft with a bunch of people screaming in your face."

"That sounds like white-water rafting."

"Yeah. Isn't that what we're talking about?"

"We're talking about parasailing."

"Oh, I haven't done that."

"Huh. Well, I might be doing it this summer, at Saranac."

"What's that?"

"A Young Life camp up in New York."

"Oh yeah. Maybe I should go, too," she offered. "There's a Young Life at Millbrook."

"Ye-e-es!" I said with effusive and completely counterfeit excitement. "That could be fun."

"When is it?"

"July."

"Oh, but . . . music camp."

"Oh, you *can't* miss music camp." I was very very concerned about her missing music camp.

"No, I'm a counselor this year."

Dodged a bullet there.

"God," she continued, "if they make us do one more Simon and Garfunkel song this year I will throw up so hard, for real."

Thank God for music camp. It was only a day camp, but it lasted for the whole month of July. If not for it and my visit to see my aunt and grandmother for the month of June, Dawn and I might have to go to third base, because what else were we going to do all summer?

"But 'The Boxer' is an awesome song," I suggested.

"No, uh-uh. Predictable. Why can't we ever do some Heart or Prince or something?"

I laid my head down on the pillow next to her.

"They'll probably make us do some Beatles or Beach Boys shit. More kids know it."

Dawn repositioned herself under her jean jacket, slapping me in the face with the sleeve.

She lay there silently, probably considering what magic the flutes could do with Van Halen's "Jump." Then she sat up.

"Wow, if you go on this trip we're not going to see each other very much this summer." She said this emotionlessly, in the same tone she might tell a stranger on the street the time. Never the most passionate of girls, Dawn had a way of sounding constantly bored, unless she was excited about something, in which case she sounded sarcastic.

"Yeah," I sighed dramatically, way overcompensating for her lack of an emotional stake in this conversation. We were quiet after that, just listening to the Def Leppard song coming from the crackly speakers on the floor of her room.

The lead singer crooned the opening line—something about love being like a bomb, so c'mon, let's get it on, shall we?—and Dawn was soon singing along.

"Pour some sugar on me," she sang, sighing listlessly.

Mmm, sugar, I thought, giving her ambivalent invitation no further thought.

—————

Brad called me to give me the scoop on the magic method for raising money for the trip. It was an insult to human dignity: I would have to sell magazines and candy bars to the public like a common street urchin.

"Oh, OK, I can do that," I said as I rolled my eyes and resisted the temptation to gouge one of them out with a spoon. I was a terrible salesman. Could never sell anything to save my life. I hated to impose on people and always preferred that they just give me money for being young and adorable. Unfortunately I was way too old now to get money for nothing, so I was forced to wander the lonely streets of suburban north Raleigh like Oliver Twist begging folks for their Christian charity. "Please, sir, can I interest you in a subscription to *Teen Beat?*"

I ended up raising only $300 for the trip after selling as many chocolate bars and magazines as I possibly could door to door and at school. Predictably, I ate some of the goods and had to pay myself back, because they were chocolate bars and they were in my backpack just sitting there not being eaten, what the hell was I *supposed* to do? So I had to resort to asking family for money. I got a hundred dollars here and fifty dollars there until, with the money I made from working extra hours at my job as a cashier at Kerr Drug, I had enough cash to commit to the trip. Paradise would be mine, and I would finally get to see Brad without that dang shirt on.

I continued attending Young Life meetings every week for the rest of the school year, doing my best to become Brad's favorite— laughing at all of his jokes, screaming "Encore!" whenever he

started to put down his guitar, standing next to him in uncomfortable silence as he engaged in a discussion with another Young Lifer
after the meetings. What was I doing, with all my shenanigans? I
have no idea, but if the fifteen-year-old me were available to answer
that question he would probably say I was laying the groundwork
for what would be an affair to remember, a passionate pairing for
the ages. You know, eventually, sometime in the future, when we
were ready. It didn't matter that Brad had an irritating habit of
mentioning his girlfriend a little too often. That was OK. When
you're fifteen and in love (though you dare not speak its name),
these kinds of obstacles are easy to ignore because your will is
strong enough to bend metal, set a forest fire, or unbuckle a leather
belt. It will just take time.

———

The trip up to Saranac Lake would be in July, and I was spending
most of June visiting my aunt and grandmother in Jamestown. It
was a perfect summer vacation: I was getting wined and dined by
the Golden Girls of Jamestown, with plenty of time to rest up and
prepare myself physically, mentally, and spiritually for what would
hopefully be the *Cabaret* of Christian camping trips.

I've already mentioned the one door I walked through up in
Jamestown that summer that I would never be able to, er, back out
of: I'd seen photographic proof that it is possible for two hot, sweaty
young men to strip down, lube up, and *get it on* with each other,
out in the open, with the lights on, gleefully, on a kitchen counter.
This was in direct opposition to the way I imagined real-life homosexuals did their dirty deeds—hiding in a bathroom stall while
constantly checking to see if the cops are coming, holed up in an
out-of-the-way motel where folks usually go to get murdered, or

weeping uncontrollably while tugging on a dude's balls in a public library janitor's closet. I can't overestimate this breakthrough. Sure, the guys in the pictures may have been lisping their ABCs while receiving their blow jobs, but here's the thing: If anyone cornered *them* in the hallway of *their* high school and called them, oh, I don't know, "Tinkerbell Tim," these dudes looked like they could and would punch back. Or whack them in the face with their rock-hard cocks, whichever.

It was sure empowering. And I empowered myself *a lot* over those June weeks in Jamestown, releasing years of sexual confusion and frustration in at *least* twice-daily batches. As my aunt and grandmother sat in the living room watching Peter Jennings on *World News Tonight,* I could be found in the bathroom jerking off with the sweaty terror, passion, and desperation of a fighter pilot landing a B-52 that's out of fuel and nose-diving into the Pacific.

About a week after my theft of the magazine, I began walking over that other threshold from which I would never return. As I said, the first indication that I'd entered a brave new world of sugar-free living was when I started waking up at night needing to go to the bathroom. On the first night, I thought maybe I had just had too many sodas during our card game or maybe hadn't peed before going to bed. The second night, I woke up at around the same time needing to pee again, and I started to think that something was weird. The third night I started to really worry that something was going wrong with my body. And naturally, I assumed it had some-thing to do with all of the . . . B-52 bomber landings I'd been engaging in recently. After all, the same part of my teenage body was in operation. Plus, there was the fact that I was *sinning like a filthy heathen acrobat* twice a day. Sure, I was asking for God's forgiveness immediately after cleaning myself up each time, but if you fully intend to commit the same sin again in a few hours or the next morning at the absolute latest, does God really even take you seriously?

I'd heard those urban myths about too much masturbation leading to fuzzy palms, but I'd never heard one thing about it leading to an overactive bladder. What was going on? Was I being punished for tainting my formerly pristine Christian soul with all of my recent indulgences? After a few more nights of the same thing, I knew what I had to do: Throw away the porno mag, stop giving in to temptation, and allow myself to once again sleep through the night. God would maybe release me from his baleful gaze, I would have fought and tamed an unchristian urge, and, most important, I wouldn't have to tell anyone that something wasn't right. I grabbed the magazine, opened it to my favorite spread, and came in for one last landing, after which I cleaned up, got dressed, stuffed the magazine in a paper bag, told Aunt Sue I was going for a walk, and took it out to the garbage.

Nevertheless, the multiple nightly trips to the bathroom in the early morning continued unabated. I was at a loss. I'd done the one thing I thought would take care of this problem. I'd cast the magazine out of my life and turned my eyes back to all that was good and pure, like watching *Wheel of Fortune* and *Jeopardy!* in the sitting room with my aunt and grandmother or reading the Jackie Collins book I'd checked out from the library. And praying mightily, with very sweaty palms.

But the fact remained: For the next two weeks I had to get up multiple times every night. My body was malfunctioning, and persistently. I didn't know why it was happening or what I could do about it, but I did know one thing: If it wasn't going away, this physical manifestation of my own moral weakness—well, I may as well go back to the newsagent and try my luck at bagging another porno mag, no?

So that's what I did. I snuck into the same newsagent one day while my aunt was at the Quality Market picking up popcorn, Hormel wieners, and ginger ale for gin rummy night. Sweating bullets, I sauntered back to the adult aisle after a few quick glances at the cashier, knelt down, and remained perfectly still to avoid detection via the all-seeing convex mirror hanging from the ceiling in the corner. My eyes roamed freely inside my perfectly still head: *Honcho, Inches, Colt, Jock, Blueboy, Torso, Stallion, Stroke.* Some really great titles, to be sure. But the options were so overwhelming that I couldn't choose, so I just closed my eyes, grabbed one, shoved it under my shirt, and scrambled over to the music magazine section, where I seized upon the latest copy of *Billboard* and flipped to the Hot 100 listing. Wiping my sweaty brow and trying to exhale without sounding like I'd been holding my breath for ten days, I smiled to see that "Alone" by Heart was still number 1. Because that song was *awesome.*

The remainder of my days in Jamestown that June were spent jerking off and peeing, jerking off and peeing, jerking off and peeing. I returned to Raleigh with a sinking sense of my spiritual doom and also with a profoundly exhausted crotch.

———

A few short weeks remained before my Erotic Christian Getaway, weeks spent (1) furiously beating off to increasingly unlikely scenes of man-on-man courtship and (2) getting up multiple times every night to pee. It was an exquisite sin cycle: sin followed by divine punishment, followed by more sin and, naturally, more late-night/ early morning divine punishment. Followed by more sin, for as we all knew, sinful thoughts are sins in and of themselves, and I was having those pretty much all day: at the grocery store, while watching *Days of Our Lives* or men's gymnastics, while doing the *TV Guide* crossword, whenever. I'd eaten Eve's apple and was now regularly fantasizing about Adam's. Mom was bound to catch me at one of the two acts at some point, and sure enough, about a week before my trip, I crept out of the bathroom after one of my late-night urination celebrations, and there she stood in the hallway, her face all squinty and concerned, her arms folded over her pink rose-flecked thermal top.

"Tim," she began in her closest approximation of a whisper, "you've been getting up to go to the bathroom a lot lately."

"Yeah," I mumbled.

"Are you just drinking a lot before bed?"

Sounded like a decent enough excuse to me. Besides, I actually *had* started drinking a lot more this week, not just before bed but all day. It was summer, I was playing a lot of tennis and stuff, I was thirsty. It was certainly an easier story to run with than "Well, Mom, actually I think it's because I've been doing so much jerking off while looking at pictures of dudes with ripped bodies plowing each other like John Deere."

"Yeah, I've been really thirsty lately."

Mom's face squinted with deepened concern.

"What?" I said, defensively.

"Oh, nothing, I'm just thinking about what it might be. You know, Uncle Ostel had a similar thing happen to him before he was diagnosed."

"Diagnosed with what?"

"Diabetes." Pronounced "dah-be-tease."

Oh, *that* awful thing. Wait, what? She thinks I have diabetes? The thing that David in second grade had?

Mom saw that she'd alarmed me. "It might be nothing," she said. "We should just, you know, maybe think about it."

I went back to bed truly spooked. I was unaware of any scientific connection between gay masturbation and diabetes. Gay masturbation and eternal hellfire, sure, but *diabetes*?

The next day—a hot, humid one—I went to play tennis with my dad, using my constant need to pee to take my game to the next level. I never stopped moving, even when tossing the ball into the air for my serve. If you never stop moving, see, you can ignore the primal need to empty a full bladder for a lot longer. Just don't even think about it as an option. Keep your feet moving, your mind on the game, your groin muscles clenched like a bitch.

Arriving home after tennis, I sprinted to the toilet and released into it a body of water that could be seen from space. My mouth bone dry, I wandered into the kitchen in search of some sort of freezing cold beverage. I opened the fridge, pulled out a full pitcher of lemonade, lifted it spout-first to my parched lips, and allowed the blissfully cold and sweet liquid to cascade down my throat and down my chin and cheeks as I grunted, groaned, hiccupped, and spat my enthusiastic approval.

I finished the entire pitcher, and stood there, eyes bulging. Almost immediately I felt in my gut the foolishness of slamming down so much lemonade in one go. My stomach churning and chugging, I slammed the pitcher down and ran back to the bathroom as quickly as my rubber legs could carry me, feeling the storm brewing and rising, up, up, up, through my esophagus and out my horrified mouth.

It felt as if the cataclysmic upchuck overtook every orifice in my head—mouth, eyes, ears, nostrils—as it spewed the acid mixture of lemonade, bile, and saliva onto every available surface. Barf splattered the walls, the toilet, the floor, the sink, my shorts, my face, the plunger, the rug. Bleary-eyed and still heaving, I rubbed my eyes and slumped down onto the tiled floor, crouching into an area that had managed to escape the wrath of my epic hurl.

Leaning against the bathtub, I looked up and rubbed away the tears that had been forced out of my eyes. There was Mom in the doorway, looking worried and slightly disgusted.

"What happened?" she said, trying not to breathe in the awful stench that had filled the room.

"I think I drank too much of that lemonade."

"How much did you drink?"

"Well, the rest of it."

"The rest of . . . I just *made* it!"

"Yeah, I went ahead and finished it." I began checking my earlobes and hair for stray bits of barf.

Needless to say, this horrific puke opera increased Mom's angst considerably, and the word *diabetes* started popping up in her speech along with the words "we'll just need to see" and "it might not be that."

I would later learn that Mom was actually seriously considering making me stay home from the Young Life trip and get checked out by a doctor. But she knew how much I'd been looking forward to the trip, so she talked herself out of it, casting her suspicions of my body's faulty engineering in vague terms, uttering them quietly lest by using too much volume she would set something in motion. But I'd already taken care of that.

For the trip to Saranac Lake we would commandeer two tour buses of Jesus-loving high school students ready to pile in, get comfortable, and sing Michael W. Smith at the top of our lungs. Setting off from Raleigh at around five thirty in the morning, we would hop on I-95 and head toward Washington, D.C., where we would spend most of the day sightseeing. In the evening we planned to venture into neighboring Baltimore to see a Baltimore Orioles base-ball game at Memorial Stadium.

Now, the Baltimore Orioles then were mired in a notorious losing streak that even non-sports watchers like me knew about, thanks to late-night comedy shows. They had begun the season with a loss and continued it with no wins and twenty more losses. The public sentiment, from what I could gather, was that the Orioles would continue to lose until there was a compelling reason for them not to, like a forfeiture by the opposing team one lucky evening. It was a law of nature now, much like gravity or Madonna. But D.C. didn't have a baseball team at the time, so if we wanted to see a game (and obviously we did) we would have to settle for the lovable losers in Baltimore. We would attend, cheer the poor suckers on as best we could, and hopefully witness our team come within four runs of winning.

In the school parking lot on the morning of our departure I got out of my mom's car, kissed her good-bye thoughtlessly as she waved to the Young Life staff standing out by the buses, and made a beeline for Brad and his clipboard.

I hadn't seen him since the end of the school year. It had been plenty long since I'd gazed into his shining eyes and seen him crack a smile that could make one, if one was not careful, break out into song.

"Hey, Tim!" he said, flashing those adorable teeth. "Good to see you!"

I blushed like a fifth grade Girl Scout, resisting the temptation to throw my bag on the asphalt and launch into my own, giddy version of "My Favorite Things."

Boys in white tank tops
With blue aqua Speedos
Flashing their ripped abs,
Pecs, glutes, delts, and . . .

Hmm, what muscle group rhymes with Speedos?

"How you been?"

How have I been, Brad? How have I been? Oh, pretty great. You see, Brad, just last month I obtained photographic proof that guys like you and I? We can make it work. Anatomically. We can make it work real good. Apparently dudes are doing it all the time. Also I'm pissing like a racehorse at least thrice nightly. But more important, Brad: you and I? It can happen.

"I've been pretty good, you know," I stammered. Brad nodded and turned his head to greet a throng of my fellow needy travelers and their question-having parents.

By the time the tour buses were an hour north of Raleigh, I had visited the bus restroom three times. My thirst seemed to be harder and harder to sate, but thankfully there was a cooler on the bus with sodas and bottled waters. An hour outside of D.C. I was on my third Coke. And in deep, deep denial.

We wandered around our nation's capital for hours in the hot July sun. I carried with me a water bottle that I continued to swig from and refill whenever possible, my thirst increasingly relentless. I tried to compose myself and not make too many obvious trips to the restroom, like, say, when standing awestruck on the steps of the Lincoln Memorial gazing into the face of the Great Emancipator, wishing to God I could be emancipated from my bladder.

We hopped around town all afternoon—from Important Historical Building to Awe-Inspiringly Phallic Monument, onward to Tragic Memorial to American Folly, southward to Hot Dog Cart, and, after lunch, up to Significant Museum, over to Site of Major Political Scandal, and, finally, to Kiosk Where You Can Buy George Washington Wigs and Tricorn Hats. The whole time I was dragging my feet from place to place and having to sit down any time a seat presented itself: next to a gargoyle outside a museum, in a traffic island, on the Mall, at the feet of a Korean War Veterans Memorial statue, wherever.

I was exhausted like I'd never been before. All I wanted to do was sit down, lie back, and have ice-cold liquid poured down my throat, preferably by Brad but I'd settle for Fred the bus driver or even my friend Ruth.

"Are you doing OK, Tim?" Brad asked me as I languorously leaned up against a section of the Vietnam Veterans Memorial wall and began sliding down, squeaking.

"I'm not sure," I said. "I feel really tired and thirsty." I turned my head and, squinting my eyes, looked at the memorial wall, trying to read the names in front of me. "Rooooooobert G. . . . Davidson . . ." I struggled to mumble.

"Hmm," he said. "I hope you're not getting heatstroke or something. We should probably get you out of the sun."

Yes, do get me out of this terrible heat, Brad, I do declare. Take me somewhere and cool me off. And be a dear and get me a mint julep. Because as God is my witness, I will never be thirsty again!

"Yeah, I feel like I just need to sit down again."

"Here, let's go over there where the benches are. You want something to drink?"

I did want something to drink. I looked at Brad and his blurry face.

"Yeah, I'm pretty thirsty."

"Great," he said, backing away toward a beverage stand. "Coke OK?"

A few more sodas later I was drifting through next-stop Baltimore in a post-apocalyptic nightmare of malfunctioning biorhythmic human machinery—at the Gallery mall, no less. My parched mouth ached for oceans of wetness; my usually nimble arm and leg muscles began to turn to molasses; my sad blue eyes struggled to see clearly anything in front of them, as if I were viewing the world from the inside of a car wash; and my hyperactive bladder demanded the expulsion of any and every liquid that passed my lips as fast as it could force me once again into a restroom.

At long last, we made it to Memorial Stadium to watch the Orioles probably lose to the Texas Rangers. We all filtered into our seats, and my body issued a pitiful "hallelujah" for the opportunity to slowly collapse into the oblivion of stadium seating.

I was a stick of licorice left out in the sun, melting into the seat. I was a pool of candle wax whose long-burning wick would soon expire. I was the watch hanging from the tree branch in Salvador Dalí's *The Persistence of Memory*. I was in desperate need of another piss. The world whirred and writhed around me as I moved in slow motion to lift the paper cup in my hand up to my cracked lips and tried to muster the superhuman strength needed to lift my body out of gravity's grip, gain control of it, and steer it toward the temporary paradise of a functioning toilet.

I stumbled out onto the main concourse and clawed my way through the crowd to the restroom. After relieving my shell-shocked bladder for what surely had to be the hundredth time that day, I exited the men's room and started staggering back to where our group was. On the way I passed by a few kiosks selling Baltimore Orioles paraphernalia and could just make out the little orange and black birdie on the jerseys.

Next to the kiosk there was a pay phone. I lurched over to it, picked up the receiver, and dialed my parents collect. My older brother Chris, home from college for the summer, answered and told me that no one was around.

"Oh, I guess I'll call back later," I said. "I think something's wrong with me."

"What's going on?"

"I'm just . . . really tired and thirsty and I can't see and I keep having to pee and it's so hot and, God, there are all these freaking people, and I'm sweating a lot and I feel like everything's melting."

"Hmm," Chris said.

"Tell Mom I'll call back in a little while."

I looked around for a drink stand, tumbled over to the nearest one, and ordered a cup of water.

"I'm still gonna have to charge you for the cup," the fat guy behind the counter said.

"I don't care," I said through chapped and brittle lips. He filled a Coke cup with ice and water from the sink.

I took my expensive cup of water and walked back to the pay phone. Checking my watch to see how much time had passed since I had last called, I realized that not only had I not paid attention to what the time was when I'd talked to Chris but that now I couldn't see the hands on my watch. I tried opening my mouth to say "Dammit" only to realize that my mouth was now so dry that my tongue was sticking to the roof of my mouth. I pissed a little into my jeans.

I was officially in the Twilight Zone. The Orioles would surely win tonight.

———

"And you've been going to the bathroom a lot?" Mom said. I'd finally reached her on the phone and had done my best to communicate my predicament through the cotton packing my mouth.

"Yeth, like every theven minuteth. And the drinkth just theem to make me thirthtier."

"Make you what?"

"Thirthtier. Thirthtier!"

" . . . "

"They jutht make me want more to drink!"

"Oh, Tim, I think you need to go to the hospital."

"I gueth tho."

"You need to get off the phone, go get one of your advisors, and bring him to the phone and call me back. I think you've definitely got diabetes."

Diabetes. Dai-ah-bee-tis. Dah-bee-tease. Diabetes.

I hung up and did the zombie walk all the way there so I could break the news to Brad or somebody (Brad) that they were going to have to drop everything and take me by the closest emergency room real quick, no big deal, just for a little checkup.

After hoisting myself along the concourse to the stands like a rubber android with self-awareness but no real muscle coordination, I found our group and caught Brad's eye with my own bloodshot devil's beams. He stood up and asked if I was feeling any better.

"I'm actually worth," my lizard-dry tongue begrudgingly allowed me to say.

"Wow, your mouth is really dry," he said, putting his strong manhand on my shoulder.

"I talked to my mom and the thaid I thould go to the hothpital."

Brad's face fell, ever so slightly, when I said this. He walked with me back to a pay phone, where we called my mom again. After dialing and thaying hello to her, I handed him the rethiever and excuthed mythelf to vithit the rethtroom.

Brad was still on the phone with Mom when I returned. He was smiling and nodding respectfully as he punctuated the conversation with "Yes, absolutely" and "Oh, is that right?" He and

Mom would really get along well one day, later on, when he and I were shacked up and having babies.

He hung up the phone, turned to me, and put that manhand on my shoulder once again. "OK, we're going to get everybody together after the game and take you to the hospital. Everything's gonna be fine. They'll check you out and we'll see what they say, OK, buddy?"

My bulging red and yellow eyes managed to focus themselves enough to make out the smile he gave me at the end of that sentence. He then walked me over to the drink stand to get me more water.

"I'm gonna still have to charge you for the cup," the attendant said.

"That's all right, I got it," Brad replied, reaching for his wallet as my heart swooned and my bladder called me back to the bathroom for a quickie.

———

Word of my freakish condition and our impending trip to the emergency room traveled fast. It took a while to get everyone corralled together and headed toward our parking spaces, and tongues were atwitter with concern and excitement over the drama. A few folks came up to me and asked me if I was OK, and I replied, "I jutht feel really weird" with my best brave/sad puppy-dog face.

"Tim!" Ruth scampered up to me as we exited the stadium. "What's going on?! I heard someone say 'diabetes'!"

"Yeah, my mom thinkth I've got it."

"Oh no, that can't be right," Ruth said. "Diabetes is a *disease*, isn't it?"

"Um, yeah, tho I hear."

"Yeah, no, you don't have that. I'm sure it's something else."

Yes, I thought, *that other thing you get when you spend the entire month of June jerking off in your aunt's bathroom to gay porn you stole from the newsagent, thereby incurring God's wrath and sending your body into a fluid-draining frenzy. What's that disease called again?*

"Yeah," Dr. Ruth continued, "I'm sure you'll be just fine. It's probably just heatstroke or something."

Ruth's optimism couldn't have been more misplaced, which was confirmed a few hours later, when I was sitting uncomfortably on an examination table clad only in a pitiful hospital gown, which is no way to face any kind of diagnosis, least of all a medical one. I had waited two hours in the emergency room before being seen because it was apparently Bloody, Uninsured, Hard-luck Zombie Night at Mercy Hospital.

Because I absolutely *hate* to cause a scene, I was simply mortified at the idea of my stupid health issue—the one that was my fault and no one else's—causing trouble for the whole group and throwing the trip into chaos. The buses were supposed to arrive at Saranac in the morning, and now it was looking like we might miss our first morning prayer-breakfast-on-the-beach.

The door opened, and in walked Dr. Vogel carrying a clipboard at which he stared incredulously. He looked up at me, obviously spooked.

"Are you . . . OK?" he ventured.

Given that I was sitting in a downtown Baltimore ER examination room wearing a hospital gown at midnight on a Friday, I couldn't help but think that the answer to that question was self-evidently "No." But since I tend to avoid conflict at all costs, I said, "Yeah, I mean, you know, I feel kind of weird, but . . ."

He consulted the paper on his clipboard. "I'm actually having a hard time believing this. Your blood sugar level is the highest number I've ever seen."

I blinked and tried to swallow.

"It's nineteen eighty."

This number meant nothing to me.

"Normal blood sugar is seventy to one twenty."

That clarified things a bit.

"Your pancreas is clearly not producing insulin anymore. We need to get you a hefty dose right now and get this number down."

Pancreas? Isn't that the thing that stores bile? No, wait, that's the liver. (Spleen?)

"I'm afraid we'll need to admit you. Your levels are really high. It's incredible. You could go into a coma at any moment—in fact, I'm surprised that you're not actually already in one. Like I said, highest blood sugar level on record."

So do I get a prize?

"And then there's the danger of ketoacidosis."

Surely he just made that word up.

Turned out he hadn't. I was in real trouble. I was not just sick. I was *diseased*. And worse: I would not be traveling the rest of the way up to Saranac to frolic in the sun and sand and roll around in the surf with Brad, kissing him passionately as the waves crashed upon us and "Love Is a Many-Splendored Thing" blasted from the camp speakers. All of that was definitely going to happen, and now it would not.

Dr. Vogel left the room to fetch a nurse, and I was left alone to contemplate the words he'd just said to me. It appeared that there were syringes in my future. Syringes full of insulin and misery.

I got up off the examination table and walked over to the mirror above the sink. I washed my hands, working that soap into as satisfying a lather as I could manage. After rinsing my hands, I splashed water on my face, then looked at myself in the mirror. I still couldn't see very clearly, but the blurry features that appeared in front of me sure looked terrified.

———

An hour later I was lying in a bed in a hospital room sucking a Diet Shasta through a straw as my blood sugar level slowly stabilized thanks to the turbo-dose of insulin I'd been given in my inaugural diabetes syringe jab. My parents had been called and had immediately gotten on the road to make the drive from Raleigh. The buses were ready to roll back onto the interstate. And it was decided that Todd would stay overnight with me until my parents got here; he would rent a car in the morning to drive up to the lake.

It was so sweet of Todd to offer to do this. So sweet. Just amazingly generous and gracious and WHY COULDN'T BRAD STAY WITH ME INSTEAD?!

Brad came in to say good-bye before getting on the bus.

"You're going to be fine, buddy," he said, flashing that smile. "We're all going to be praying for you that your stay here is short and sweet."

I nodded and took another long suck on my Diet Shasta, emptying the can.

"You're going to be OK. We'll get together and play tennis or something when I get back, OK?"

"Sure, that'll be fun." Not as fun as swapping slop on a sandy beach, but OK.

And with that he was gone, leaving me alone with a new, dreadful disease that prohibited me even drowning my sorrows in a bowl of freaking Froot Loops.

"Want to watch TV?" Todd asked, coming into the room with some snacks he bought at the vending machine down the hall.

"Yeah, let's turn it on," I said. "Oh, and would you mind getting me another one of these?" I asked, pointing to my empty Diet Shasta can.

I was still very thirsty.

The teenage boy is sleeping peacefully in his bed at home.

Listen to that dulcet hacksaw snoring erupting from his giant nose, sounding like cutlery being thrust into a blender in front of a microphone. But despite this veneer of elegant slumber, all is not well.

First there's a quiver. Then a twitch. And a jerk of the head.

Maybe he's dreaming about being slapped in the face? More quivers. And twitches. Another jerk of the head.

Now it seems that a thousand beads of sweat have popped through the surface of his skin, blending to cover every inch of his body in a clammy glaze.

A few more twitches. Another couple of jerks.

He's dreaming that he's alone on the floor of a brightly lit bedroom that's not his, kneeling on a brilliant light-green shag carpet and looking out the window as his aunt and uncle get into their car and drive away. Casey Kasem is on the radio reading a long-distance dedication. The boy is amazed by the brilliance of the green of the carpet, and really wants that shade for his room. He pulls at a clump of carpet strands, and Casey Kasem tells him, "Needs mowing." He jerks his head around looking for the lawn mower. He doesn't see it anywhere in the room, but his head keeps jerking and shaking so it's hard for him to see. The brilliant green of the room is soon pierced with snatches of black as his eyelids repeatedly pop open, then close again. He slowly slips out of the green room and into the darkness, twitching all the way.

The bed is soaking wet now, and its occupant—not to put too fine a point on it—appears to be somewhat possessed by the devil.

Twitchjerktwitchjerktwitchjerktwitchjerktwitchjerktwitchjerk-THUDwhackCRACK-CRACKCRACKCRACK.

Yikes. He has left the bed and fallen nose-first onto his hardwood bedroom floor. Couldn't have been pleasant. And what is that he's doing now? Is that . . . swimming? Yes, he appears to be trying to swim freestyle on his hardwood floor. He was never a very fast swimmer, but he's really going for it right now.

There is more cracking and whacking of his head and limbs against the floor for a few minutes. He's trying to get back into that green room. God knows why; that carpet was hideous.

Ah, a light! Now we're getting somewhere. The boy's mother and father have rushed into the room and turned on the light. The mother says something to the father—I can't hear what because of all the whacking and cracking. She's left the room, and the father has crouched down, taken hold of the flailing boy, and is now trying to turn him over onto his back. It's not an easy task—the father has to grip the boy harder than he would like and force him to turn over, all the while deflecting blows from the boy's crazy spastic spider arms.

At last the mother returns with a container in her hand—it's a plastic bottle in the shape of a bear. A squeeze bottle. That's a funny phrase to say: squeeze bottle. Squeeze bottle. Squeeze bottle. *The more you say it, the funnier it sounds, no? Anyway, what's in it?*

The mother screams at the father to hold the boy down, and as he does that she lifts the container to the boy's mouth. Ah, I see, it's honey. She's squeezing honey into his mouth. And around it. And above it. Basically it's going all over his cheeks and hair is what I'm saying.

"TIM! TIM! TIM!" The sound of his mother's screeching into his bouncing young face appears to be tugging him loose from the spotty netherworld he's in. Am I right? He looks to be opening his eyes a little more often now. Yes, he's now back with us, his eyeballs flitting to different spots on the bright white of his bedroom ceiling. His head is still banging against that floor, and his face and hair are just slathered with honey. If you rolled him in nuts you could sell him at the state fair.

"TIM! Can you hear me?!" His mother has, it appears, turned the volume up to 11.

"Drink the honey, sweetie! Drink it! Drink it! Honey, hold him!!!"

The boy twists and shakes. His arms flap and flail. It's like he's trying to do the hand jive but instead of doing it in a gymnasium at a 1950s school dance he's doing it on his back, in his bedroom, while his mother covers him in honey, intermittently hitting the bull's-eye of his open fishmouth. The mother tells the dad to hold him and leaves the room. The boy, even from the twitchy dimension he's currently in, can hear her yelling into the phone, and he even recognizes the human English word "diabetic," though he can't recall what it means. A minute later she's back in the room, still wielding the honey bear.

The boy gurgles and moans as his body, minute by minute, calms the hell down. Slowly the jerks become less jerky, the floor thwacks less thwacky. As his slippery body begins to reach the mechanical balance of a normal, nonpossessed human (give or take a few persistent twitches and jerks), his mother mercifully turns the volume down to about 8 or 9.

"Tim! Tim? Tim? Can you hear me? Can you understand me?"

The boy breathes deeply, and his eyes flit from his mom's face to his dad's face and back to his mom's face. His parents hover over him like stunned scientists over a newly unfrozen alien specimen.

"Buddy? You there?" his dad says.

The boy blinks and turns his head to look around his room. He discovers that he's lying on the floor. That he's sticky. And that his nose is hurting like a bitch.

A siren sounds outside the house. The dad leaves the room and goes downstairs. The mom strokes the boy's head.

"Tim? Can you hear me? Say something if you can hear me."

"Mmmmeh," the boy says, his honey lips smacking, his synapses finally starting to synapt again. He struggles to lift himself up. He falls back down and thwacks his head again.

The sound of multiple footsteps on the stairs reaches their ears, louder and louder.

The boy tries again to summon the strength to sit up on the floor and get himself back into bed, and makes some headway this time. He's covered in sweat and is feeling a chill. He flops onto the bed and quickly pulls the covers over his wet body before the footsteps turn into people. He's in his underwear, you see, and he doesn't want to be seen by strangers in his underwear. (This will change.)

The three paramedics make their dramatic entrance. The boy is still confused and doesn't understand why three hunky firemen (are they firemen?) have entered his room. He sits bug-eyed and breathless as one of the handsome brutes comes over and takes his hand. Not, sadly, to ask him out for pancakes, but to test his blood sugar. He grabs the boy's index finger, swabs the tip with an alcohol wipe, and jabs it with a lancet. He squeezes out a drop of blood, turns the finger over, and transfers the blood to a test strip. The boy lies back with his arm outstretched, surrendering to the manhandling like he's on the cover of a romance novel.

After two minutes, the glucose monitor gives its reading: 34. Very low. But after all that honey, it is certainly on its way up.

The mother chats with the paramedics for a few minutes, and the boy sneaks a quick look underneath his blanket: Thank God, no boner.

Ten minutes later, after checking his sugar again, the calendar boys depart. The exhausted boy, his body ravaged by adrenaline, slips back into sleep.

He will not dream about a bright green carpet. He will dream about crash landing on a snow-covered planet and being attacked by a clown with pinwheels stuck into his wig.

He's had a lot of sugar.

CHAPTER 2

THE HONEYMOON PERIOD

Knowledge is power, this is a certainty. Thing is, I've never been particularly power hungry, and my knowledge of the world's realities had always been a little skewed. For example, when I was a paranoid youngster, I'd thought that Olympic events decided geopolitics. So if the Russians beat us in, say, the pole vault, we Americans would all be sent to labor camps. I learned later on this was not the case, but that was probably only because the USA beat the Soviet Union in hockey. The point is, I had no idea how the world worked.

In the weeks after my diagnosis, I felt completely and utterly power*less*. I needed to regain some semblance of equilibrium, to fill in some of the gaps in my understanding of the world o' diabetes so I could go back to living my life half awake rather than completely passed out. For example, why did I have such a lazy pancreas?

"Type 1 and type 2 diabetes have different causes, yet two factors are important in both," my informational pamphlet from the American Diabetes Association proclaimed. I was sitting at home on the couch watching *Days of Our Lives* and wondering (1) how I ended up with this disease, (2) if I did anything to cause it, and (3) if Calliope was ever going to get a decent storyline. The latter question would be answered in time (no, and the answer was because daytime television writers didn't know what to do with funny women), but the first two questions were really bothering me. I'd never gotten a very good answer from anyone at the hospital about why this had happened. I needed to know that it wasn't my fault; that I was just an innocent babe in the woods whose destiny it was to have an insulin deficiency.

"First, you must inherit a predisposition to the disease. Second, something in your environment must trigger diabetes."

Something in my environment, something in my environment, hmmm. Trying to think. What in my environment changed in the past month or so? I got a haircut, but that's never triggered diabetes before. I swallowed a watermelon seed at a picnic a few weeks ago, but that doesn't lead to diabetes, that just leads to germination of a new baby watermelon in your stomach. *Oh, I know, I'd pleasured myself constantly to magazines swiped from Satan's own porn closet. COULD THAT BE IT?!* I needed the good people at the American Diabetes Association to tell me that that was not it.

"One trigger might be related to cold weather," the pamphlet continued unhelpfully. "Type 1 diabetes develops more often in winter than summer and is more common in places with cold climates." Well, that was certainly the exact opposite scenario from the one I'd just experienced. Got anything else, ADA?

"Early diet may also play a role. Type 1 diabetes is less common in people who were breastfed . . ."

OK, stop right there. I was breastfed plenty. I loved the teat. Was all over that shit. Mom was actually still weaning me off my pacifier when I was four, that's how much of a nipple fanatic I was. I'm gonna give you one more shot, diabetes pamphlet.

"In many people, the development of type 1 diabetes seems to take many years. In experiments that followed relatives of people with type 1 diabetes, researchers found that most of those who later got diabetes had certain autoantibodies in their blood for years before."

Oh, so it's the autoantibodies, thank *God*. Science sure cleared that one right up.

———

In the weeks after my Baltimore meltdown and my initiation into the lifestyle of a two-injections-and-five-finger-pricks-a-day diabetic wunderkind, I found solace in the two small blessings that such a terrible new existence allowed: sympathy and diet soda. Preferably at the same time. Diet Coke just tasted better when it was sipped while chatting with a visitor who was looking at me with pity. (Did I encourage their pity with an evocative expression of plucky bravery? Maybe.) And it was downright delicious when sipped while staring into the dreamy eyes of a visitor such as Zach, a player on the Sanderson soccer team who had been on the Saranac trip and had stopped by to see how I was.

"That must have been really scary," Zach said, sitting on my couch wearing sexy soccer shorts.

"Yeah, it was kind of scary, but, you know, I was lucky. I could have *died*." The day would eventually come when I would have to stop using that reference to death as a way of getting hearts to bleed. That day was not today.

"Wow," Zach responded, looking into my brave face.

"Yeah, it was crazy. But, so, tell me about Saranac! Do you want a Diet Shasta?"

Yes, diet soda had entered my daily life in a big way. Though my taste buds recoiled in horror at first, after being force-fed Diet Shastas in the hospital in Baltimore for a few days, and another week of them when I was moved down to my local hospital in Raleigh, my revulsion subsided. I got used to the fake taste, and I started liking—even craving—it. And it didn't take me long to place the limited choices available to me on a continuum running from "crisp and delicious" to "wholly, irrevocably unacceptable": Diet Coke? Sure, bring it on. Fresca? OK, that's pretty refreshing— it's right in the name! Diet Pepsi? If there's absolutely nothing else. Diet Rite? (Eye roll, stink-eye.) Tab? Fuck that bullshit.

Mom never bought us sodas when we were growing up—we were raised on sweet tea, naturally, because it was healthier—but after my diagnosis she started buying the *hell* out of some diet sodas. It was like she felt they were the one thing she could allow me to indulge in without sending my blood sugar levels into conniptions. And though these fizzy saccharine bombs were probably giving me cancer, I guess we just figured we'd cross that bridge when we came to it.

Plus, I needed something to take the edge off. Not only had my nontropical-but-still-sun-drenched vacation in upstate New York been thwarted and my doomed romantic hopes of seeing Brad's fuzzy navel also crushed, I was looking at spending my summer giving myself tutorials on the best places on my body to plunge a syringe into twice a day. Really, if I didn't deserve a diet cola and some sympathy, then who did?

So it came as a little bit of a surprise when my girlfriend Dawn, who by all rights should have been first aboard the Empathy Express, broke up with me while I was in the hospital. She didn't call, because that would have been too awkward. She sent a sympathy card, with a lengthy note of explanation written on loose-leaf paper, which basically boiled down to: *I'm, like, so messed up, and I met Roger the College Freshman, and I'm really sorry for your situation, but I've got to do what's right for me.*

This was just a terrible development. Not the breakup; sure, it was unfortunate, but our relationship was obviously going nowhere—well, you know, no place that Roger couldn't take her much more enthusiastically. What really galled me was that, in breaking up with me via Hallmark card, she didn't allow me the dramatic hospital room breakup scene that would have made the whole relationship worthwhile. You know, something like:

[Dawn enters Tim's hospital room from stage right, wearing sunglasses, a tiara, and that stupid jean jacket.]

Dawn: Tim, my sweet Tim. You look so weak. Have you lost weight?

Tim: Yes, Dawn. Probably a whole waist size.

Dawn: Oh, that's just wonderful.

Tim: Yes, I'm pretty thrilled.

Dawn: But Tim, your body is a wreck. It is immobile and powerless. How will you ever satisfy my needs?

Tim: Your needs? What do you mean? You're not making any sense. It's like you're speaking a foreign language. Can you get me some Nabs?

Dawn: I need a man, Tim. A man who can sweep me off my feet and paddleboat me around Shelley Lake.

Tim: But Dawn, I almost die—

Dawn: Shhh, Tim, don't speak. I just can't commit myself to a man whose pancreas is shooting blanks.

Tim: Dawnie! Friend, Roman, countryman. My pancreas is fine. It's just slowly dying is all.

Dawn: I need a man with a fully functioning endocrine system, you know that.

Tim: And I suppose Roger has one?

Dawn: Yes, he does. [gestures toward the door and beckons Roger in] Come in, Roger darling. It's OK. I've told him.

[Roger enters wearing aviator glasses, a leather jacket, and white tennis shorts.]

Roger: Hi, Tim. Sorry about your pancreas.

Dawn: Roger is a freshman at State, and he's currently taking care of his general college requirements before deciding on his major.

Roger: I took a lot of AP classes, so . . .

Tim: Wow. All that and a working pancre—

Dawn: And he drives a Trans-Am.

Tim: I'm getting my permit in October.

Dawn: Too late, Tim. Too late.

[Dawn and Roger slowly back out of the room, gazing into each other's sunglasses.]

Tim: But Dawn! What about my Nabs? And what about your brother?! Is he back from basic training yet?! Dawn! Tell him I said hi! . . .

[And scene.]

This was the closure I needed, and I was robbed of it. From my girlfriend I received no sympathy, not even a packet of cheese crackers with peanut butter in them. And I never saw her again. Since she went to a different school, there was no reason for me to. For all I know she and Roger robbed a bank and then paddleboated their way to the border. Which border? I guess I'll never know.

———

I'd had to digest a lot of information during that week at Rex Hospital in Raleigh—especially when, by all rights, I should have been sunning myself on an upstate New York lakeshore instead of lying in a hospital bed in Raleigh learning which of my fingers would deliver the best blood specimen. (The middle one.) Thankfully I had an excellent target for my scorn and teenage hatred during that hospital stay: my day nurse, Kimberly.

Kimberly was my very own Nurse Ratched. She could not care less that I was terribly unhappy and lonely and sexually frustrated and also scared and newly diabetic. Didn't give a *fuck*. She found me and my tedious emotions exceedingly boring.

I knew I hated her from the very first time I pressed the CALL NURSE button and she stormed in and said, "What do you want? I'm busy!" This was a woman who didn't let herself get too emotionally involved with her patients. Also, this was a woman who had a fuse as short as her unibrow was long.

One morning she brought me a packet of information spelling out the indignities I was going to be subjected to for the rest of my life, beyond just the pricking of the fingers and the injecting of the insulin. This packet spelled out the *lifestyle* changes. The dietary restrictions, the daily regimen of prickings followed by shots followed an hour later by eating, the reduction in salty and potatoey snacks, the regular visits to medical specialists, the need to maintain consistency every day in what I ate, what I did, and the insulin dosages I took so that I wouldn't throw my young but vulnerable body into a mad whirlpool of circulatory confusion.

Kimberly stood next to me as I flipped through the packet and its various papers, and she answered my quivery questions with the compassionate concern of a Venus flytrap.

At one point, I became overwhelmed with all the information coming at me, and I started tearing up. Yes, crying like a soft little girl. Kimberly sighed and handed me a tissue. As I wiped my eyes and tried to get my lip-wobbling under control I began to feel that maybe this would be our breakthrough moment. Her heart would be touched by my show of young fragility, she would take my hand, look into my eyes, and say, "Tim, it's going to be OK. You're going to get through it. And I'm going to help you."

Instead what I got was:

"Well, you're just going to have to get used to it. It's your life now. The sooner you suck it up and face that, the better off you'll be."

She did look me in the eyes, at least.

Even as I looked around for something to throw at her as she left, it occurred to me: Wow, I'm *really* getting on her nerves. And as much as I hated to have to say it: That raging hell bitch was right. Basically, there was no way around it: I have a disease, a disease that used to kill people just a few decades ago but that now folks are able to live with relatively healthily if they take care of themselves. I basically needed to buck up, learn what I needed to learn, and stop whining.

During the week I was at Rex I simultaneously loathed Kimberly and appreciated her honesty. Sure, she had an irritating tendency to roll her eyes and sigh whenever she entered my room, but she would kind of justify her existence at least once a day, like when she commented upon my stress eating by saying, "You know, just because your mom brought you three packets of Nabs this morning doesn't mean you have to eat every one." My response to this type of thing was usually just a silent dimming of my eyelids, because the lady spoke the truth.

"Hi, honey." Mom walked into the room just as Kimberly left one day. "Oh, hi, Kimberly! You've been so good to us, thank you so much." Mom's effusive courtesy toward Kimberly was really starting to become a problem. Kimberly nodded and replied, "Oh, you're welcome" in a singsongy voice, as if she were Julie freaking Andrews all of a sudden. She then contorted her mouth into the shape of a human smile, turned, and walked out.

"Here," Mom said, turning back to me. "I got you some sugar-free chocolate. They had some at the Diabetes Center."

She placed the chocolate bar on the tray next to my bed. *See, Tim?* I thought. *When God shuts a chocolate door he opens a sugar-free chocolate window.* I picked it up and opened the wrapper.

"It doesn't look too bad," Mom said. "But the lady at the store said you shouldn't have more than two squares at a time, otherwise it'll really mess up your stomach."

I settled for one square. It was gross.

———

"Timmy, I've come to the conclusion that I was wrong about the whole diabetes thing," Ruth the terrible prognosticator said as we sat on the deck in my backyard sucking glasses of Fresca over ice through straws. "In fact, I think you may actually have it. You know, *diabetes*."

I finished arranging my blood sugar testing kit on the table in front of us, jabbed my finger, got some blood, placed it on the test strip, and started the timer. "Yes, Ruth, you could be right," I replied. "I mean, who's to say, though, really? Doctors? Blood tests? Deadly, record-breaking blood-glucose levels? *Pfff.* I need *proof.*"

"Yes, well, it's pretty likely that it was more than just heat-stroke. I mean, the doctors have put you on insulin, and you're having to do all these blood tests all the time with the finger pricky things. Probably time to start considering the possibility that, you know, you may be diabetic after all."

Beep. Beep. Beeeeeeeep. This series of beeps signaled that it was time to wipe the test strip of the unsightly blood droplet and stick it into the machine so it could give me a reading after another dang minute.

"I'm really sorry for the error," Ruth continued. "It was very hot that day, and I obviously wasn't thinking clearly."

"Oh, don't worry about it. I mean, look on the bright side. Would we be sitting here in this beautiful weather having so much fun talking about me if you didn't feel horribly guilty?"

"That's a good point."

"There's a bright side to everything. Praise the Lord. So how was Saranac?"

Beeeeeep. The time was up, and the monitor had rendered its verdict: 134!

"Wow, Ruth, I've got an amazingly normal blood sugar for such a freak of nature. What say you we celebrate with some Nabs?"

The Nab—that exquisite marriage of peanut butter and inexplicably orange cracker—had become my favorite nibbly thing. It was the kind of snack that my doctor approved of because it contained carbs and protein, which would help keep my blood sugars stable during the first year when I'm figuring out the best dosages of insulin to give myself. Because the first year after a type 1 diabetes diagnosis was pretty much designated "the honeymoon period." And I was smack in the middle of it.

During the honeymoon period, a newly type 1 diabetic's pancreas is likely—albeit sporadically—still producing and secreting small amounts of insulin. Eventually, the pancreas will be completely "insulin deficient" (such a sad phrase), and the person will then be completely "insulin dependent" (also sad). So I was struggling to figure out the balance between enough insulin and too much.

I was on a regimen of two insulin shots a day. Those two shots, taken before breakfast and before dinner, each contained two types of insulin: regular, which would start to work in about an hour and would stay in my system for a few hours after that; and lente, which was a long-lasting insulin that didn't start for about five hours and would carry me through the day or the night. All of this insulin was harvested from other humans somehow. Gross, yes, but better than the previous alternative, pig insulin, which was just insulting.

Apparently the trick of dealing with this new, dreadful disease was maintaining a balance between diet, exercise, and insulin dosage. If this balance was not maintained there would be trouble. If, for example, I decided to just say "screw it" and eat Twinkies for breakfast every day and not compensate for all that sugar with a crazy exercise regimen or extra insulin, I would probably have to have a foot hacked off by the time I was thirty-five because of circulation problems resulting from chronic high blood sugar levels. On the other hand, if I was constantly careless and didn't eat enough to cover the insulin I'd given myself and the amount of physical activity I was regularly engaging in, I would have a low-sugar attack, stagger around zombie-like, do embarrassing things in public, and then collapse in a puddle of sweat and idiocy. The former was a more long-term concern; the latter, a daily danger.

I'd already had a few attacks in the middle of the night when my blood sugar went dangerously low and I started convulsing and seizing up. Professionals had to be called, and I still had a bruise on my swollen nose from slamming my face against the floor, which didn't make me look tough so much as it made me look like I slammed my face against the floor.

As a result of these early attacks, my number one biggest fear in the world changed from being caught by my mom jerking off in my room to an International Male catalog to finding myself alone somewhere (or in the middle of nowhere with a group of people) with a plummeting blood sugar level and no snacks to save the day. I would face this fear often in these early years because, you know, life is hard and there's a lot of things to remember and keep track of and sometimes you just forget to put the dang Snickers bar in your backpack and STOP JUDGING ME.

It was a frightful learning curve. I was worried about my ability to manage this disease, because science and math were my weakest subjects and who wants to spend all day reading dreary magazines like *Diabetes Forecast*? But there were moments when I felt I had control of the situation, however briefly. Like at that moment, as I sat with Ruth, on the deck in my backyard, basking in the summer sun, munching on Nabs: I was safe for the time being and in no danger of tweaking out. My blood sugar was normal, and I could drink in as much of Ruth's delicious sympathy as I wanted.

"It's sad that you couldn't go to Saranac," Ruth said. "But you did get a free week at the hospital. You shouldn't forget that."

"Yes," I agreed. "And lots of pretty flowers."

———

Brad came to visit a few times that summer. His visits meant a lot to me because obviously it was his sympathy that I wanted more than anyone's.

"How you feeling, buddy?" he asked the first time he came over after I was out of the hospital. "You look good!"

It felt amazing to hear that from his strong lips, even though I knew I looked like hell because I'd been holed up in a hospital bed for more than a week living on crackers, saccharine, and angst. When a handsome man tells you after you get out of the hospital that you look good, you don't argue.

"Ready to play?" he smiled.

Boy, was I. We had a tennis date, and I was ready to play. To bounce some balls. To volley. To go deep. To receive his backhand. To return his serve. And if there was a God, Brad would get too hot to keep his shirt on and would have to just tear it off with his bare hands and fling the hot 'n' soggy thing at my face, while biting his lip.

There was no God. Though it was a typically brutally hot North Carolina day in July, Brad showed no signs of even beginning to break a sweat. And I was, of course, the exact opposite, my shirt drenched and clinging to my gangly frame after a mere ten minutes.

After playing a full set I began to realize that I wasn't just wet from the heat. I seemed to be playing worse than normal during that last game. In fact, I couldn't remember successfully hitting the ball once. The last score I remembered hearing (did I say it?) was "forty–love." I bent forward and put my hands on the top of my knees to catch my breath.

"You OK, Tim?" Brad said with concern on his face, wiping the almost invisible dots of perspiration on his forehead.

"Yeeeeeaaah," I said very slowly. "Neeeeeed tooooo siiiiiiiit dooooooooooowwwwwn." I stumbled over to the grass and slumped down onto it, reaching into my pocket for the glucose tablets I'd brought for just such an emergency. Glucose tablets were horse-pill-sized edible sugar tablets that tasted like chalk but didn't melt, so they wouldn't turn to slop in my pocket. I pushed one of the tablets out of its container and started chomping as Brad came over and sat down on the grass beside me.

"Is it your sugar level?"

I nodded, finishing the first tablet and starting loudly on a new one. An insulin reaction brings out the ravenous beast in a person—it's not unlike the effect that marijuana has—a compulsion to eat powerful enough to make you combine foods that wouldn't normally go well together. I'd already experienced one in the middle of the night during which I dunked Oreos into a glass of orange juice and enjoyed the *hell* out of it.

"So does this happen often?"

"Na na tha mu js win I do too muts . . . stuff," I explained.

Brad nodded. "I was wondering if you were getting tired. You didn't seem able to, you know, hit the ball much that last game."

"Js, y'know, shə ga thn."

"Yeah. I guess we should have taken a break a while ago, huh. You know, Tim, God really had his hand on you that day in Baltimore."

I wanted to say, "I know, I could have died" but couldn't form the words.

"I'm so glad that we got to the hospital in time. My girlfriend is a nurse, and she said she can't believe your blood sugar was that high. She's heard of people dying when their blood sugar is, like, six hundred."

Stupid girlfriend.

"But you made it. That's just a miracle."

I liked where he was going with this.

Brad kept talking, about miracles and the grace of God, then about Saranac and the ropes course and the parasailing and the singing and the testimonies and the sunny weather and the swimming and all of the etcetera. I was doing my best to listen, but I was zoned out, still ravenous, and waiting for the sugar I'd ingested to start doing its work. In the interim I was a pretty useless conversation partner. I tried to stay focused by staring at Brad's hairy, muscular thigh. I really wanted to pour some powdered sugar on it and lick it.

". . . and I think the Sanderson gang had a good time. We all missed you, though."

Brad and I sat for a little while on the grass. I slowly came back to myself and realized where I was and what had happened. As would always happen when I came to after an insulin spell, I felt a great, overwhelming embarrassment. I hoped I hadn't said anything inappropriate out loud, like that I wanted to eat his hairy, muscular thighs.

"God, I'm sorry, Brad, that was so weird."

"That's all right, man. No problem. I think your body's still getting used to being diabetic."

"Yeah."

We stood up and walked back to his car. I was so tired from the adrenaline that had surged through my body during the reaction that I felt like I was navigating through a strong ocean current.

"Do you mind if I lie down in the back, Brad? I still feel kinda weird."

"Sure, that's fine. You do what you need to do."

I opened the passenger door of his compact car, flipped the seat forward, and wriggled into the backseat. Brad sat in the driver's seat and turned on the engine. The vinyl of the backseat was hot from the sun, and it felt nice on my face. I could see the back of Brad's head, the tufts of his dark hair.

As I lay there, I tried to remember anything from the conversation we had while we were sitting on the grass. I could just recall snatches of stories about Saranac. Then I fell asleep for the rest of the drive home. Pretty sure I dreamt about tennis balls and tufts of soft hair.

———

Mom decided I should go to a diabetes summer day camp for a week. This did not appeal to me. What on earth was there to do *all week* at a camp for diabetic teenagers? Sure, there would probably be diabetes instructional videos and activities, some diabetes nutrition workshops, and a few panel discussions on the best diabetes paraphernalia to have in the house. But what were we going to do the rest of the time? Would there be some diabetes-related arts and crafts?

"What's this clay sculpture you've made, Tim?"

"It's my dead pancreas. His name is Fran."

Perhaps a diabetes fashion show.

"Christine is wearing a peach fleece hoodie from L.L.Bean. It's a cotton/polyester blend and has three sleeves—two for her arms and one special one sewn into the back to hold all the diabetes stuff she has to cart around with her all day, every day, forever. Dazzling!"

Or a diabetes open-mike comedy jam.

"So I was goin' down on this fat diabetic midget, and . . ."

"Oliver, off the stage!"

I couldn't imagine what I was going to get out of this camp that I couldn't get by just staying at home reading the stupid packets the hospital had given me and feeling sorry for myself.

"You're going," Mom said in the tone of voice she uses when she's not going to take any more bullshit whining from you.

The first indication that something was not quite right on the first day was when Mom and I entered the building to check in and saw that the room was full of kids who were at least five years younger than me. The second indication was when we found out from one of the camp directors that Mom had mistakenly signed me up for the wrong camp. This one was for diabetic kids aged six to ten. This was great news because there were several boxes of Nabs in the cupboard and a six-pack of Fresca in the fridge at home, and if we hurried we could make it in time to watch *The Love Boat* reruns they play on TBS before the soaps start.

"Oh, I'm so sorry, I didn't realize that!" Mom said to the director. "Can he still participate? He's really been looking forward to it, and he was just diagnosed a few weeks ago!" Mom was clearly playing hardball. I rolled my eyes and sauntered away, slumping into a chair at a table in the corner, watching six-year-olds chase each other around the room screaming and laughing, blissful in their ignorance of how complicated life gets when you're midway through the first set of double digits.

Mom came and sat down, letting her purse slide down her arm and land on the tabletop.

"They said it's fine for you to stay, so I'm just going to leave you to it," she said. I rolled my eyes again, and when I was finished rolling them I pointed them at her. She met my gaze, and I looked away, sighing again and sucking my teeth. The director clapped her hands to call everyone to attention. I couldn't believe I was having to spend my day with these kids. I was Molly Ringwald in *The Breakfast Club.*

"Excuse me, sir? I think there's been a mistake. I know it's Diabetes Day Camp, but I don't think I belong in here."

Mom was quiet. I looked over at her a few moments later and saw that she was crying. Now, that is something I have never been able to take, Mom crying. There's no worse sight that a son's behavior can bring about. It hit me in the gut, and I immediately felt like an ass.

"Mom," I whispered, trying to be discreet lest we draw the attention of all the elementary school imps in our midst. "It's OK, really. It's fine."

"I'm just trying so hard, Tim," she sobbed. Yes, she was sobbing now. "I thought this would be good for you and that you'd enjoy yourself. I didn't know that . . . this." At "this" she looked over at the gaggle of young hobgoblins, one of whom was picking his nose and wiping his finger on the rim of his glasses.

"Mom, really, I'll stay. It's fine. I'm sorry. I just, you know, was hoping there'd be some kids here my age." Like the platonic ideal of the clueless teenager, I was only now realizing that it wasn't just me who had gone through an upheaval in recent weeks. Mom had also been shaken to her core by the experience of having her youngest child so close to death (I almost died!), and she was struggling to adjust to the new reality of what this disease meant for me and for her. And I wasn't helping things by being such an asshole. What would Nurse Kimberly say if she saw me now? Something inappropriate and mean, but also something with a real underlying truth to it, buried deep beneath its sneering contempt. Something like "So I see you've made your mother cry again. What happened, did she find out about your crush on Kevin the serial killer on *General Hospital?*"

"I know," Mom said, still blubbering a little, wiping her tears and her nose with a tissue she grabbed from her purse.

"Just go on home, Mom. I should probably go join everyone else."

So Mom stood up and prepared to leave. She probably wanted to give me a hug good-bye, but I was still a fifteen-year-old in a public space, so that wasn't going to happen.

"I'll see you at four," she said, and she walked out. I nodded and walked over to join the others. There were about twenty kids total, and they were sitting at tables with their blood glucose testing equipment and their glucose diaries out and ready to be filled in with their mid-morning blood sugar levels. I sat down at the end of one of the tables, flopped my diabetes case onto the table, and retrieved from it my glucometer, finger pricker, and diary.

"Hi," a little girl with thick glasses sitting next to me said.

"Hi," I said. "What's your name?"

"Amanda. I'm eight. How many shots a day do *you* take?"

"Two. How about you?"

"Eh, I take four, sometimes five. Depends."

I nodded my head. "Wow. That's a lot."

"Yeah, but I'm used to it. I give them to myself."

There's nothing like being shamed by an eight-year-old girl into feeling like you're making out pretty well, all things considered.

Kimberly would have said as much, if in slightly less polite terminology and while also suggesting I was probably too old to be hanging out with such young children.

Amanda pushed the button on her finger pricker and sprung it into action against her index finger. The blood specimen she squeezed out was judged too paltry, so she cocked the pricker again and chose a different finger, not missing a beat.

Inspired, I picked up my pricker, placed a new lancet in the chamber, and placed it against my middle digit. Then, in communion with twenty six- to ten-year-olds, I proceeded to stab myself in the finger with a souped-up thumbtack and squeeze out some blood as a sacrifice to the God of Diseases You Can Live With.

The boy is making pancakes. They smell great, all buttery. He's getting ready to test out his new sugar-free pancake syrup, so it's an exciting morning for him. He's also frying up some bacon, because why not?

His older brother is in the living room reading the newspaper. He just stopped by to get some food because he's in college and doesn't have any of his own. There's no one else home.

The boy has just flipped over the three pancakes in the pan and is now flattening them with the spatula. He's pretty hungry, hasn't eaten yet this morning, though he's taken a few chomps of bacon here and there. He's been holding back, though, because he wants to wait and eat everything at once, on one big plate. He took his insulin shot about an hour ago so his body should be ready to receive.

It's kind of hot in the kitchen, he starts thinking. He turns on the fan above the stove to disperse some of the smoke rising from the pan of bacon. He wipes some sweat from his brow and his cheek and his nose, then saunters into the hall bathroom to do something. Let's follow him in there.

He turns on the shower. That was unexpected. Now he's gone over to the sink and is looking at himself in the mirror. Strange, but he doesn't seem to actually see *himself. He just stares blankly, as if he's looking at the wallpaper in the reflection behind him. He goes back out to the kitchen, returns to his skillets, and flips the pancakes and the bacon again.*

He's really sweating now, so he backs away from the stove, bumping into the kitchen table. He ungracefully moves around it with his hands on the tabletop and sits down in the first chair he comes to. It's a good call on his part, stepping away from the heat of that stove, but it probably would have been a good idea for him to turn that burner off before adjourning to a seat. He's sitting now with his sweaty head in his clammy hands, while just a few feet away, pancakes and bacon are starting to burn. Damn, and those pancakes were just about perfect a minute ago, golden brown and ready for more butter and then some syrup. And the bacon was nearly done, too; crispy but not too crispy. But now it appears both are quickly passing through the threshold separating "delightfully edible" from "carcinogenic." Smoke is rising from the pans more and more furiously, and oh, shit, where'd he go?

He's back in the bathroom. He's turned off the shower and is now just sitting on the toilet with the seat down. Steam from the shower has filled the room, so he's a little hard to see now. OK, his head is in his hands, but now instead of resting in them it's kind of bobbing around on them like a buoy on the surface of a lake after a motorboat drives past it.

"Tim! Tim?"

His brother is calling him. The brother's just caught a whiff of that burned pancake smell. He gets up and walks over to the kitchen, where a smoke monster is throwing a tantrum on the stove. He turns off the burners, and looks around for the boy, who was just here a minute ago, humming to himself and getting his breakfast ready.

The brother walks down the hallway and stops at the doorway to the bathroom, seeing the boy and his bobbing head.

"Tim! What's going on?"

The boy whips his head up as if his power switch has just been turned on. He turns and looks at his brother. He's just realized something: He's absolutely starving and is really really REALLY craving something sweet. Needs something sweet. If he doesn't get something sweet right now he will absolutely die of disappointment (and a seizure). Crunch Berries? *he thinks.* Do we have Crunch Berries?

The boy stands up and walks straight past his brother and back into the kitchen, where delicious pancakes and mouthwatering bacon go to die. He throws open the cupboard to see what cereals are on offer. His movements are overdone, like he's not fully in control of his limbs and so is approximating the correct gestures. Sadly, there aren't any Crunch Berries, but there are some Oh's, so he pulls the box out, tears it open, grabs a bowl and spoon from a drawer, lifts the milk jug out of the refrigerator, and sits down. His brother stands off to the side, watching him do his weird Kabuki with anthropological interest. It's like a monkey playing Ping-Pong: kind of human, kind of not.

The boy has quickly prepared his cereal and is chomping down on those Oh's like he has not eaten in weeks. It's delicious. But wait a minute. Something is weird. It tastes good, but it also tastes weird. Mmm, *he thinks,* this cereal is good! But it's weird.

The boy looks at the gallon of milk on the table. It's some weird-looking milk. He squints at it. Oh, OK, see there? That's why that milk looks weird. It's a gallon of water.

He looks down at his bowl of cereal. The Oh's are still piled high in the bowl even though he's had several mouthfuls. He digs his spoon in and chomps down on a few more. The pile of Oh's is going down now, and the boy is starting to see the cloudy H_2O peeking through the gaps in his cereal.

Water? Is that water? *the boy is clearly thinking.*

His brother sits down next to him as he finishes the bowl of Oh's. "Are you all right, man?"

The boy is chomping and isn't able to answer yet. He'll need a few more minutes before he's communicado.

In the meantime, he'll just keep eating. He refills his bowl, then takes the gallon of water and pours more of it onto his cereal.

Because it was weird, but it was kind of good.

CHAPTER 3

THE BOY WITH THE THORN IN HIS SIDE

I was lying on my back on our carpeted staircase, my feet up the stairs from me and my head on the bottom step, listening to the music coming out of my sister's first-floor bedroom. The room had French doors made out of plywood left over from a renovation job we'd done in the living room, and they didn't fit together all that well. Hollow and flimsy, they would do absolutely nothing to save you from, say, Jack Nicholson in *The Shining*—in fact, they'd surrender quite willingly—but this meant that they formed a negligible barrier between me and the New Wave stylings of whatever fey and sexually ambiguous band was coming out of her speakers at any given moment.

Two years older than me, Laurie was a full-fledged New Wave chick, a tall, thin waif with effortless style and long, naturally curly blonde hair; a thrift-store maverick who wasn't afraid to go to school wearing a tuxedo shirt, a paisley vest, a calfskin miniskirt, pinstriped purple tights, and monkey boots. Or just a black cotton dress and no makeup. I longed for that kind of bravery. I'd never been able to really dress myself properly, and when I was gearing up to go to high school the year before, Laurie had taken it upon herself to attempt a makeover of her sloppy younger brother.

Part of this involved convincing me to grow my hair out a little bit and get some wingtips, button-up shirts, and tasteful vests, as well as introducing me to the world of what she called "progressive" music. She got my feet wet with gateway bands, like REM and The Cure, and I was a little slow on the uptake. I'd spent my entire life listening to Top 40 and John Williams movie soundtracks, and had recently, of course, been on a Christian rock kick. Laurie was up against years and years of my devotion to Cyndi Lauper and Madonna and Exposé and The Pointer Sisters and Juice Newton. Those ladies wouldn't go without a fight.

Laurie had one tool in her toolbox she wasn't even aware of, though—her boyfriend Brian, who was a freshman at UNC–Chapel Hill with an awesome coif and a smashing wardrobe. He had the appearance of an MTV-ready New Romantic, and if he wasn't wearing a skinny tie, he always looked like he should be. I coveted his black cardigan and his houndstooth slacks. He'd recently made Laurie a few mixtapes that he had titled "Numerous Dandy Tunes" and "Even More Dandy Tunes," and these tapes were constantly on her stereo system. Even though she'd made me my own copies, whenever the hollow-cheeked echo of the mixtapes reached me up in my room, I went out to the top of the stairs and listened, falling hard for the majesty that was Love and Rockets, The Smiths, The Mighty Lemon Drops, Echo and the Bunnymen, New Order, The Psychedelic Furs, XTC, The Icicle Works, The Cult, The Jesus and Mary Chain, and Modern English.

Though I'd been passively listening to her music for a year or so, it was only that summer that those mixtapes really made an impact on me. They also made me realize that there was a Morrissey-shaped hole in my life that I had been futilely trying to fill with Michael W. Smith. Best known for his anthem to chaste Christian love, "Friends," Smith also had a slew of fun Christian-themed electro pop songs and kind of looked like New Wave Jesus. It had long been my firm belief—and if not a firm belief, then a powerful fantasy—that if there was a man in the world who would ride into my life on the back of a white horse and carry me away to his castle, he would be carrying around his neck a Casio CZ-1000 keyboard and playing the synth line from "Cars" by Gary Numan. Michael W. Smith had lots of Casios, I was sure. Also, he could read me Bible verses while we made out, which might help neutralize the damnation that awaited us later on.

Behind Laurie's closed doors, Morrissey crooned something about me not having earned it yet, baby.

Oh, I thought. *I must suffer and cry for a longer time? Yep, sounds about right.* It was the first Smiths song I'd ever heard, and it forever altered the things I would demand from my music. How on earth could Michael W. Smith's Christian bromides possibly compete with the hard truths of "Shoplifters of the World Unite"? Morrissey's palpable, comic bitterness made me wonder if he had recently been cruelly diagnosed with type 1 diabetes as punishment for having dirty fantasies about hot gay surfer orgies. Because it felt as if he were singing directly at me, knowingly pointing his index finger at my troubled face, barely able to hold his hand up with his limp gay wrist. I hadn't earned it yet, baby, and he knew because *he* hadn't earned it yet, either, baby.

As Morrissey continued over-enunciating his Portrait of the Artist as a Gangly and Unlovable Freak who must stay on his own for slightly longer, I continued to lie there, upside down on the stairs, nodding my head to the beat. This charming man certainly didn't have all the answers, but he did ask better questions. Like "What Difference Does It Make?" and "Is It Really So Strange?" and "How Soon Is Now?" As the blood rushing into my head threatened to start seeping out of my nostrils, I wondered to myself, "How soon *is* now?"

But Brian's mix wasn't all bleak: The next song on the tape was pretty much the antidote to Morrissey's dreary "life's a bitch and then you cry" sob story. It was Sinéad O'Connor's "Mandinka," and its message to me basically boiled down to "Fuck all y'all, I ain't sorry."

Atop a driving drum beat and a snarling guitar lick, Sinéad screeched into her no-doubt-petrified microphone about not feeling no shame and not feeling no pain, visiting several octaves in the process. This pale, bald woman was sure pissed about something, and it sounded marvelous. Who was this Mandinka guy, and what did he do to this woman? Or maybe Sinéad has also been cruelly diagnosed with type 1 diabetes after having fantasies of hot gay surfer orgies? Hers was a Catholic God, after all, and That Guy sure knew how to instill the guilt. But Sinéad was having none of it.

In any case, I envied Sinéad's ability to emote artfully, and longed to be like her—unapologetic, ferocious, and able to flaw-lessly pull off a shaved head. Sadly, my head was not the right shape for any of that, and I was also a weak, self-pitying moppet, so ever since Baltimore I'd been languishing indoors, slouching from room to room staring at walls, looking with bitterness at the refrigerator that housed my insulin vials and the sweet tea that I could no longer drink, and sitting in the living room watching TV, getting ever so slightly turned on by the dude who hosted the *Bodies in Motion* exercise show on ESPN.

Or lying upside down on the stairs listening to the jams explod-ing out of Laurie's speakers, playing air keyboard, and waiting for my knight with a shiny Casio to come riding in and play me some-thing I could dance to.

━━━

The summer had turned into a major fiasco. It had started with the promise of sun, sailing, and soapy showers with boys: It was stiff, locked, and loaded. Ready for takeoff. Fit to burst. Pulsating. The beginning of summer 1988 was a throbbing teenage hard-on, is what I'm saying.

And here I was just two short months later, limping toward the end of August, battered and bewildered, and facing the specter of another year of school without having done anything of note over the summer besides acquiring an awesome new disease and a hilariously callous break-up letter from my girlfriend.

The point is, I was due for a little tantrum. Kimberly the nurse would have disagreed, saying something along the lines of "You know, Tim, it may seem right now like the weight of the world is on your shoulders and that there's no light at the end of the tunnel and that God is punishing you for something and that you are all alone in the world, but you know what? It is, there isn't, he is, and you are." But Kimberly had no idea that she was talking to a grade-A top-shelf drama queen, and that I didn't *care* that she didn't care, I was ready to hurl a coffee mug on the floor, break it, and then feel stupid and toss it in the garbage can before anyone saw what dumb thing I'd just done.

Mom and Dad could see that I was having trouble adjusting to my new diabetic lifestyle. For one thing, I was rolling my eyes and doing that annoying teeth-sucking thing in response to things they said, more than usual. One night they were out on the deck in the backyard, sitting on the patio swing in the pitch-black darkness because the deck light had burned out, and they called me out to talk to me.

"Tim," Mom began, "you've really got to get a handle on yourself. You're just staying inside watching television all the time. I know you're upset about Dawn . . ."

Upset about who? Oh yeah, Dawn, my now ex-girlfriend, who would have broken up with me via text message if the technology had existed. Yeah, I guess I was supposed to be upset about that whole thing. But somehow I wasn't really.

"But we're worried that you're just spending too much time alone, at home. You should be out more. School's coming up. I know you've been through a lot with your diabetes, but we feel like you are not adjusting as well as you should."

At that, I rolled my eyes.

"Tim, don't roll your eyes at us," Dad admonished, without missing a beat.

How he could have known I rolled my eyes is beyond me, since it was as dark as the dickens out there. But he knew. God, not only was I irritating, I was also predictable. How is a snotty teenager supposed to respond to being called out like that? If I'd been more like Sinéad, I would have raised up my hand, looked pensively at the floor, and said something like "Don't know no shame, don't feel no pain." Except maybe when I prick my finger in the same place twice in a row. Otherwise I'm a strong, proud, bald Irish woman.

But really I was just a delicate little mini-Morrissey wannabe, with a twee little chip on my shoulder and a full head of lustrous hair. If I could have verbalized what was in my head, I would probably only have been able to quote Morrissey lyrics, because I was no poet and I sure did know that thing.

"I've seen this happen in other people's lives, and now it's happening in mine." Something along those lines.

But Mom and Dad, like most other humans, wouldn't have understood any of these non sequiturs, because what on earth did they have to do with my diabetes diagnosis or my breakup? And besides, Mom might say, there are plenty of other girls out there besides Dawn. There's plenty of time to find love. And Mom would have a point. There *were* plenty of girls out there. Plenty. Lots. Way too many, in fact.

Anyway, it was decided that Mom, Dad, and I would go on an outing to Kerr Lake the next day. Dad would take the day off from work, and we'd go waterskiing in our new used motorboat, which we kept parked at Presbyterian Point, a campground on the lake near the North Carolina–Virginia border that was owned by our church. It wasn't nude parasailing at Saranac Lake with Brad, but at least I could pretend I was one of The Go-Go's in the "Vacation" video as I skied around the lake behind a boat pulled by my dad and in the back of which my mom sat enthusiastically waving at me. Surely that was the next best thing.

On the drive up to Presbyterian Point, I was able to force my parents to listen to the "Dandy Tunes" collections. We had just crossed the Virginia border and were midway through the first tape when I found myself wanting to hear something more visceral, more tied up in knots, more offensive to my parents. I got Sinéad's *The Lion and the Cobra* out of my plastic bag of cassettes. On this album, old baldy was unhinged, raw, crazy, possessive, horny, schizophrenic, and pissed, much like myself. She beautifully verbalized and gave voice to the bilious stuff swirling around in my head and stomach. Mom and Dad would take one listen to the songs on this album and realize the pain I was in.

By the third song, "Jerusalem," Mom had made up her mind about the quality of the music coming out of our Chevy Corsica's speakers.

"Tim, she's just *screaming*. This is terrible."

"What?" I said, turning the volume up.

"How can you enjoy something like this?" But Mom's screaming was drowned out by Sinéad as she spat something about next time being the last time and you better not two-time if you want the best time 'cause there ain't gonna be a next time.

I dimmed my eyelids and looked at my mom as if to say, "Whatever can I add to that?"

We got to Presbyterian Point, lugged the boat to the water, and sputtered out into the middle of the lake. It took me a while to hit my stride on the skis. The first five or ten times I either fell forward, fell sideways, fell backward, or lost a ski as I attempted to rise like a phoenix out of the water. I was exhausted by the time I managed to stand upright and make a single swing around the lake. Naturally, I fell while attempting a Belinda Carlisle wave in the direction of the imaginary camera off in the distance. It seemed like a good time to take a break.

I flopped into the boat, breathing heavily.

"You should probably test your blood sugar," Mom said, looking into her day-bag to fish out my black diabetes case.

I snarled like Billy Idol and prepared to let out a rebel yell. I was not in a blood sugar testing mood.

"Oh, I'll do that a little later, I just want to relax right now," I said, putting on my sunglasses and lying back on the cushioned row of seats in the back of the tiny boat. I watched out of the corner of my eye as Mom, wearing her blue visor with the message TODAY IS THE DAY THAT THE LORD HATH MADE stitched into it, looked back at me, disgruntled. She sat holding the black case, concerned but not wanting to push it, since I was being such a petulant imp these days and it sure didn't take much to set me off.

I continued sunning myself, but because I'm such a pushover and could see through my sunglasses that Mom was still holding the black case in her hands a few minutes later as she stared off into space, I sat up slowly and, with the requisite huff, held out my hand and waited for her to deposit the diabetes equipment into my palm.

I unzipped the case and got out the glucometer, placing it precariously on my knee. God, I hated this thing. With its smug, know-it-all digital display and its oversized buttons and its beeping. The way it existed to bring me irritating news about how I've been failing in my diabetes regimen. And the way it had to be coaxed into giving me the information I needed from it—not only did this bloodthirsty glucose robot insist that I stab myself in the finger to get a specimen, it also demanded that I feed it with a large enough blood droplet to satisfy it, which meant milking my finger for blood as if it were a cow's teat, which it most assuredly was not. Then I had to maneuver my blood onto the test strip, press the timer on the meter, and wait for a minute before being prompted by three beeps to blot the strip and stick it into the meter so it could be read after another minute. Sometimes after all that the meter would not even give me a number, it would just say ERR, meaning "error," which translated to "You've done something wrong, you idiot, try again." And I'd have to start over.

Mom hovered over me like a parole officer. She was not doing this to be a scold. She was concerned. She was curious. She wanted to make sure I was not about to die again. But I didn't appreciate any of this at the time. I just wanted to be alone with my glucometer, do my business, and put the damn thing back in the case without making a big production out of it. But there Mom was, leaning forward to get a better view of the big production.

I took a stupid alcohol swab out of the damned case and then took a dumb-ass test strip out of the infernal container and cocked the shitty lancing device and looked at my frigging fingers to decide which of my dumb digits would get the jab. The index finger on my left hand wasn't too scabby from pricking, so index finger it was. I massaged the finger for a minute—milking it, as it were—then swabbed it with the alcohol wipe. I waved the finger around to dry it, then pressed the lancing device against the pulsating finger, and pressed the trigger.

Boing!

"Ow, fuck!" I said, shaking my finger furiously and sprinkling blood droplets onto my face. The lancet felt like it had hit bone, though my finger was probably just raw from all the recent pricks it had been enduring as the nipple of choice.

I looked at Mom and realized I had just said the f-word out loud.

"Uh, sorry. That really hurt," I said, wiping the blood off my forehead. Mom remained silent.

If Kimberly the nurse had been on that motorboat, she would have narrowed her eyes and said, "Man up, Nancy," then slapped me with a rubber flipper, because she would have just had one handy.

Thankfully, I had enough blood still oozing out of my finger even after losing some of it to my face, so I was able to squeeze out a healthy droplet, lift my finger up and over, and place the droplet onto the dual-tiled strip. I touched the button on the glucometer to start the timer, and sat back and held the strip in my fingers as the digits on the screen counted down.

"Is your finger OK?" Mom asked, still registering disappointment on her face over my f-word slip.

"Yeah, it's just sore 'cause I use that one a lot," I said, trying to segue into Reasonable Tim mode, knowing full well that I'd been swimming in incredibly bratty waters for the better part of the day.

Beep. Beep. Beeeeeeeep.

I dabbed the strip, wiping it clean of blood, and inserted it into the glucometer for final judgment, which would arrive after a minute-long intermission.

"Thanks for bringing me here today," I said, looking guiltily down at the floor of the boat.

"Well, we're glad we could all be together," Mom said. Translation: "You're welcome, now stop your cussin', and can you please quit pouting like a little bitch?"

"Yeah," I said.

Beeeeeeeep.

It was time to read the verdict. Mom leaned forward.

God, please don't let it be in the 200s, God, please don't let it be in the 200s, I kept thinking, my eyes closed. I *really* want a snack.

I opened my eyes and calmly gazed toward the digital display on my lap.

ERR, it said. Error.

This is when things started happening in slow motion. When I saw that message staring me in the face, my eyeballs filled with flames, and smoke shot out of both of my ears. My eyeballs bulged, threatening to pop out of their sockets, my head twitched, my throat tightened, and my hands seized up as I received signals from the devilish voices in my head to *Kill. That. Glucometer. Kill it.*

With a Grendel-like growl, I picked the glucometer up in a slow and drawn-out fashion, and threw it down on the floor of the boat.

This act of devastating violence and sabotage took about five minutes to play out in my head. In Mom's and Dad's, it took about five seconds, I'm pretty sure.

"Tim!" Mom said, crouching down to grab the machine.

"Tim, what are you doing?" Dad said, whipping around from his perch at the steering wheel. "What happened?"

I sat back against the cushioned seats, staring at the floor. Mom picked up the glucometer, which was, amazingly, still in one piece. Because even when I'm having a monstrous fit, I still can't break a piece of equipment about as indestructible as a TV remote.

Mom pressed the power button on the machine. "Well, it turns on," she said.

She handed it to me, and I looked it over. The display, once a perfect rectangle with a pristine gray screen and digits formed by sharp, blade-like strokes, was now warped. A plastic piece inside was now bending upward into the screen, clouding the digital display. But it still worked.

Dammit.

So I went through the bloody ritual once more, swabbing a fingertip, jabbing myself, squeezing the blood out, placing it on the strip, waiting, blotting, inserting the strip, waiting, hoping, praying.

ERR.

I rolled my eyes. Then I looked quickly over at Dad to make sure he hadn't seen me do that.

"It says 'error' again," I said.

Mom looked at me and then at the glucometer.

"Well, I guess we'll have to take it in to the Diabetes Center and get a new one," she said. She shot me a look that conveyed in no uncertain terms that she was embarrassed for me.

"I'd better eat something, just in case," I said, avoiding her gaze and tearing open a packet of Nabs.

"You ready, honey?" Dad asked.

"Oh yeah," Mom said, putting on her life vest. It was her turn for a wipeout in the water. Dad revved up the boat engine again, and Mom jumped in.

Dad put the boat in gear, and we blasted off. After a few moments, Mom rose triumphantly out of the water, effortlessly gliding upon the surface like an only slightly drunk Rockette. We went around the lake, and she remained regally upright, sprays of water shooting up all around her like she was some Busby Berkeley water dancer. I excitedly waved to her. She waved back, then lost her grip on the rope handle, and sank into the wake left by our boat.

———

Debbie, the lady at the Diabetes Center, sat down with me in the back of the shop to give me a little pep talk.

"Here you go," she said, handing me a new glucometer. "It's got a new battery in it already, so you don't need to worry about that."

"Thanks a lot." I wondered if Mom had had to pay for this one. She was browsing in the front of the shop.

"Yeah, hopefully this one will last for you. I know that these things can get frustrating sometimes, especially when you're new to the whole thing."

I thought Mom and I had agreed that we wouldn't tell the good people at the Diabetes Center that I'd had a major freakout and hurled my defenseless glucometer onto the floor of a motorboat in hopes of shattering it into a million pieces, managing only to warp it a little. But it seemed like Debbie, though she wasn't saying it outright, knew the truth.

"You know, one of these days," she continued, "maybe they'll come out with a way of testing your levels by just, I don't know, licking a test strip and waving it in the air."

"That will be a great day," I said.

"Yeah. But, you know, for now, just try to be careful with this one. OK?" She smiled.

I nodded, chastened.

"Great! Well, you look like you're doing great, and you and your mom should definitely call us if you have any problems with this one or if you just have some questions. Oh! And here, have a bar of this new sugar-free chocolate we got in." She handed me a sample.

"Thanks," I said, feeling I'd seen this particular candy before.

"It's pretty good, better than most sugar-free stuff, I think," she said. "Just make sure you don't eat more than two squares in one sitting. It'll give you pretty bad diarrhea."

The young man is lying on his bed in the dark with his black light on, staring up at the brand-new Sinéad O'Connor poster hanging above his bed on the wall. It's . . . interesting. It features the singer's pale bald head in immense close-up, glowing like a supernova. She's staring off to the side and upward, and she looks like a giant showroom dummy with a major chip on its shoulder. The young man thinks she looks tough, probably because she could easily kick his ass, but a Cabbage Patch doll could easily kick his ass, so he's not the best judge of what's tough, let's face it.

God, that bald amphibian head is bright. How can he even look directly at it without burning his retinas and singeing his feminine lashes? But he just lies there, eyes wide open, recklessly drinking in the glowing white light, waiting to go blind.

He's a little spooked right now, having just watched Fatal Attraction *on video with his sister. Though he would never ever advocate sneaking into someone's house and boiling their pet bunny in a pot, he couldn't help but admire Glenn Close's spunk and stick-to-it-iveness. But he found himself unable to sleep afterward because Glenn Close was also terrifying.*

So because he couldn't get out of his head the image of Glenn losing her shit, he'd reached over and turned on his black light, igniting the ghoulish bald head that now glowed in front of him. For some reason he finds it soothing.

— His eyes are glazed over, his mind a kaleidoscope of unrelated images, the kind of manic slide show you experience in dreams when you pass out and your brain is just too tired to even bother with a storyline. But he's awake, wide-awake and drunk on images floating

in front of his face, images of Fruit Roll-Ups, eternity, Brazilian soccer player Pelé, robots, deep space, beach parties, Marlon Brando, gravity, and chopsticks. What ties all of these things together? That's right: mystery. They're all mysteries wrapped up in plastic enigma bags. Or maybe nothing ties them all together, who knows?

He's sweating mightily. He's sitting up now and clumsily getting to his feet. He's standing up on the bed, stepping forward toward the poster, and is now head-to-head with Sinéad. He presses his face up against hers, moving it from side to side against her giant paper cranium. It's a true meeting of the minds. It's also a useful way for him to rid his face of all the sweat, his primary objective.

The poster is damp now. The young man is blotching up Sinéad's giant pristine alabaster pate with his sweaty teenage face. But that's a lot of sweat, even for a fifteen-year-old. Yeah, he's having another one of his cute little attacks that take him forever to realize he's having. Let's watch.

He backs away from the poster and stares at it. Ah, he's noticed the blotches. He reaches out his fingers and runs them over the damp parts, which are now softening up and wrinkling a little. He tilts his head as if to say, "Did I do that?"

He's struggling to remain standing. Yep, knees are going all wobbly. He manages to lean down, grasp the headboard of his bed, and shakily lower himself down, accidentally sitting Indian style on his pillow briefly before falling backward onto his twisted-up sheets. He enjoys the softness against his rubbery skin only fleetingly before tumbling from the bed onto the floor. That smarts. Looks like he landed on his Walkman.

He rolls around trying to figure out which way is up for a few moments, which is just adorable. Finally he picks himself up and leans against his bed, trying to figure out his next move. Should he start picking at his hangnails? Should he stand up and stare at himself in the mirror for a while, enjoying the way his braces shimmer under the black light? Should he pass out?

Looks like he's becoming self-aware, like all great androids. He wipes his sweaty brow with his clammy hand, an action that drives home the point that he is a sebaceous mess and needs sugar now.

His eyes flicker with a realization: He has some glucose tablets in the bedside drawer. He opens the top drawer and fishes them out, rummaging through papers and magazines and Kleenex and years of Soap Opera Digest*s. Does he never throw* anything *away?*

Finally he arrives at the box of tablets. He struggles to open it up with his wet hands, and eventually just grabs the end of the box and tears a portion of it off, like the Incredible Hulk would if he were a frail, skinny, white teenage homosexualist with diabetes and few working synapses. The box spills its contents, and the boy tears into the packaging, determined to put something, anything in his mouth pronto. He finally frees a tablet and clumsily shuffles it into his mouth.

His teeth crunch, pop, and grind against the giant tablet.

He quickly devours the first one and tears another one out of its aluminum cage. Crunch. Pop. Grind. Sigh. Wiping of the brow.

The boy eats the entire box of chalky tablets, leaning back against his dresser, staring up at the beacon of hope that is the glowing head of the hairless woman on his wall. Does she stare down at him benevolently and tell him he will be OK, that one day sugar-free candy won't make him have to vomit and shit at the same time, and that his destiny is not necessarily the piping hot punishment of eternal damnation just because he'd rather tongue-kiss Scott Baio than do just about anything else ever?

No, she doesn't. But with all of the adrenaline coursing through his system right now, he's hearing what he wants to hear.

CHAPTER 4
GETTING AWAY WITH IT

I stood in my bedroom looking into the mirror and admiring the new piece of jewelry hanging from my neck. Well, "jewelry" might be too strong a word. It was certainly a necklace. But you wouldn't find yourself surprising your girlfriend or boyfriend with it and a box of chocolates on Valentine's Day, unless you were being really ironic.

What I was so prominently displaying on a chain that hung over my crisp white button-up shirt was my official medical tag. On one side was a snake wrapped around a staff—the Rod of Asclepius, the symbol of medicine. The other side was more prosaic. Just one word, short and sweet: DIABETIC.

I wasn't sure about wearing this thing at first, and I especially hadn't intended to go around flaunting it. But then my sister and her friends—all vintage-store-shopping dynamos—were all "Oh, it's so cool, you should wear it on the outside of your shirt with a vest!" and I was therefore convinced that this diabetic necklace might possibly be considered a bold fashion statement.

I was really getting into vests, like any New Wave newbie worth his Orchestral Manoeuvres in the Dark cassettes. Laurie was wearing them, and fabulously. So was Brian, sexily. So was Laurie's best friend, Alison, with panache. I wanted to break me off a piece of that pie, so I went on down to the Goodwill and got myself a smashing collection of vests no doubt infested with traces of rat droppings, lice, and human blood. And there I stood in front of my mirror, in a thin blue paisley vest, a white button-up shirt with extra-long cuffs, and the glistening, sun-kissed disease advertisement hanging around my neck. Fetching as all heck.

I was on my way to my part-time job at Kerr Drug at Eastgate Shopping Center, a dreary, half-dead strip mall in North Raleigh. I was returning to it after a little time off during my diagnosis, convalescence, and cathartic series of temper tantrums. School had started again, too. It was time to go back to the real world of autumn after the Summer of the Failing Pancreas and test my diabetic training wheels in a less controlled environment.

I worked the front register at the drugstore, ringing folks up for cigarettes, candy bars, ugly but cheap lawn furniture from the seasonal aisle, shitty eyeglass frames, cosmetics, and impulse buys like the *Enquirer*, *Weekly World News*, and Big League Chew. It was a great job for a new type 1 diabetic in the thick of the honeymoon period, because I had all of the emergency sugar I could possibly need. Right across the counter from me was a wonderland of 5th Avenues, 3 Musketeers, Snickers, Milky Ways, and Mounds. If I felt a low blood sugar attack coming on, I was well defended.

It was the least glamorous job a boy could have, but this boy didn't know that. I wielded power at this job. Because this was in the days before the price scanner, I was able to charge folks whatever I wanted for whatever they wanted. This meant that my friends/people I wanted to impress from school could come in and buy a pack of cigarettes and I could give them a reasonable discount. I wouldn't give it to them for free, because that would have been wrong, perhaps even sinful. But God probably didn't have a problem with, say, twenty to thirty percent off, did he?

The uniform for men at Kerr Drug was slacks, shirt, and tie. The uniform for the ladies was decidedly less strict; whatever they could find to barely cover their sexy bodies was fine: skirts, short skirts, miniskirts, blouses, tight-ass blouses, low-cut T-shirts, heels, sandals, bikinis, thongs, whatever. I thought this double standard was unfair, so I had slowly started flouting the rules and dispensing with the tie. I was starting to enjoy the idea of standing out from my peers anyway. In years past I had always wanted to be a coolio, walking around school wearing a letter jacket, high-fiving other good-looking coolios in the hallways, and getting blow jobs from soccer players under the bleachers at halftime, while crying, like in the 1950s. But as I entered my second year of high school, it was painfully clear that this was not going to be happening, ever. For one thing, I didn't like sports. And it's incredibly difficult, even impossible, to be a good jock if you don't play, much less even appreciate, sports. Sure, I kind of liked tennis, but you didn't even have to wear an athletic supporter for that.

So it was a good thing that I was getting a little more comfortable being a weirdo, because the time I spent hunting for hot threads at the American Way Thrift Store and Goodwill meant that I was more and more often showing up to work as if I'd just left the set of *Beyond the Valley of the Dolls*. It was all tight, spastically patterned polyester pants, increasingly blousy and/or country-western shirts, and, of course, vests, vests, vests.

And compared to the staid dudes that worked with me at Kerr Drug, all of whom looked as if the most sartorially transgressive thought they'd ever entertained was whether or not to wear a pink necktie, I was a fairy princess. But that changed ever so slightly when I went back to work and found that there was a new employee in town manning the pharmacy register: Josh Epstein, who, like me, didn't fit the Kerr Drug mold.

It wasn't because I got strong gay vibes off him. No, Josh broke the mold in a very different way: first and foremost, because he was all Jewey, in direct opposition to the decidedly Anglo-Saxon character of all the other guys working there. He wore thick glasses, had an awkward gait, didn't seem comfortable interacting with the public—or other humans generally—and he had a marvelously large Jew-fro that he wasn't afraid to wear at maximum capacity. Though from the neck down he wore the costume of the establishment (shirt and tie), there was always something slightly askew about his presentation: tie crooked, Batman undershirt clearly visible through his yellow shirt, dirty sneakers on his feet. The boy was a social disaster, and I loved him for that. And I had an excellent view of it from my perch at the front register. I could stand at my station and stare across the store at the pharmacy on the opposite end, and there Josh and his fro would be at the pharmacy register, wordlessly ringing up a customer or filing away a newly filled prescription into the trays. I was intrigued by his matter-of-fact approach to his self-presentation. He wasn't trying to hide anything, wasn't trying to impress anyone. And he was getting away with it, as far as I was concerned. Though by any conventional measure, Josh was not a looker, he had something going for him that I couldn't put my finger on. I hoped to one day put my finger on it.

I would stand at my register—ringing up, say, a creepy regular customer who came in every day for cigarettes wearing a blond Don Johnson wig, mirror shades, and a five o'clock shadow that appeared to be painted on—and all the while would be staring at Josh up at the pharmacy counter as he leaned against the register, adjusted his enormous glasses, or stared quizzically at a customer as they talked at him. I had a crush.

Eventually, after a full shift of my gawking, Josh got wise to me, and he started staring back. Not with any malice or irritation.

Just with a blank, curious face. We would just stand at our registers between customers and stare at each other, me chewing on a Snickers bar, him looking up from his homework and pushing part of his fro out of his face, or me eating some corn chips and him running a customer's credit card through the machine and waiting for him or her to sign it. We were making a connection. The more we stared, the more convinced I was that we would eventually share a meaningful fifteen-minute break in the back of his parents' station wagon, which he drove to work and parked out front. Whenever he would leave for his break and would have to pass by my register, he would nod and smile, his eyes lingering on me just long enough to make it pointed, and I would smile, watch him leave, and try to determine what fresh fruit his round butt most resembled under those khaki slacks. A pair of Granny Smith apples? Two shaved peaches? Couple of cantaloupes?

It was mild, mysterious flirtations like this that helped get me through my twitchy days as a sophomore at Sanderson High School. Well, that and the fact that I could use my new disease as a reason to get out of school when things became too much for me, be they geometric proofs, the scientific method, or the sight of Darryl McClintock's rock-hard abs in the locker room after gym. The first few times I left early were legitimate. I'd had low blood sugar attacks in class, flooded my body with adrenaline, and felt exhausted as a result, rendering myself useless to my teachers. After the first attack, Mom had decided to sign a note that the attendance ladies could keep on file, saying that I could go home whenever I needed to.

In a different teenager's hands this could have been a dangerous thing indeed. Another lusty young closeted gay boy less concerned with keeping his GPA up and getting into a decent college might have used this as a way to ditch school all the time and go to Crabtree Valley Mall to visit the men's restrooms and read all the dirty messages on the stalls. Not this lusty closeted gay boy. I only left when I absolutely needed to. Like if I'd forgotten to do my homework or left my lab report at home or wanted to take a nap.

———

One thing that I was finding myself ditching more and more was Young Life. Sitting in some schoolmate's living room with a few college kids strumming guitars and singing squeaky-clean pop songs or Christian rock favorites no longer held the appeal it once did. The summer had really changed things. My world had shifted, and I couldn't go back to the age of innocence I'd pissed away all over Washington, D.C., and Baltimore. Life was so much more dirty and complicated than Michael W. Smith or Amy Grant had communicated to me.

This wasn't to say I didn't still adore Brad and resent the hell out of his girlfriend. But I was coming to the slow realization that maybe I was barking up the wrong strong, supple, sexy tree, and that my dream of one day getting Brad drunk enough to get naked with me might have been a bit unrealistic—especially for someone who was still five years away from legally drinking. And besides, booze doesn't make you gay. Sometimes gayish, maybe. But not gay. And I think deep down I knew this.

Not that I was even remotely ready to admit the truth of myself to myself. This was 1987, and we were neck-deep in AIDS fear and paranoia. The last thing you wanted to reveal in Ronald Reagan's and Jesse Helms's America was that you were a boy who liked boys. It was hard enough to admit you were a boy who liked soap operas. So I sublimated. All this angst went into growing out my bangs, writing terrible poetry, picking out Smiths songs on the violin, and amassing an enviable collection of post-punk and New Wave cassettes.

If you were a pale dude who wore eyeliner and had an equally unhappy band of moppets slinking around your videos on *120 Minutes*, I wanted to hear what you had to sing about. (Also if you were Siouxsie.) I was transforming into a terrible, angsty teenage goth monster. Worse, a goth monster who, given the opportunity, would happily go down on David the student council president. How could Jesus love such a thing? How could such a thing love Jesus?

And anyway, I was now stepping out with my new New Wave friends, like Heather, my only new New Wave friend, who I met at a Sanderson football game. She complimented me on my black cardigan and Sugarcubes T-shirt, I complimented her on her brown cardigan and Smiths T-shirt, and the rest was history. She started showing up at Kerr Drug Eastgate to get her friendship discount on cigarettes, and in return she would let me smoke one in her car and then drive me home as we listened to her Gene Loves Jezebel tape all the way to my house.

It was Heather who would escort me to a party at which my diabetes would collide cataclysmically with my warped hormones. My blood sugar and barely suppressed gayness would be let off their leashes to flail across the grounds of a country farmhouse in some neighboring town where a huge throng of Raleigh high schoolers were gathered to drink a sugary, fruity, blood-red alcoholic punch. This party would cause the world to shift on its axis and alter forever the music of the spheres. Things would get sloppy.

———

A beige 1986 Toyota Camry pulled into the Kerr Drug parking lot one Friday night and stopped in front of me where I was sitting on a bench outside the entrance.

"Hey, this is Sarah," Heather said from the passenger seat, pointing at the girl behind the steering wheel. We had plans to go to something called a "PJ Party" out in the sticks somewhere. I'd never been to one of these types of parties, but some kids had been talking it up at school, and I'd overheard them, so I had some firsthand secondhand knowledge. It apparently involved a big vat of red Kool-Aid augmented with vodka and Everclear, whatever that was.

"Hey!" I said to Sarah, thinking, *So this is the girl who sluts it up all the time.* Heather had told me about Sarah and her amorous ways with boys at Sanderson. It was kind of a shock to hear this kind of talk about her, because I remembered Sarah from middle school, and she'd worn glasses back then. People sure changed when they switched to contacts. But I was all for reinvention and was certainly excited to finally be face to face with someone near my age who I knew for a fact had had sex. I'd heard a short list of dudes she had banged, and it was very impressive. Not the number, although that was quite staggering as well. It was the quality of dudes. All hot dudes. Smoking hot dudes. There was not one dude among them who I would not have allowed/paid to take me behind the ESL trailer at school to diagram a few very long sentences.

"Hey," Sarah said in return, her eyes hidden behind her Madonna sunglasses.

"We're staying at her place tonight. Her parents are out of town."

"Cool."

We went over to dump our stuff at Sarah's house before heading out to the barn in the middle of nowhere where this PJ thing was happening. I tried to make conversation with Sarah so she would start to feel comfortable talking to me about all of her sexy hookups, but she wasn't a terribly chatty individual.

"So have you been to one of these PJ parties before?" I asked Sarah while Heather was microwaving ramen noodles in the kitchen.

"Yeah," she said. "Or actually, maybe not, I can't remember. I've had PJ before, though."

The sun was setting as we headed out of Raleigh toward Creedmoor, where this legendary barn sat in the middle of a field surrounded by rolling hills, beckoning to the hedonist high school students from the surrounding counties to stop by and taste the devil's favorite fruity cocktail.

On the way there Sarah and I had decided to sip on some of her Jack Daniel's to wet our whistles. It was disgusting, and terrible for the diabetes, but I couldn't get enough.

"So Sarah," I said after slamming a swig of Jack directly from the bottle, "are you gonna hook up tonight?" I was living vicariously through the only slut I knew.

"Uh . . . I don't know, maybe," Sarah said, laughing dismissively and looking at Heather as if to say, "Why is he talking to me so much?"

"Cool, cool," I said, nodding my head, lifting the Jack Daniel's bottle to my mouth, and hitting myself in the teeth with it as I tried to take another swig.

It took about a half hour to get out to the barn, and by the time we got there the party was thick with depravity. The barn was actually a cabin house, and the cabin house was full of crazy kids on a bender. Who were all these people? Whose cabin was this anyway? Nobody cared, because holy damn, look at that big vat of PJ in the kitchen!

We all lined up to ladle out a plastic cup of the poisonous punch for ourselves, and things pretty quickly turned into Swirl City. This stuff was good! Murder on the blood sugar, but hell, it was Friday, I could take one night off from my monastic and joyless diet plan. I'd just let my hair down this once and give my taste buds a reason not to cry themselves to sleep.

I'd never really been drunk before, so I was in virgin territory that night. I'd had enough beers to get happy and dumb on a few occasions, but I'd never really just stone-cold ignored the voice in the back of my head telling me, "Whoa, sister, you've had enough now, I think." But I was different now. I was getting away with things. I had sloughed off my former squeaky-clean self and was trying on a new persona: careless idiot. I'd been getting pretty good at drawing out insulin into a syringe and jabbing myself with it, one-handed, while driving. My new favorite thing to do was to take out my glucometer, prick my finger, and test my blood sugar while, say, sitting in a crowded Taco Bell. (Or while driving.) In short, I was a rebel, a teenage tough, a boy unafraid to wear tight polyester pants to church. So this was the first time I'd ever be getting full-on sloppy drunk, and I was planning to be good at it.

After a few cups full of the red elixir of destiny I was quite chatty. I talked to strangers. I talked to people at school whom I hated for some reason. I talked to people who had their backs to me. I followed Heather around for a while to see if I could talk to some of the people she was talking to, then got lost and couldn't find my way back to the PJ. Thankfully, I talked a person into escorting me back to it.

I was now fuzzily drunk enough to start walking around trying to find people who couldn't possibly be at the party. The person I wanted to find? Fellow outside-the-boxer Josh Epstein, from work. He had to be here somewhere.

I staggered around looking hither and yon for Mr. Epstein's Jew-fro. On the back porch I thought I caught a glimpse of it, but then realized it was just a potted fern hanging from the ceiling.

Then I saw Ruth, of "diabetes is a *disease*, I'm sure it's just heat-stroke" infamy. She was standing with Kathleen from homeroom, who not only had a bitching Metallica necklace around her neck every day, she also had the most winning metal hair in all the land.

"Tim! Tim! Oh my God, I didn't know you were going to be here!"

We rushed to embrace, slamming our sloppy bodies against each other.

"Are you drinking PJ?" she asked.

"Of course!" I said, raising my plastic cup as if to toast Ruth for noticing.

"Yay!" Kathleen shouted, raising her cup and clinking mine.

"You know," Ruth said with her concerned face on, "PJ has a LOT of sugar in it. You better be careful." Kathleen looked much less concerned as she tipped her cup to her mouth and PJ onto her face.

"Oh, Ruth, I'll be fine, I'm cool, no problem," I somehow made my mouth say, knowing full well my blood sugar was on its way to the ionosphere. "I haven't had that much and are you ready for more 'cause I kind of want some more it's really good!" My mouth was already starting to get dry and sticky from the hyperglycemia. "Have you seen that guy Josh?" I ducked inside in order to avoid any more of the diabetic inquisition, and refilled my cup. It was then that I noticed a tub in the kitchen. Somehow I hadn't seen this before. Inside it was a girl with a mohawk wearing an Exploited T-shirt lying down drinking Boone's Farm.

"You really should put that down and come get some of *this*," I said to her rolling eyeballs as I lifted up my filled plastic cup. To my amazement, she didn't tell me to go fuck myself or start quoting X-Ray Spex lyrics to me. She delicately placed her bottle of terrible wine on the floor, stood up in the bathtub like a lady, and stepped out and over to the vat of PJ, taking my advice to heart.

"You're probably right," she said, her tone serious and, ironically, sober.

There was Heather talking to a guy with a mohawk and an Exploited T-shirt on. I floated over and said hello to Heather, then turned to her friend.

"I just met your girlfriend in the bathtub," I said, pointing to his twin over by the PJ, who had started drinking straight out of the ladle.

He looked at her, looked at me, then said, "I don't know that girl."

They really should meet. Wait, what was I just obsessing about? Oh yeah, Josh. None of the people in that kitchen looked anything like him, so I trundled back onto the porch. Then I saw him. Not Josh, but him.

He was standing outside in the crowded front yard among a small cluster of guys. Tall and lean, with bedhead and a handsome face. He wore a long unbuttoned black trench coat that opened to reveal brown corduroy pants and a dark red sweater. His hair was brown and wavy, and he smiled when he talked, often raising his eyebrows in a friendly expression of sincere interest in whatever bullshit the person in front of him was saying. Oh, how I wanted him to feign interest in *me*.

As I stood on the front porch gawking, Heather bounded into me from behind and shook me out of my daydream, clucking, "Having fun?!"

"Yes! Where's Mr. Exploited?"

"Oh, I think he went to the bathroom."

"And Mrs. Exploited?"

"Back in the tub."

Heather wandered down the steps and into the front yard, where she floated over to a group of girls chatting next to the guy in the trench coat. So I followed and sidled up to her, trying to listen to their chatter while also eavesdropping on what the dudes next to us were saying and whether they might have said something about the guy in the trench coat liking to kiss boys. They seemed to be just talking about weed. I looked over at the girls, and they were all staring at me, expectantly. Had one of them asked me a question?

"What'd you say?" I asked, taking another sip of PJ.

"Do you know anyone here?" a girl with a thick mane of curly locks in the shape of a big furry parabola asked. She was holding a plastic cup of blood-red bubonic juice, and her big, pin-up girl lips seemed to be coated with the stuff.

"I don't know *you*, do I?" I queried.

"I'm Jennifer," she said.

"Nice to meet you."

"So," Jennifer asked for the third damn time, "do you know anyone here . . . *besides* me?"

"I saw my friend Ruth, and I think someone from my church might be here? Also, I know Heather."

Heather and Jennifer nodded silently, then shook hands and exchanged pleasantries and cigarettes. ("I've been wanting to try these," Heather said about Jennifer's Benson & Hedges DeLuxe Ultra Lights 100s.)

"Excuse me, do you have a light?" someone next to me asked. I turned and, Lordy be, it was the guy in the trench coat, smiling big and holding in his hand what appeared to be an illegal thing that one might smoke if one had something to light it with.

I didn't have a light, but I poked Heather to get hers from her. I presented it to him as if it were placed delicately upon a small silk pillow.

"Thanks," he said, expertly lighting his doobie. "You want a toke?"

I've never once said no to that question in the years since this party, so it makes sense that without any hesitation I said "Sure!" and pivoted away from Heather and Co. over toward the trench coat guy's merry group of pot-smoking ruffians.

As we passed around the joint the guys continued their conversation, which was about the band INXS, which had recently played the Civic Center.

"I love the drummer!" I said, way too enthusiastically. The guys looked at me with curious expressions and nodded absently. "I mean, you know, he's a really great drummer." And he has an amazing body.

"You play the drums?" the trench coat guy asked.

"No, I just really like drummers." Particularly that one.

"For my money, nobody beats The Smiths," he said, taking another toke and melting my heart. "Johnny Marr is a genius."

"Oh yeah," I nodded, "and of course, the singer is hilarious."

"Yeah," he said.

And what, I wanted to ask, do you make of the singer's . . . inclinations? One of his buddies started talking about Amsterdam, which renewed the talk of weed. I stayed where I was, downed the rest of my PJ, and watched the trench-coated dreamboat's face as he talked. The weed was mixing with the PJ in my blood to send messed-up signals to my brain about him. The more I watched his mouth move—sugary lips curling, tongue gliding across teeth—the more convinced I was that this guy had stuck his tongue down a guy's throat once or twice. Maybe we could take a walk behind the house and I could be the second or third.

He handed me the joint again, and I took a particularly long tug on it and handed it back. When he took it from me his fingers brushed over mine, sending an electric shock through my entire body.

"Hey, anyone want another cup?" I asked. Because when in doubt, offer to bring people more alcohol. It makes them like you. (I think I read that in *Tiger Beat*.) Nobody answered, so I bounded back inside and into the kitchen, where the crowd had grown even denser around the vat. I grabbed two paper cups and squeezed my way into the center, where one person was ladling punch into the cups of whoever stuck theirs out. As drunk as I was, I was remarkably adroit in my quest for more booze. I steadily stretched out one hand, got one cup filled up by the wandering ladle, then pulled my hand back and switched the full cup to the other hand and sent the empty cup in for more. I then withdrew my arm from the center and carefully backed out of the kitchen with two cups of blood-red sugary death syrup for me and one other person to enjoy outside.

"More PJ?" I said to trench coat guy when I returned to the smoking circle outside, holding out the cup for him.

"Oh," he said. "Uh, thanks." He moved the joint he had in one hand to his other hand, then took the cup from me and gulped some of it down. He leaned over to listen to one of his friends, who was saying something I couldn't hear. Trench coat guy had an adorable little puddle of red liquid clinging to his not-quite-there blond moustache. I managed to get his attention and signaled to him that he needed to wipe his mouth. He smiled and did so, then continued listening to his friend's story.

I took a few swigs of PJ and looked around at the little clusters of partygoers standing outside and chitchatting.

"Have you seen Sarah?" Heather's disembodied voice said behind me suddenly.

"Uh-uh," I answered.

"Oh my God, if she's left with someone I'm gonna be so pissed," Heather continued. "How will we get home?"

"I'm sure she's here somewhere. It's still early." I had no idea what time it was. "You should check inside."

Heather looked at me. "Be right back."

"Hey, man, can I hit that again?" I said to trench coat guy, pointing to what was left of the joint in his hand. Actually, I was swaying so determinedly that I pointed at his cup, pointed at his friend's stomach, then pointed at the joint on the way back up.

"Sure, here you go."

I toked on the doobie until my eyes crossed, then, after offering it to his friend's stomach, handed it back to him and said thank you.

I was now well and truly wasted beyond all justification: bombed out on Everclear, stoned as a wombat, swaying from side to side like a melting metronome, and with a blood sugar level that was no doubt creeping dangerously into "drop face-first into a coma" territory. So naturally I was in the mood for love. And at that point, with the trench coat guy so close to me, I made a terrible, terrible error in judgment.

I swayed close to him and grabbed his crotch.

"Get away from me, man," trench coat guy said. Not angrily, but quietly, adamantly.

[SCREAMING, INSIDE MY HEAD.]

I forced myself to laugh and swayed away from him, but I didn't bother to wait around and see if my action had been seen by his friends or by anyone else outside. I backed away, turned around, and bolted into the darkened field where all the kids had parked their cars.

Oh my God, oh my God, oh my God, my life is over, I've been found out, I'll never work in this town again. I stumbled toward the darkness, desperate to disappear, to be invisible; to dig a grave for myself, dive in, and tunnel my way to Beijing.

I reached the rows of cars and kept moving, looking for a good one to duck behind and get out of sight. By some miracle I spied the vehicle that had brought me to this den of sin: Sarah's car. Scuttling over to it, I crouched down, and sat on the back bumper. I looked back at the farmhouse and the kids on the lawn, which was lit by a single porch light—I couldn't see anyone, which meant that no one could see me. Leaning back against the trunk, I remembered that Heather had given me her cigarettes to hold because she didn't want to bring her purse in to the party. I reached in my pocket, retrieved a Camel Light, and lit it with the lighter she always kept in her packs.

I exhaled a plume of angst and smoke, playing over in my head the scene that had just gone down over at the farmhouse. OK, OK, let's see, I had a little PJ, had some pot, talked to Heather, talked to Ruth and Kathleen, talked to a girl in a mohawk in a bathtub, talked to a guy in a trench coat, oh, and I JUST GRABBED HIS CROTCH WITH MY WHOLE HAND. Not secretly, in the woods, on the outskirts of town, with a Richard Nixon mask on my face. No, it was at a high school party, in front of a bunch of people, while rip-roaring drunk, in front of the guy's friends. I tried to remember who else could have possibly seen it. When the guy told me to get away from him, he didn't shout it, he said it almost under his breath. A good sign? Maybe. He wasn't giving the go-ahead to his friends to come after me with knives, I guess. At least he didn't go to my school.

Just as I had decided that perhaps—PERHAPS—I might live to see another day, the car started moving. Not forward. Not backward. Kind of up and down. I sat there for a minute, slowly registering that the movement of the car was not just me being wasted, but because of something actual that was happening outside my miserable head.

Yes, it was starting to bounce up and down, ever so slightly. It was like the car was trying to seduce the ground it was parked on, lowering its rear half teasingly before whipping it back up, then repeating the action again. I got up from the bumper and slowly turned around, then leaned over to see if I could make out anything through the rear window. The palm of a hand suddenly slapped against the window from the inside, then snapped back into the darkness. I leaned in closer, because damn if that wasn't scary and alluring at the same time. I squinted to see inside and all of a sudden realized what I was looking at: Sarah's upside-down face. Yes, that was Sarah, on her back, in the backseat, with her eyes closed, getting plowed mightily by some dude on top of her who hadn't even had the decency to take his shirt off.

I backed away and crouched down a few cars over, continuing to watch the car bounce up and down, up and down, up and down. It bounced faster and faster and faster, just going to town on that grassy knoll, which was surely now turning to a desperate and sweaty mound of mud. Finally the car came, shivering, to a halt. I weakly stood and wafted back to the party, hoping against hope that the trench coat guy and his friends had either left or gotten so high that my little indiscretion would just be a cloudy memory that they couldn't really recall through the wildfire of weed smoke burning up their frontal cortexes.

I saw a couple of shadowy people walking toward me and feared the worst. But then I saw a big parabola head and realized it was just Heather and Jennifer.

"Hey, you ready to find Sarah and hit turbo?" Heather said.

Yeah, she was probably zipping up and finding her car keys as we spoke.

I looked around everywhere for the trench coat guy, but he was gone. My heartbeat settled down a little at the thought that maybe nobody had seen my scandalous crotch-grab. Perhaps I was in the clear.

"Where's my Boone's Farm bottle?" came a shrieking voice from the direction of the house. Looking over, I saw the blurry figure of mohawk girl, standing on the porch in her bra and under-wear, holding up her bottle of Boone's Farm in the air like it was a tomahawk. Yeah, it was time to go.

We somehow all got back to Sarah's house and crashed on various pieces of furniture down in her parents' basement. I woke up the next morning feeling raw and sticky, the sinfully high amount of sugar in my blood lowering my life expectancy by the minute. I stood up from the La-Z-Boy I'd passed out on and swayed as I tried to stop the floor from moving out of sheer will-power. Hobbling over to the staircase, I steadied myself with the railing, and slowly padded up the carpeted stairs leading up to the kitchen.

I immediately gagged after stepping onto the linoleum. It was a very small kitchen, and there was no avoiding the horrific diorama on the table: a half-eaten Big Mac, a scattering of fries, and a hot fudge sundae container on its side that had spilled its contents onto the Big Mac wrapper. I didn't remember a trip to McDonald's, but I guess it happened.

I sat down at the table, grabbed my backpack, and took out my insulin vial and a syringe. I wasn't even going to test my blood sugar, because it would probably break the machine. I drew out ten units and jabbed myself in the stomach, all the while trying to think of what awful thing had happened the night before. I knew it was rotten, knew I had done something incredibly dumb and life-threatening, but what the heck was it? I looked at the revolting burger in front of me, visible teeth marks and all. I picked it up, turned it around to the unbitten side, and shrugged.

Well, whatever it was, I assumed I'd gotten away with it. I took a bite of the burger, then went and threw up.

———

It wasn't until Monday that I remembered in a flash the humiliating thing I did at the party. I walked into homeroom that morning, still delicate from the weekend's activities, and slumped into my chair. After a few minutes I lifted my head up, and there was Kathleen, her hair looking admirably gravity-defying for a Monday morning.

"Have fun at the party?" she murmured, visibly stoned.

"Yeah. Don't remember much, though."

"Did you see that chick take all her clothes off?"

And then it hit me. I worked backward from my last memory. Mohawk girl on the porch in her bra and panties holding a bottle. Then there was Heather and Jennifer's big parabola head walking away from me toward the house, me watching Sarah's car bumping and grinding on the ground, then me moving toward the car, seeing Sarah's upside-down face in the backseat underneath an unidentifiable dude, then me sitting on the trunk, followed by me walking backward toward the farmhouse and hearing a guy in a trench coat say "Get away from me, man," and then my hand moving away from his crotch and taking an outstretched doobie from him and putting it into my mouth.

"Oh, my God," I said.

"Yeah," Kathleen said. "It was pretty hilarious."

I went to my first few classes trying to avoid the gaze of anyone who might have possibly been at the party. Surely there was someone who had seen me do what I'd done and was spilling the beans all over school. Sure, being talked about can be nice, but not really if it involves the words *Tim, wants, to, grab,* and *dicks.* My paranoia escalating, I saw Heather in the hall.

"Hey, lady," I said, sidling up to her. "Heard any terrible rumors?"

"Sadly, no," Heather yawned.

"Is this a conglomeration of pukey drunks I see before me?" Jennifer cooed, running up and jumping right in front of us. She laughed and took off her headphones, from which one could hear, if one was listening, the first song on The Cure's *Disintegration,* blasting celestially.

"Oh, shit, I remember you!" I said. "You smoke Benson and Hedges."

"DeLuxe Ultra Light One Hundreds," she clarified.

"Let's go out to lunch today," Heather suggested absently.

"Sure, OK," I said. That was a thing we'd been doing, sneaking out through the woods to go out to lunch, because we were rebels, just like all the other underclassmen who did it. "Jennifer, you wanna come?"

But she already had her headphones back on and was backing away to get to class. She saw me looking at her quizzically.

"YEAH, IT'S AWESOME! I CAN'T STOP LISTENING TO IT!" she assured me.

Heather and I ended up at Wendy's on Falls of Neuse Road. At no time did Heather give any indication that she'd seen me do anything untoward at the party, even when I gave her an opportunity to tell me.

"You know, I don't remember a lot about Saturday. I hope I didn't do anything embarrassing!"

"Sarah fucked some dude in her car," Heather said in response, sounding jealous. "And I think she stole my Gene Loves Jezebel tape."

Had my power grab somehow not been witnessed by the teeming masses at the party? If they'd seen it, they hadn't told Heather yet.

That's when I saw him. Again. He walked into the restaurant with a group of friends and got in line. He was in his trench coat again, looking even more handsome by daylight.

"Wasn't that guy at the party?" Heather said, pointing her head in his direction and sipping on her Frosty.

"Uh, I don't know. Was he?" I tried to stick a french fry in my mouth and succeeded only in brushing it against my cheek.

"Yeah, he totally was," Heather continued. "I remember seeing him out front. He's cute."

Trench coat guy and his group walked toward us carrying their trays and looking for a table to sit at. He saw us and locked eyes with me. A spark of recognition.

"Shit," I couldn't stop myself from saying.

"What?"

The group sat down at a table near us. I couldn't look. I could see his face out of the corner of my eye. I nervously flashed my baby blues in his direction for a fraction of a second, but he was talking to a friend and eating, not paying me any mind.

"Nothing," I said. "Just, I think I do remember talking to that dude. He had pot."

"Speaking of," Heather said, "guess what I've got in my glove compartment."

"Isn't that kind of risky?" I asked.

"Eh, it's just a roach, and it'll be gone soon enough. Like, before our next class. Let's go."

We stood and walked past the trench coat guy's table. He glanced up at me with a blank face and stared for just long enough to communicate that he remembered, then quickly darted his eyes away. I wanted to jump in his lap and cover him with kisses for not telling anyone about me grabbing his jock at the party, but that would have been counterproductive, to say the least. Heather and I emptied our trays into the trash and left.

———

I went to work that afternoon wearing my new favorite vest, one of Laurie's that I'd found on top of the washing machine. I was finally recovering from the trauma of the weekend and feeling like maybe I wouldn't have to go into hiding after all. So why not wear a black velvet vest over my new pristine white tuxedo shirt and augment it with my diabetes necklace hanging like a talisman around my neck? It's called living out loud.

I was looking forward to exchanging meaningful glances with Josh, my favorite awkwardly alluring Jew at the pharmacy counter. It was time to go back to harmless flirting. Enough of being so drunk and grabby.

I walked into the store, clocked in, and took my position behind the front register, replacing Joy the day cashier. Once she left and the coast was clear, I visited the candy bar shelf a few steps away and brazenly swiped a 3 Musketeers bar, because whipped chocolate.

Looking up at the pharmacy counter, I saw Josh talking with Ron the store manager. It appeared to be a serious conversation. What on earth about?

A line started forming at my register, so I dutifully rang up folks for their cigarettes, hair clips, Cheetos, greeting cards, romance novels, baby oil, condoms, Dark and Lovely hair products, and panty hose.

Then the cops came. Two robust-looking gentlemen made a beeline for the back counter. I kept intermittently looking back at the pharmacy while ringing folks up, watching as the cops spoke to Ron and looked solemnly at Josh.

"He's apparently been stealing pills from the pharmacy and selling them as a kind of side business," Agnes the cosmetics lady whispered, having sidled up beside me behind the register. "And he looked like such a nice boy."

Indeed. The kind of boy you would take home to Mother after jerking him off in his station wagon. I walked in front of the register so I could turn and look at the mirror that ran across the entire front of the store just below the ceiling as a theft deterrent. I saw Josh being led by the uniformed butch brigade up toward the front, in handcuffs. Rushing back to my register, I turned around in time to see Josh and the officers rounding the corner toward me and heading toward the exit. Josh looked at me and flashed an embarrassed grin.

Wow. Josh had done something dishonest and, even sexier, illegal. Not to mention entrepreneurial. And now he'd been caught. He'd thought he was getting away with it, but now here he was, being led away like a common criminal, his crooked clip-on tie clinging precariously to his collar. That fresh nerdy face and luxurious frizzy hair would never survive for long in the slammer. It was depressing, watching him humiliated like this. Had he really been hurting anyone? Probably, but with their consent, surely.

I walked out to the automatic door to watch him being put in the back of the police car. Returning to my register, I looked down at the 3 Musketeers bar on the counter, picked it up, and returned it to the shelf.

In conclusion, I found out later that night when I came home from work that it wasn't my sister's black velvet vest I'd been wearing. It was my mom's.

The oily young boy with the short hair and the curly bangs swirling over his forehead like an out-of-control plane spiraling toward earth has been browsing at the Tracks record store for what seems like years, looking to fill in the gaps in his tape collection. Is it gonna be some Siouxsie and the Banshees? Through the Looking Glass *or* Join Hands? The Peel Sessions *or* Once Upon a Time: The Singles? *Or hey, maybe he wants some Joy Division, Depeche Mode, Kraftwerk, or some other Teutonic nonsense?*

Make your decision, young man. Because hear this, your blood sugar is ready to dip like raw vegetables on a party tray. And everyone knows that the likelihood of you making a good decision under that circumstance is on par with the likelihood that you will not embarrass your parents the next time they have friends over from church. You don't want to walk out of this store with a cassette you will regret, like Wang Chung or T'Pau. It's the late eighties, after all, and the line between delightfully tacky and god-awful is fine indeed.

Finally, FINALLY, he catches a glimpse of himself in a glass partition and discovers that he's sweaty and stupid, and realizes that maybe that is why he's having trouble deciding. He resolves at that moment that he can only spend a few more minutes choosing which cassette to buy before heading over to the Fast Fare to buy some sweets. After another half hour of useless internal deliberation and endless walking of the pop/rock aisles, he closes his eyes, clicks his heels together three times, and pulls one cassette out from the others he's gathered. Hurrah, it's Burning from the Inside *by Bauhaus, time to go. He hobbles over to the cashier and prepares to pony up his hard-earned $8.99.*

At first he attempts to pay with his driver's license. The cashier—a charming young lady with an earring in her nose and hair the color of vomit—indicates with a cold stare that Tracks does not accept that form of payment. He then starts just pulling things out of his wallet that could possibly be mistaken for legal tender by, say, a newborn baby: a torn piece of paper with a phone number on it; a Red Cross CPR certification; a small collection of wallet-sized school portraits he was given by class-mates, all stuck together. But none of these are satisfactory to the cashier, who just keeps narrowing her eyes, repeating the amount he owes, and pointing to the amount helpfully displayed on the register screen.

Suddenly the boy's face brightens as his instincts kick in and he realizes that what he needs to give the nice lady is money. Cash money. Not photo IDs or paper clips, but American dollars. He pulls a twenty out of his wallet and hands it to her with the magnanimity of Daddy Warbucks serving slop at a soup kitchen. So generous of him, to offer the woman money for a product/service she's providing.

He stumbles to his car with his new purchase, trying in vain to get the wrapping off the cassette so he can listen to it immediately and make sure he made the right choice. He quickly gives up and tosses the Tracks bag on the passenger seat of the 1977 Plymouth Volare that he inherited from his grandfather. It's a huge, four-door vehicle that comfortably seats six, uncomfortably seats about twenty, and would easily survive a nuclear holocaust or any type of run-in with another vehicle. So, in short, a great car for dangerous diabetics in distress and a terrible car for everyone else.

He takes his keys out of his pocket and looks at them intently, studying every ridge and slit of each key. One of these makes the car go vroom vroom, *he probably thinks. Locating the right one, he sticks it into the ignition, starts the car, and pulls out of the parking space like a cat pulls out of a full bathtub it's just been thrown into. He just has to get to the Fast Fare across the street. Across the very busy street.*

He sticks the nose of his Plymouth out into traffic, the better for passengers in oncoming vehicles to see how they will meet their deaths. He needs to turn right and then immediately get in the left-hand-turn lane so he can swerve on into the Fast Fare parking lot. He pulls out onto Six Forks Road and lumbers across the street to the convenience store as horns honk and expletives fly. Panicked drivers swerve gracefully around the Plymouth and magically avoid piling up on each other in an orgy of death. Our hero makes it across without so much as a scratch and parks the car, naturally, in the handicapped space, diagonally, because fuck it.

He enters the shop and once again gets sucked into a Black Hole of Impossible Choices. Twenty minutes later he's still looking over the selection with an extremely Libran indecisiveness. He's now pacing back and forth, up to the Twizzlers, Gobstoppers, and SweeTarts, and back down again to the Reese's Pieces, Kit Kats, Milky Ways, and 5th Avenues. What will he choose? Candy or chocolate? Nuts or nougat? Why not both?

It's very exciting, like watching two turtles play table tennis.

Uh-oh, something has caught his eye. He's moving, mesmerized, to the end cap, where the cheap candy hangs from pegs, packaged in clear plastic bags stapled closed by a label that says CANDY CORN, BUTTERSCOTCH, CIRCUS PEANUTS, or GUMDROPS. He walks straight up to the selection and pulls two bags of giant orange gumdrops in the shape of orange slices off their pegs.

Legs tingling from the adrenaline surging through his bloodstream in order to keep him standing upright, he pivots to the poor cashier, who is now tasked with executing a transaction with the equivalent of a somnambulant circus monkey. But just when you think he's ready to wrap this safari up, he decides he should probably get reinforcements just in case the two bags of orange corn-syrup-infused sugar blasts aren't enough to bring his blood sugar up to normal human levels and beyond.

He tramps back to the candy aisle, walking as if trudging through a dense thicket of rosebushes, and picks up a Mars bar, a Whatchamacallit, a Butterfinger, and two Almond Joys. With any luck he'll get some of this stuff into his mouth before toppling face-first onto the floor and giving the poor lady behind the register one more spill to clean up. All the young man has to do now is pay.

He pulls out of his pocket a crumpled-up gum wrapper and places it on the counter.

Ugh. We're going to be here for a few more minutes.

CHAPTER 5

I STARTED SOMETHING I COULDN'T FINISH

"My little sister would totally go out with you," a classmate of mine, Ashley, told me at lunch in the cafeteria one day. "She thinks you're cute and thinks the whole diabetic thing is . . . intriguing."

Hmm. I doubted that sentence had ever been uttered before in the history of time.

"Because she thinks she's diabetic, too. She's always having low blood sugar spells when she doesn't eat."

"Hmm, well that's probably hypoglycemia, not diabetes," I explained. "She probably just has an overactive pancreas, or maybe her metabolism is—"

"Anyway, you should ask her out."

Oh, OK, I was done talking. And yes, I supposed I should consider asking Ashley's freshman sister out. I sure didn't have girls banging down my door, and definitely none for whom my status as a diabetic was part of the allure. Since Dawn had pulled that comfortably platonic rug out from under me, I hadn't thought much about trying to get a date. Perhaps I needed to get out there and find some poor unsuspecting young lady to take me as her secretly gay boyfriend. Get back up on that horse that I was so terrible at riding. Sure, on the inside I was a pulsating maelstrom of homo terror, but there was no way in hell that I was anywhere close to being ready to declare that openly. I was barely ready to declare my love for hair mousse openly, and I wore that every day. The experience of doing something so reckless in public at the PJ party had shocked me to my core, and I was ready to run for the hills of heteronormativity, however inaccessible the entrance, across the deep river of denial. And I needed a girl to be my raft. Or something.

And hey, maybe there was a nice girl out there who could turn me around? And maybe that girl was a diabetic enthusiast with a sister who was in my algebra class?

In any case, I'd recently drawn a dramatic line in the sand, one demarcating the division between myself and terrible, horrible, no-good, very bad gayness. I'd jumped across it and sworn to God, Jesus, and the Holy Spirit that I would not ever ever ever cross back again. After a final bout of self-pleasuring while alone in the house one Saturday, I took the magazines I'd stolen from newsagents and hidden under a rug in my closet—*Honcho*, *Bolt*, and *Torso*—and ceremoniously burned them in my tin Charlie Brown trash can.

I tossed the magazines in the can one by one. When it landed, the *Bolt* issue opened to a photo spread of about eight dudes playing "Whose Pickle Is This?" I lit a match and ignited the corner of the mag, its glossy pages only too willing to give themselves over to the flames (they'd been burning hot for so long). I died a little inside as the sweaty orgy scene before me darkened and curled into ashy nothingness before my eyes.

I did keep one tawdry publication: the *International Male* catalog. In case I found myself in need of a pirate blouse or gauze overalls.

———

Ashley's sister Dani, a fourteen-year-old freshman, was a hot little number. Even I knew that. She had legs that went up to here, long brownish-blonde hair, a full set of strong teeth, and a confident swagger. I called her one afternoon after getting assurance from Ashley that Dani would indeed be home and would indeed say yes if I asked her out.

"How's it going?" I asked nervously.

"Oh, fine, you know, pretty good."

"I got your number from Ashley. I hope you don't mind that I'm calling."

"Oh, no, it's cool. She, you know, uh . . ."

"So, I was wondering if you wanted to maybe I don't know go out or something like to get some food or you know whatever I don't know."

"Sure, that sounds awesome."

We made a date for Friday night, and I hung up as quickly as possible because who wants to just sit there and talk on the phone to the girl you've just asked out? Not me.

Immediately after getting off the phone, I entered the planning stages of the date, a stage that no real heterosexual teenage boy has ever embarked upon in the history of the world. Any other lover of the ladies worth his raging libido would probably not plan a date several days in advance and, worse, decide upon taking her to Darryl's because it's classy. No, that boy would probably just take his girl out for a quick ice cream so they could hurry up and get down to the proper point of a date: humping feverishly in the back of his car. I was clearly a different breed of boy, an old-fashioned type with a powerful respect for women, an abiding interest in their wants and needs, and a willingness to hear all about them while sharing a titanic plate of Darryl's Signature Loaded Smashed Potatoes.

OK, so we'd go to dinner, chitchat about school and music and movies and diabetes and boys. (No! Not boys!) No problem, I can do that stuff in my sleep. But what would we do after that, after we'd finished stuffing our stomachs with cheesy buttery bacon-and-scallion-covered carbs? I had no idea.

"Just take her to the record store," my sister, Laurie, advised as we sat in her room. I'd invited myself in because I knew that she'd just bought Morrissey's first solo album and I could hear the fey strains of "Everyday Is Like Sunday" moaning gaily through her closed door. In short order, she asked me what I was going to do on my date and I said I HAVE NO IDEA PLEASE HELP ME.

"It could be a cool way to just, you know, browse around and talk about bands and stuff."

"Oh yeah, we could do that," I said as I unfolded the sleeve of the *Viva Hate* cassette and looked at the liner notes. "And there's a Schoolkids Records right down the street from Darryl's," I added. It was destiny.

"It's a shame about that car of yours, though. Wait, you're going to Darryl's?"

Laurie didn't approve of my dinner plans, and she definitely didn't approve of my Plymouth. She had told me long ago, before I started high school, that one thing I absolutely had to do when I got a part-time job was to save money for a decent car, because girls liked cars. But I hadn't taken her advice. After my grandfather died I got his car—my giant, proud, gray Plymouth Volare—which was good enough for me. I wouldn't have dreamed of wasting money on some beat-up car when I already had one, and when there were so many albums and vintage threads to buy. And why not wallpaper my walls floor to ceiling with Morrissey, Siouxsie, Ian Curtis, Sinéad, and, I don't know, a bunch of blue whales? No reason not to. And that costs money.

"Yes," I said, defensively, before telling a bald-faced lie. "And guess what, Dani *likes* my car."

"No she doesn't," Laurie quipped.

"Something, something, nuclear bomb," Morrissey said.

———

Friday came, and it was time to step out into the suburban North Raleigh night. It was early October, still sort of warm, but with a slight chill in the air. Perfect weather, in other words, for my new trippy polyester ball-hugging wonderpants. These trousers had a hypnotic black-and-orange pattern that undulated alluringly as I walked and under the right conditions had the power to give kittens the power of human speech and smack Earthbound asteroids back into deep space. It was predestined that I would wear them on this date, along with my green button-up army shirt and my favorite black cardigan. Dani would expect nothing less.

And what would she wear? I was dying to know. I stepped up to her porch and rang the doorbell. Ashley answered the door and smiled.

"Hi, Tim! What's up?"

"Hey, I'm, uh, here to, uh, pick up, you know . . ."

Ashley cocked her head to the side.

"To what? To pick up whom?" she chirped in an elegant/insufferable *Masterpiece Theatre* accent.

"Oh, Ashley, stop being mean," Dani said as she emerged from behind the partially opened front door. She stepped out onto the porch, and we sauntered to the Plymouth.

"You kids have fun, don't do drugs or anything," Ashley shouted from the doorway.

"No promises," Dani said without looking back. Shit, was I supposed to bring drugs?

My momma raised me right, so I escorted Dani to the passenger side, opened the door for her, and shut it behind her. She appeared befuddled by all this forced chivalry, but she rolled with it, offering awkward "thank you"s as we tried not to step on each other's feet during the whole clumsy teenage tango.

As I walked around to the driver's side, I had to admit that she was a stunner—a vision in a white peasant blouse and some tastefully ripped-up and faded-out jeans. Around her neck hung a necklace made out of apple seeds, and she carried a brown leather hippie/saddlebag purse that, I hazarded a guess, she bought at the Disabled American Veterans Thrift Store. Together we were a late-'80s alternative rocking New Wave power couple.

I circled my giant gray tank out of her cul-de-sac and started in with the small talk. We established early on that she liked school OK, her classes were fine, she had hated middle school, and she had an abiding love for Don McLean.

"Hmm, who on earth is that?" I asked, dumbfounded that the breadth of her musical knowledge was larger than mine. I was a year older than her, after all.

"Oh, you probably know his song 'American Pie,'" she said. "He's a big old hippy who got started playing on boats."

"On boats?"

"Yeah, on boats. On the Hudson River."

I nodded, clueless.

"New York City."

"Oh, I see. That's cool. By the way, did you know that 'American Pie' is the longest song ever to hit number one?"

"I did not know that," she said brightly.

"It's true! Very true. I've got lots of stuff like that up here," I said, pointing to my crusty, moussed head.

"My dad loves him, so I grew up listening to 'American Pie' all the time."

Wow, such different parental guidance she'd had. Unless she also grew up listening to a lot of Lawrence Welk and Rodgers and Hammerstein.

We arrived at Darryl's—"I love their homemade crackers," Dani said—and I tried to get out and over to her side of the car quickly enough to do the whole chivalry thing again, but she hopped out before I could. Dani was clearly a modern, independent woman who waited for no man and who was also probably hungry.

We were shown to an intimate table in the corner of a room with only one other incredibly large and loud family present. Our dinner conversation was easy, breezy. We talked about it all: more Don McLean, Janis Joplin (another of her favorites), Echo and the Bunnymen (*that's* the stuff), Violent Femmes, how she likes to make clothes out of old upholstery fabric, what it's like to drive a huge, glamorous Plymouth, what it's like to have to prick your finger all day, every day, forever, what it's like to give yourself a shot, what it's like to give yourself a shot while you drive a huge, glamorous Plymouth—all of it.

"Do you wanna see how I prick myself?" I asked in a husky, James Bond voice.

"Of course I do!" Was she serious? It's so hard to detect sarcasm this early in a date.

So I happily took out all of my instruments—glucometer, finger pricker, test strips, syringe, insulin vial—and placed them all on the table just in time for our perky waitress to approach us and ask if she could get us started with some drinks.

"Oh, don't worry about this stuff," I assured her. "We're not doing drugs."

The waitress forced a laugh out of her mouth.

"No, that's *after* dinner," Dani assured her. "Out in the parking lot. Can I get a Diet Coke?"

"Yes, yes, I'll have what the lady is having!" Ugh, did I just say that?

The waitress smiled, nodded, and scuttled away to the bar.

"So," I continued, presuming Dani's unwavering interest in my diabetes, "you just take one of these out, then you take this thing and you cock it, then you place it against your finger, then . . ."

Dani was doing a heroic job trying to look interested, but I could tell that, like any good hypnotist, I was making her very, very sleepy.

"So, how come you think you're diabetic?" I asked.

"Well, if I don't eat for a long time I get all weird and confused and clammy."

"Hypoglycemia."

"Yeah, that's what it's called."

"Don't you get the biggest craving for Pop-Tarts smothered in hot fudge and then dipped in Cool Whip when that happens?"

"Hmm, nah, I tend to just go for stuff like grapes or something."

Grapes? "But there's no chocolate in those. You know that, right?"

"Yeah, doesn't bother me, really. I mean, don't get me wrong, I'll happily dip a grape in chocolate. I just don't really *crave* that."

"Amazing."

The waitress came and delivered our sodas, and we finally got around to ordering. The lady ordered a French dip, and I ordered a cheeseburger with fries as I sheepishly put my diabetes supplies away into my case.

As I put it on the chair next to me, I saw out of the corner of my eye a handsome man rounding the corner and walking toward us, his golden, tightly combed locks glistening in the dim lights of the dining room. He was staring straight at me with his bedroom eyeballs, his lips curved into a smile. He approached our table gingerly, looking around at the other empty tables next to us and at the loud family nearby, and knelt down between us as if he were about to whisper into our ears North Raleigh's sexiest secrets. Who was this mysterious man interrupting our heterosexual date with his handsomeness?

"Hi, good evening," he said in a hushed tone.

"Hi," Dani and I said in unison.

"My name is Chuck, I'm the floor manager here. I have a proposal for you."

Go on.

"And I'll go ahead and tell you," he went on, "it involves free dessert."

It was all I could do not to slap him and say, "We'll do it!" But I had to give Dani a chance to weigh in. Also we needed to know what the proposal was.

"We have a large party that's come in, and this is really the only room we can fit them in. I'd love to buy you guys dessert if you'd agree to move to another table, in the other room."

I shot Dani a look that said, unequivocally, "Oh, *hell* yes." She shot me a look back that said, also unequivocally, "OK, but aren't you diabetic?"

"I can take some extra insulin, no problem," I assured her. "We can't say no to free dessert."

"OK," she said. "Let's do this."

"That's great, thank you so much," Chuck said, clapping his hands together as we gathered our things, followed him to another room, and sat down at a smaller table.

"It's kind of a shame," Dani said, as we got comfortable. "We won't be able to hear that obnoxious family all the way over here."

As if on cue, the screams of an antsy toddler erupted from the room we'd just been in.

"Oh, sure we will," I said. "Now, what should we get for dessert?"

———

The date was going pretty well so far. We had an easy rapport with each other, and nothing disastrous had happened. I had gotten on that horse again, and we were trotting around the course and clearing at least half of the hurdles.

Sometime between the burgers and our free dessert—Charleston Chocolate Chip Pie—Dani said something that shocked me to my very core.

"Nah, I don't really believe Jesus is the Son of God."

I'm not sure how we arrived at a conversation about the historical Jesus after a discussion encompassing tattoos, Pop-Tarts, and hypoglycemia, but I guess it kind of makes sense.

"You what?"

"Yeah, I mean, I think Jesus was great, you know, and he had a lot of good things to say and interesting ideas. But I just don't buy the whole 'Son of God' thing, you know?"

"But what about . . . I mean, do you pray?"

"I guess, in a way. More like talking to whatever's out there. My mom says I'm just lazy."

"Too lazy to believe in Jesus?"

"Yeah, well, like a lazy thinker, I guess. She says it's just easier for me not to believe than to have faith." Dani took a big swig of her Diet Coke.

I couldn't believe what I was hearing. Jesus wasn't the Son of God? He was just some guy? Hanging out with twelve other guys, preachin'? Dani was the first human I'd ever known who had expressed skepticism of Jesus's divinity. I'd always assumed that everyone just naturally believed this, like they believed in the existence of the moon, or heaven, or the magic of Christmas.

"Don't get me wrong," Dani continued, noting my stunned surprise. "I believe that, if he existed, he was a great man. But, you know, I don't think he was . . . what is it? Divine."

If he existed? She was blowing. My. Mind.

"Wow, that's really wild," I said, thinking that *it was absolutely insane.* Sure, I had withdrawn from Young Life, and sure, I didn't spend much (any) time reading the Bible or reflecting on whatever lessons I'd learned at the previous Sunday's church youth group gathering. But I still believed. In Jesus, in God, in prayer. If I didn't believe in prayer, what would I do about the weird desires for my fellow man that had been keeping me up nights? How would I be assured that these embarrassing yearnings would go away, or would be conquered, as long as I wanted that badly enough? I would have nowhere to turn.

I was sure that, eventually, Dani would believe, too. Why? Because she just would—everyone would. Because it was the truth, and it would be self-evident. Wouldn't it?

But I held off on preaching to her that night, because no one wants to be saved while trying to enjoy free pie. We continued our complimentary dessert, switching to talk of books. I was currently reading *The Vampire Lestat*; she was reading the collected works of

Dorothy Parker. I complimented her on her taste and made a mental note to look up who Dorothy Parker was at my earliest opportunity.

I paid the check, and we made our way out to the Plymouth. It was time to do the next thing. It was only eight thirty, the night was young, and we were young and immortal.

Everyone knows that dates should have three acts. This was taught to us by Shakespeare, or *Sesame Street*, or maybe *Falcon Crest*. (*Love Connection*?) The man and woman go to dinner, the man and the woman do something else after that, during which they might kiss, then the man and the woman either go home together or go their separate ways after an awkward good-bye because the kiss was gross.

So after a spirited and eye-opening first act, it was time for the second. As planned, I proposed we go record shopping, an idea that Dani was shockingly cool with, so we headed down Falls of Neuse Road to the Schoolkids Records at Quail Corners strip mall, where we could engage in more witty banter as we browsed through all the Monty Python posters.

I pulled into the shopping center and circled around to search for a parking place near the store, and my heart sank: The store was closed. This was not part of the plan. What on earth would we do now? I had no backup plan. There was an ice cream shop open, but we'd already had dessert.

"Shit," I said.

I circled around again as I tried to figure out what we should do instead—go to the mall? The park? A last-minute movie? Finishing my final lap around the parking lot, I turned to head out to the exit, and all of a sudden brakes squealed, an angry horn blared, and headlights shined into our surprised eyes. We had just almost crashed into a car that had the right-of-way, and now the person in that car was waiting for me to proceed, now that I'd made him squeal to a stop. And he was pissed.

As if by instinct, Dani looked out her window, lifted her hand up, and flipped the guy the bird with a haughty scowl. "Fuck off!"

Now he was really pissed.

I skidded out in front of him and bolted for the exit, turning right onto a back road. My eyes widened when I looked into the rearview mirror and saw that the car had also turned right and was following us.

"Oh my God, I think he's chasing us!" I shrieked.

"Oh, shit!"

"OK, OK," I said, breathless with fear. "I'll just . . . I'll just . . ." I slammed on the gas and skidded down Country Ridge Road until it dead-ended. In the rearview mirror I could see the guy was barreling toward us, probably cocking his firearm with his free hand while getting a hand job from his cousin. I didn't bother to stop at the stop sign, just swerved to the left to turn onto Tremont Drive, my poor Plymouth's wheels squealing out in pain. I accelerated again, checking my rearview mirror and, sure enough, the guy was in hot pursuit. Dani sat with one hand over her mouth, constantly turning around and checking to see how close he was to us.

It was here where my experience driving the back roads of North Raleigh worked to my advantage. Like my dad before me, I always took the long way to wherever I was going, and I knew these back roads like the front of the back of my hand. I'd be damned if I was going to let some jerk my date had just flipped off punk me on this turf.

We flew down Tremont until we hit Indian Trail. A screech, some more tire spinning, then it was Hiddenbrook Drive. Hiddenbrook to Hemingway, Hemingway to Quail Hollow, Quail

Hollow to Compton, *screech squeal shriek*, Compton to Latimer, Latimer to Duke, Duke to Sweetbriar, and Sweetbriar to, finally, Millbrook Road. I stopped at that intersection, put the car in park, checked my rearview mirror again, and declared, tasting adrenaline in my mouth, "I think we lost him." I felt like both Bo and Luke Duke. And how was my Daisy doing?

"Oh my God, I'm so sorry, that's totally my fault," Dani said.

"Oh no," I said, trying not to tremble visibly, "don't worry, that guy was obviously an asshole." I was still out of breath. I looked over at her, and we both laughed. At this point in a normal date, there would probably have been a kiss, and possibly a major detour into Gropeytown. But we didn't kiss; I was convinced that a kiss should happen at the end of a date, as a kind of down payment on the next date. Just like they did in biblical times. But that's because I was not being led around by my pelvis. If I'd been out with a dude I would probably have nose-dived into his lap to celebrate our survival. But poor Dani didn't even get an appreciative grope of her outer thigh.

As we both recovered from the scare, it dawned on me how close we were to my house. I checked my watch. It was just before nine now. I really wanted to get off these roads in case we happened upon Night Rider again.

"Hey, I live close to here—you want to go to my house?" I said.

"Sure, that's cool."

I don't know what I was thinking or how she took this proposal. Did she think we would be going up to my room? Did she know I'd never had a girl up to my room? Did she realize how terrified I was of trying to kiss her? Did she know that my mom would probably bring up Jesus?

I had no answers to these questions just yet. But I had basically decided that we had screeched and skidded our way to the end of the date's second act. It was time for the hilarious third.

———

We walked into the living room, where my dad sat in his La-Z-Boy watching Larry King on CNN. Mom washed dishes up in the kitchen.

"Hello!" I said, as Dani shyly walked behind me, smiling and nodding hello.

"Mom, Dad, this is Dani," I bellowed and gestured toward Dani, as if I were Vanna White.

"Hi!" Mom said, reaching a hand out from her dishtowel to shake Dani's. "Honey, you are gorgeous!"

"Oh, thank you," Dani said, thrilled by the compliment. I quickly realized: I hadn't even told Dani how good she looked. Not once did I shower her with empty but well-meant flattery. What a fraud I was.

Dad shook her hand, too. "Has anybody ever told you that you look like Geena Davis?" he said. Oh, he was good.

"Actually, no, I've never heard that, but thank you, that's quite a compliment!" My parents were wooing her better than I ever could.

"Oh my gosh, you really do," I said, trying to piggyback on my dad's line. "*Beetlejuice!*"

Mom asked the obligatory questions about Dani's family and chitchatted for a few minutes before she and Dad made themselves scarce and went upstairs to leave us in peace.

What on earth were we going to do down here? I HAD NO IDEA.

"Is this you?" Dani asked, pointing at a picture in the framed collection of photographs on the wall. Every year Dad always collected the best family photographs of the year and made a collage of them to give to Mom for Christmas. This one was from 1972, the year I was born.

"Yep, that's me. I was obviously more of a jock back then."

The picture showed me as a little blobby baby, the shape of an egg, wearing a sweatshirt with a picture of a football on it. The only time in my life I ever wore such a thing.

"You were a fat baby!"

"Yeah, the fattest one in the family."

It was then that I knew what we should do: look at photo albums! What beautiful young lady out on a first date wouldn't want to sit next to her suitor and peruse page after page after page of family photographs? Trips to Kerr Lake, trips to Disneyland, Thanksgiving dinner at Grandma Ruby's, Christmas morning in our pajamas, it was all there for the seeing. Somehow Dani managed not to melt into the carpet at my suggestion.

My parents were dedicated family photo scrapbookers, and the bookshelf in the living room was lined with them. I picked a few off the shelf and joined Dani on the couch. That's right, I said I picked *a few* off the shelf.

Dani faked interest in our family albums like a true champion, remarking on many of the photos we looked at ("Oh, I loved It's a Small World!" "That looks like a really great Thanksgiving spread!" "Did you catch any fish?" "A baby alligator, really?") and generally indulging my need to tell embarrassing family stories, like the time my mom accidentally got so drunk on screwdrivers on my uncle's boat in Florida ("I couldn't taste the vodka!") that she threw up over the side, then fell in the water.

"We should get her to tell us that story," Dani said. *Seriously?* I thought. 'Cause we could do that.

Dani was too indulgent. Her agreeable reaction to the terrible photo album slide show lulled me into a false sense that hey, I was killing it. This was a slam-dunk. She was enjoying herself. She was satisfied. There was nothing she'd rather be doing on this couch at this very moment than flipping through multiple books of pictures of my family members blowing out birthday candles, posing with the Easter Bunny, and dancing with mops.

Which I guess is why I decided it would be a good idea to show Dani my Snoopy doll. *I did what?* Yes, flipping through the photos, we came across a picture of me as a five-year-old holding a brand-new stuffed Snoopy. How I loved that Snoopy when I was a boy. Loved him so deeply. Slept with him every night. Dressed him in different outfits.

"Oh, that's a cute one of yo—"

"I still have that Snoopy!" I couldn't help myself. As Dani sat on the couch with wide eyes that I mistook for genuine curiosity, not dread, I went over to the closet where I had a shelf of items from my boyhood, and took him out. He was still dressed in his red nightgown, his white fur discolored from the years of being boy-handled.

I brought Snoopy over to Dani and introduced them. She took him from me and gave him the once-over, looking like she wanted to ask him for a ride home.

"I still have all of his outfits! There's a disco one and an Uncle Sam one and an airline pilot one, and . . ."

"A disco outfit, huh?" she said. "That's pretty hot."

All of a sudden, all became perfectly clear. I realized—observing Dani's expression of mild concern—that the date had kind of gone off the rails, and not in a good way. In a weird way. It could have been weirder, sure. Like if I had decided to put on one of my mother's dresses and start reciting the Pledge of Allegiance to the hydrangeas over in the corner. But just because it could have been weirder didn't mean it wasn't already weird enough.

"Um, it's, like, nine thirty, and my curfew is at ten, so I kind of need to go," Dani said, leaning her head to the side to soften the blow. She probably wanted to nip this thing in the bud before I got out my full collection of paper dolls and my sister's Holly Hobbie house and demand that she and Snoopy join us for a tea party. In any case, my flailing attempts to do ANYTHING with Dani on that couch but make out with her had gotten ridiculous, and Dani, bless her, knew when a thing was not going to happen. (She also knew, at this point, that she didn't really want a thing to happen.)

I awkwardly put my Snoopy back into the closet (that damn closet) and collected the photo albums and stacked them back on the shelf, as Dani visited the bathroom and probably laughed until she cried and then said "What?" to herself a lot while staring at her reflection in the mirror.

I drove her home and walked her to the door. It was apparent to both of us that there shouldn't be a kiss, there really really shouldn't. Still, a trace of awkward will-we-or-won't-we uncertainty remained as we said good-bye on the porch. The front door was open, and through the storm door we could see Ashley on the floor of the living room watching TV. She waved. We were both relieved that she was there, because that meant it was too late to steal a kiss.

"Thanks a lot, I had a great time," Dani said with a perfectly straight face.

"Yeah, we should do this again," I said perfunctorily.

"Oh yeah, totally, awesome, yeah," Dani concurred. We hugged briefly, and she walked inside.

I walked back to my Plymouth and turned on the car. "What on *earth*, Tim?" I asked myself. In a few short months, Dani and I would see each other again at a party, bond as we took shots of Jack Daniel's, and quickly become lifelong friends. In a few short months we would go to a Mojo Nixon concert in Chapel Hill, and I would be schooled by Mr. Nixon on how a real man treats the ladies—in this case, he jumps off the stage and cuts a flirty hillbilly circle around Dani while singing "Stuffin' Martha's Muffin." But that was later. Right now, in the aftermath of our date, I felt I'd been found out to be a huge weirdo. This night had been, oh, what's the word?

"Fiasco," I said to myself, fixing my curly bangs in the rearview mirror with one hand as I shoved the cassette into the stereo with the other. The first strains of The Smiths' "That Joke Isn't Funny Anymore" escaped from the car speakers, and I turned it up. What do *you* think, Morrissey?

He crooned that I should park the car at the side of the road.

"Yeah, I've done that already," I said. "Then what?"

Slow like syrup, he emotes a few more notes. Ugh, get to the point, Morrissey.

Morrissey then gets to the point: Apparently, time's tide will smother me. Thanks, Moz! Anyway, yeah, total fiasco.

Also, Jesus might not be real.

Raleigh's Shelley Lake Park is, during the day, a manmade pastoral wonderland of hikers, bicyclists, picnickers, skateboarders, Frisbee throwers, paddleboaters, soccer players, and sunbathers of every size and description. A place where families go to frolic, where couples go to hold hands and perhaps give each other innocent pecks on the cheek, and where dogs go to chase things and whiz on trees.

When the sun goes down, though, Shelley Lake turns into a rotten, sulfurous underworld of sin and debauchery, a ghastly hellscape where sordid fornicators, uncouth youths, and drug smokers gather to bow down to their demonic idols, swear everlasting oaths to their fiery protectors, and huddle within the acrid purple dry ice of the dead to tug on joints and pass them around like a bunch of giggly retarded gargoyles.

Take, for example, the gaggle of teenage idiots clustered around this picnic table in the heart of the park. A serpentine trail of smoke cuts through the night sky above them, a sinister, immaculate trail punctured only by the coughing of the guy with the hilarious curly bangs.

"You OK, Tim?" his lady friend Dani, in the flannel shirt, blue jeans, and cowboy boots, asks him. Marcus and JJ, the other two in the group, who appear to not have showered since before their last Metallica concert, look on, giggling.

"Yep. Yep, I'm fine," the young man answers, lying through his braces. Because he's not fine, though he doesn't really know it yet. Sure, he feels soft and spongy, and his brain is enjoying an exhilarating ride on the Tetrahydrocannabinol Train, but the THC he's been sucking into his clammy adolescent body is quite strong—the boy keeps seeing the face of the scary clown from Poltergeist *in the clouds. The evil weed is also masking the fact that his blood sugar level is nose-diving to a*

dangerously low number. The preventative signals his body usually gives him that danger is lurking—confusion, perspiration, tingling fingers, inability to communicate effectively—are easily ignored by both him and his degenerate friends as they descend into a murky swirl of psyche- delic dreamscaping. Yes, that pot was laced with some terrible bullshit.

"Wow, it's . . ." the young boy comments before losing his train of thought and bending over in an embarrassing fit of feminine giggling.

"Dude, he's, like, . . ." JJ starts to say before forgetting what he was going to say.

"Fucked up?" Marcus finishes for him.

"That sounds right," Dani declares.

All four of them are overtaken by the compulsion to laugh. Just laugh it all out. Laugh at the way the trees look like Smurf heads against the sky, laugh at the very concept of a picnic table, laugh at the thought of Marcus going into a life of politics, laugh at Dani being in a band and refusing to play tambourine, laugh at the boy and his crusty hair.

"Wow, I think there was something in that stuff," Dani says after taking a breath from all the laughing and inhaling a clump of her hair. She's thankfully talking some sense. "Who'd you get this from? I feel like a laser beam."

"You what? I what? He what?" the young diabetic says before shouting "Ahhhhh!" He looks at the sky again. The evil clown face is gone now.

"I got it from Jeremy," Marcus explains. "You know him. He's got a . . . car."

"Yeah, yeah, dude," JJ says. "I've been in Jeremy's car. Like, in it."

The young boy is now sitting down on the ground picking up blades of grass and tickling his ear with them. He starts sniffing them.

"Tim, you OK?" Dani says. Someone needs to give this young lady a citizenship award.

"I'm . . . you know . . . um," he responds.

Dani continues to look at him, crouched on the ground. "Tim? Tim?"

The boy lets out a snort, then wipes his nose with his muddy hand. He stands up, and Dani gets a good look at him. It looks like a squirrel has just taken a whiz on his face. She leans forward and, in the glow of the moonlight, gets a glimpse of his glassy eyes.

"Uh-oh, I think he's low," Dani says. "C'mon, Marcus, we need to get to the store. He needs sugar."

"What, it's a diabetes thing?" JJ asks.

"Yeah, he's got to have some sugar. Tim? Tim! Do you have any sugar on you?"

He lifts up his hand and opens it to show Dani the blades of grass he's been holding.

"OK, that doesn't do much for us, Tim. We've got to go to the store. I've got the munchies anyway. Who wants doughnuts? 'Cause I fucking do."

"Yeah, dude, doughnuts, yeah, what?" JJ says, even though his blood sugar is fine.

The four Musketeers, stoned as sea cucumbers, wade through the darkness, finally arriving at the parking lot and Marcus's Mazda. From a distance, you would be hard-pressed to point out which one of them is currently in the throes of an epic blood sugar plunge; they all look like zombies, hungry for brains and Hostess CupCakes.

They get in the car and Marcus drives them with all due haste to Sav-A-Center, the closest grocery store. Dani gets out of the front seat and helps the young marionette out of the back. She walks with him to the entrance as if she were escorting her grandmother to the early bird dinner at the K&W Cafeteria.

Dani's been through this drill before—being out somewhere with the boy at a rock show or a party or the Starcade and seeing his face go

*blank and clammy, then having to rush out and get him something
from the DJ Cinnamon's Bakery or the Fast Fare or the Food Lion
before he collapses onto the floor because, dammit, he never brings any
freaking sugar out with him.*

*So Dani was prepared to walk the grocery aisles with her friend,
only worried that he not enter the Vortex of Indecision she knows he's
prone to falling into when they're wandering in the land of Way Too
Many Choices.*

*The boy's eyes expand as he enters the wide-screen Technicolor
Land of Oz that is the Sav-A-Center. He pivots left, knowing full well
in which direction the bakery resides. He now stands at the edge of a
yellow brick road that leads directly up to the pastry case against the
far wall.*

*"Ahhhhhh, look at all the glorious pastries!" the boy exclaims, the
first full sentence he has uttered in about an hour.*

*"They are pretty good lookin'," Dani agrees as they march onward
to the case. Dani turns her head around to see if Marcus and JJ are
nearby. They are both thumbing through magazines at the racks back
by the checkout lines. She turns back around, only to see that the diabetic slob she arrived with has disappeared.*

*Ice cream aisle, she knows instinctively. She scurries to the frozen
foods section, and, sure enough, sees the boy clumsily stuffing into his
gaping mouth a Klondike bar he has pulled out of a box.*

*She walks up to him and takes the torn box out of his hands, looks
around, and puts it back in the freezer. While she's doing this, he's
already moved on to a box of frozen Butterfinger ice cream bars. Judging from the way he's messily shoving one of them into his mouth, they
are wonderfully edible.*

*"OK, Tim, you have to stop doing that," Dani says, taking the
Butterfinger box out of his hand and hiding it under a stack of other
ice cream bars. He stumbles and upsets a stack of ice cream sandwiches,*

133

and they come crashing down, flopping out onto the floor just as Dani finishes saying, "Let's go get some doughnuts or something."

The boy sets off, dashing over toward the forgotten pastry case and leaving his friend to pick up the pieces in the frozen food section behind him. He turns and glides along the floor of the cereal aisle, his bright eyes taking in all of the delicious options—Lucky Charms, Cookie Crisp, Apple Jacks. If only he had a bowl of milk handy. He turns right at the end of the aisle, looks down, and sees that somehow he has a Hostess cherry pie, a bag of Hershey's Kisses, and a Little Debbie Star Crunch in his hands. He shrugs and soldiers on until, finally, he comes face to face with the glass pastry case of his dreams.

He presses his nose against the glass and takes it all in: There are bear claws, cream cheese Danishes, Boston cream–filled doughnuts, regular glazed, chocolate glazed, chocolate cream-filled, oh, it is all there and more. But now he must decide—how many, and which ones?—and, dear baby Jesus, that is the last thing he is equipped to do.

By the grace of God, Dani is there to save the day. She trots up to the case, nudges him to the side, takes a white paper bag from the stack, grabs the tongs, and starts putting pastries in the bag.

"OK, I think we have enough, Tim," she says after filling the bag to capacity. She guides him back toward the checkout stand, where Marcus and JJ are still flipping through their trashy supermarket tabloids and learning about Elizabeth Taylor's latest marriage, to Michael Jackson's chimpanzee.

The sugared-up supercouple make their way up to the checkout. Dani takes all of the items out of the boy's hands and places them on the conveyor belt. The unfortunate young cashier begins ringing him up, the poor thing.

"That's $8.79," she says, expecting a normal human response.

The boy pulls some crumpled paper out of the pocket of his unnecessarily tight corduroys. There's a dollar bill, a school note, and an empty and sticky Klondike bar wrapper. He offers all of these to the nice cashier, who narrows her eyes and looks at Dani for a lifeline.

"Sorry, he's diabetic," she says, then turns to her friend. "Tim," she says in crisp, clear English, "give me your wallet."

Still able to respond to emphatically delivered demands, he squeezes his billfold out of his cords and hands it over. Dani pulls more dollar bills out and hands them to the cashier as the boy licks Klondike ice cream off his hands.

"OK, guys," Dani says to Marcus and JJ, who now are fully up to date with Donna Rice's diet secrets. The kids all leave the Sav-A-Center and walk back to the car, many many pastries in their possession and probably only a few items stolen.

Did the manic scramble to get to the Sav-A-Center and the bright fluorescent lights of the store kill their buzz? Never mind. Marcus has another joint in his glove compartment. So it's back to the moral vacuum that is Shelley Lake at night, where they can stay for a while, because now they have snacks.

For now, at least. There's a boy in the backseat eating one of the cream-filled doughnuts, and he will soon move onto the bear claw. And he's not really in a sharing mood.

CHAPTER 6

MEET ME AT THE COTERIE, WHERE WE WILL ENJOY AVOCADOS, THE VILLAGE VOICE, AND BEER OVER ICE

There comes a time in every person's life when he encounters electrifying things he never knew existed before, and he excitedly engages in the blissful process of adapting this new information into his understanding of the world around him and realizes that he can never go back to the boring and lifeless days of yore. Like when Britney Spears discovered Daisy Dukes and pole dancing, or Rush Limbaugh found out about bacon and spittle.

At the squeaky age of sixteen, I landed a job at a bakery/used bookstore that, after a rocky start, ended up becoming surely the best job I would ever have. It opened up brave new worlds for me, worlds that hinted at the wild and wonderful universe that was out there for the taking once you got beyond the straitjacket of your own mega-normal upbringing. It also had the added benefit of providing easy access to lots and lots of homemade cookies, cakes, pastries, and other fine baked goods.

The bakery was called the Coterie, and it sat in Greystone Village Shopping Center in North Raleigh between a surf shop and a dog-grooming salon. It was run by an ex-hippy named Will who spent some time in Canada and jail during the Vietnam War and these days spent as much time as possible golfing. So already he was the type of human I'd never encountered in my life, and someone my parents weren't sure they really approved of. Laurie had worked there before me, but when she quit her senior year, she told me that she would talk to Will about hiring me to replace her. One evening, she came into my room to tell me the great news.

I was on my bed reading, toggling between Stephen King's *It* and a diabetes pamphlet Mom had picked up at the pharmacy and forced upon me when she got home. Both were horrifying, so whenever one of them became too much for me, I would put it down and pick up the other. *It*, of course, featured a murderous clown who loved to eat children, and the diabetes pamphlet covered in explicit detail all the possible complications that could arise later in life for a young diabetic who didn't take care of himself: glaucoma, cataracts, foot infections and disorders, hypertension, heart disease, impotence (what's that?), nerve damage, and amputation. And, obviously, depression.

People with diabetes are far more likely to have a foot or leg amputated than other people. The problem? Many people with diabetes have artery disease, which reduces blood flow to the feet. Also, many people with diabetes have nerve disease, which reduces sensation. Together, these problems make it easy to get ulcers and infections that may lead to amputation.

So if I'm not careful, I could lose a foot. Duly noted. But could this pamphlet possibly drive this point home with some useful visuals so that I'd be under no illusions that feet problems are at all attractive? Why, yes, it could. I shuddered and dry-heaved a little when I saw a giant photograph that showed a real live ulcer on the underside of some poor tramp's swollen, diseased foot.

Good *Lord*. The ulcer was the size of a fifty-cent piece, it was the color of zombie blood, it had flecks of scabby pus along its periphery, and it was surrounded by yellowy, cracked skin that appeared ready to cede its territory to the expanding ulcer at the earliest opportunity.

Breathlessly I put the pamphlet down and picked *It* back up, needing a little palate cleanse. I'd had my fill of the American Medical Association's diabetes horror show and felt the need to turn to some lighter material, say about Pennywise the clown going medieval on some Vermont schoolchildren. Then I thought maybe I should just, you know, check my feet real quick. Mom was always going on about how I needed to take care of my feet, and I usually just ignored her, but there was no ignoring the photo I'd just seen. Perhaps I should just have a look, give them the once-over, you know, just to make sure my feet *haven't been eaten alive yet by the pus-seeping ulcer monster.*

I sat up and swung my legs over the bed and onto the floor. I lifted up one foot to the opposite knee and examined the underside: It was supple and pristine, like a newborn baby diabetic's bottom. But wait, what's that tiny pinprick of discoloration? It's . . . blue, yes, it's blue. What might it be? Hmm. Maybe *the subepidermal glow of an ulcer fetus that will soon explode through my foot like a hungry alien*?

"Hey, Tim," Laurie said as she poked her head into my room.

I gasped audibly and turned to her.

"I talked to Will about you, and he said to come by this week to talk about the job."

"Cool, thanks," I said.

"What's that?" She pointed at the diabetes pamphlet featuring photos of outtakes from John Carpenter's *The Thing*.

"Oh, this?" I said, picking it up. "It's just, you know, a new Stephen King diabetes pamphlet I've been reading. Did you know that my feet are going to eventually look like two little Elephant Man twins?"

Laurie's eyes narrowed. "Hmmmm. No, that's probably a worst-case scenario."

She was probably right. Anyway, I could easily get hit by a bus before that happened. In the meantime, I was excited at the prospect of having a hip new job. I needed this change of scenery. After my hilarious foray back into high school dating, I had a few more girlfriends, and things predictably didn't work out. With poor Lisa, whom I started seeing a few months after my date with Dani/destiny, it was because we were always exasperatedly yelling at each other—a trend I continued even after we'd broken up and Lisa had matured, stopped yelling, and moved on to other, much better-looking dudes. I just couldn't stop yelling at her whenever I saw her. In the hallways, in the school parking lot, at a party, at the Taco Bell. Yelling at Lisa became my thing, and I couldn't give it up. Sample argument, while I was driving us to some rock show or other during happier times:

> Me: *You don't like The Primitives? What's wrong with you?*
> Lisa: *I don't know, I just don't like them.*
> Me: *Have you listened to their album? Do you know their songs? "Stop Killing Me"? "Spacehead"? "Way Behind Me"? Are you deaf?*
> Lisa: *I just . . . I just don't like them, I don't know.*
> Me: *But you like Jesus and Mary Chain! You like Blondie, don't you? You like the Buzzcocks! And The Smiths! What do you have against The Primitives?*

> Lisa: *Nothing! Nothing, Tim, I just don't really care for their*
>   *music! It doesn't appeal to me! It's just not my thing!*
> Me: *Why?!*
> Lisa: *I think they're kind of boring!*
> Me: *God, I can't believe you said that, you are such a bitch!*

I was an angry, angry little hobbit, and angry hobbits yell at ex-girlfriends because they are also often secretly gay little hobbits. (I'm so sorry, Lisa.)

With Zoe, my next, *extremely* short-lived girlfriend, things didn't work out mainly because I think she couldn't shake the idea that there was some problem with our chemistry. Can't imagine what it was. But when it came to the romance, things were just not happening, even though she was a stunning beauty with alabaster skin, full red lips, and an award-worthy wardrobe of secondhand French dresses. When we kissed for the first time, it was soft, sweet, and, for me at least, a little too wet. After the kiss she looked at me with narrowed eyes and tilted her head slightly, as if she just couldn't put her finger on something. Something missing. She would proceed to do this after every kiss.

"What is it, the thing that is missing?" she always appeared to be asking herself as she looked at me in the pale afterglow of our passionless liplock. Our hangout sessions went on for a few months until we finally just evaporated into a puff of sexless smoke in her living room, like the dry ice at a Bauhaus concert. No, that's too sexy. Like the dry ice at a Peter Cetera concert.

So I would be leaving my great job at the drugstore, where I had access to any and all Hershey products I could ever possibly stuff into my greasy face (under the necessary circumstances, of course), and trade that for a new job at a bakery where the selection of suicidal sweets would be epic. I looked back down at my foot, and at the suspicious blue mark on the underside that might possibly one day explode with bloodred lava and gooey pus. I rubbed the mark with my thumb, and it disappeared. Oh. Probably not an ulcer, I guess. Yeah, a pen mark. It was a pen mark.

I laid back and picked *It* back up, able to comfortably settle back in to this tale of fantastical child murder now that I was sure that my feet wouldn't need to be lopped off, for today at least.

———

One might think that a bakery would be one of the worst places for a newly diabetic teenager to be working, especially one with a fearsome sweet tooth and a particular weakness for salmonella-rific delights like cookie dough and cake icing. Sure, I can see your point. But consider this: It was also one of the best, because since I was still in the throes of the honeymoon period—which, unlike real honeymoons, can last up to a few years—my blood sugar level was always threatening to plummet at any given moment if I wasn't super-vigilant of what my levels were (which I wasn't). It had quickly become my biggest fear that I would find myself somewhere—a desert island, a campsite, the boiler room of a naval vessel—with plunging blood sugar and no Double Stuf Oreos to combat it. So it was always best to err on the side of deliciousness.

I went into the shop one Saturday soon after my powwow with Laurie and met Will, because I wouldn't just get the job without a thorough examination of my credentials, obviously. That just isn't how things work in our merit-based system of nepotism and crony capitalism, come on. This is America.

I walked in during the early Saturday morning rush, and the place was buzzing. Folks, most of them at least middle-aged, sat at little circular tables drinking coffee, chatting, and munching on their sweet and/or savory breakfast goodies. Many tables were taken up by older couples who didn't have the good sense to sleep in on a Saturday morning. At one table sat two men, both looking to be in their sixties. One of them was bearded and grumpy-looking, and his name was probably Leopold; the other was the pretty one: He was clean-shaven, tanned, and he wore short white tennis shorts and a white T-shirt, against which his pectoral and arm muscles pressed with admirable persistence.

The shop smelled unbelievably delicious, a mixture of fresh-baked muffins, coffee, cakes, burnt cheese, and used books. NPR's *Weekend Edition* program played on the speakers, and books lined the walls of the place, hardcovers and paperbacks great and small. On a shelf by the front windows sat copies of the *New York Times*, *Barron's*, the *New York Review of Books*, and the *Village Voice*. I'd heard of all of these but had never seen them face-to-face, much less cracked the pages of any one of them. Mine was a *Saturday Evening Post* kind of family. The most explosively liberal publication we consumed was the *News and Observer*, Raleigh's daily newspaper that we got every morning in spite of the fact that it had, in my mother's opinion, a terrible liberal bent, as evidenced by the endless stream of unflattering photos of Jesse Helms it was always running. (These were very funny photos.) In short, this was the most highfalutin establishment I'd ever stepped into. I could feel myself getting smarter and more insufferably smug the longer I gazed at the covers of these new elitist publications before me, not to mention the shelf upon shelf of books—Godless novels by the likes of Norman Mailer, Gore Vidal, and some guy with the unlikely name of Truman Capote. Imagine what I'd be like after a few *months* in this joint.

Will was a big, burly guy with a full head of graying hair and a wonderfully bushy and equally graying moustache. He stood behind the counter in a white apron cutting up vegetables for the soup of the day. He looked me over, asked if I could work weekends, noticed my ridiculous/impressive curly bangs swooping down into my face like a weeping willow, and said, "OK, start next Saturday morning, but you'll have to keep that hair out of your face somehow."

"Oh, sure," I said, having no idea how on earth I was going to accomplish that. There was nowhere else for my luxurious bangs to go but down into my face, really, cascading over my forehead in tight curlicues, and often swirling directly into my eyeballs. These hair shoots were a force of nature, and they could only be tamed by lots and lots of mousse. They were also a major part of my public persona—I was known for them, like Ayn Rand was known for her boobs or Jayne Mansfield was famous for her fountainheads. Many of the black kids at school referred to them as "Jheri curls" and complimented me on them quite frequently, not always with sarcasm. I supposed I could tease them over to the side by using extra mousse and maybe some Aqua Net, but the very idea of doing that felt like selling out. Anyway, I figured I'd cross that bridge when I came to it.

I would be a counter worker, waiting on customers, making sandwiches, making and pouring coffee, cleaning and busing tables, and, restocking sodas, beers, and cookies. I arrived at eight a.m. the next Saturday wearing my best vest and my shiniest patent leather shoes, and there was Will behind the counter chatting with a customer about his golf game. The same regulars sat at their tables around the shop, including the gay couple. It was the first day of the rest of my life.

I had managed to stretch my curly bangs to the side of my head, gather them into one big swirly clump at the end with the assistance of gobs of mousse, and hook them around my right ear. Not all of them could make the journey; the ones on the left couldn't stretch far enough, so I just tucked them up under the others and hoped for the best.

I went around behind the counter, and Will stopped his conversation to say hello. He looked at my hair and tilted his head, trying to make sense of it. He then looked at my outfit and probably wondered why I was wearing my sister's clothes.

"How you doing?" he said.

"Good, good," I said. As Will turned to wash his hands, a tendril of hair popped out from behind my ear, bouncing and dangling in front of my eye. I quickly stretched it back and hooked it again, then pretended it never happened when he turned back to me and wiped his hands on his apron.

"OK, let's show you all about where the magic happens," he said, clapping his hands together and walking down the narrow area behind the counter to where the glass cases holding the pastries and cookies stood on both sides of the corner register.

"Pastries and breakfast stuff is here," he said, gesturing to the case on the left. "The prices are in the front of the tray, but you'll learn them soon enough. Over here are the cookies. We bake a bunch in the morning and just keep 'em stocked up all day."

The pastry case was a flakey, aromatic utopia. Everything you could ever want was there: cream cheese Danishes, blueberry and cream cheese Danishes, croissants, ham-and-cheese croissants, bear claws, cheese straws, banana nut muffins, chocolate muffins, blueberry muffins, carrot raisin muffins, strawberry croissants, EVERYTHING.

And just when I thought that this heaven I'd entered couldn't get any more scrumptiously obscene, I stepped over to the cookie case, and my knees buckled. Many of the cookies were nearly the size of Belgian waffles. There were deluxe chocolate chip, chocolate chocolate chip, oatmeal raisin, chocolate chip shortbread, peanut butter, peanut butter chocolate chip. I never wanted to come up for air. I was home.

Will took me into the back where the large ovens and the racks of newly baked cookies were. He had a row of large plastic containers out on the counter space, where he was doing what was called "setups" for the next morning's muffin baking: basically mixing together all the dry ingredients for each muffin so that all he had to do the next morning was toss in some milk, butter, and eggs, mix, and put the trays into the oven.

Around the corner was Leslie, the cake decorator, who came in mornings to work on the custom cake orders for the day. The one she was working on at the time was a big sheet cake with a picture of Chip 'n' Dale, the Disney chipmunks, in the center. Both looked delicious.

We walked back out to the front, and soon enough I was having a go at helping folks, ringing them up, refilling their coffees, and eyeing their Danishes as they took them away to their tables. Every time I bent down I rewrapped my bangs around my ear lest they pop out with a *boing* and unleash pandemonium in the bakery.

I quickly began to feel as if the regular Saturday morning customers didn't know what to make of this gangly new thing with the sticky hair and the ugly brown pants and the Siouxsie T-shirt underneath his sister's vest. When they came up to order something from me, they approached me cautiously, intermittently looking over at Will with mild discomfort, as if they didn't want to agitate the unsightly young vampire who should probably be asleep in his black-lit coffin rather than serving the early birds of the upper middle class Greystone Village cohort. I felt on display in a way that I hadn't been as a cashier at Kerr Drug. Maybe because this place had a hint of class, refinement, and exclusivity that Kerr Drug, which any old hobo might enter to buy cigarettes and suppositories, completely lacked. I felt a little out of my league. I mean, I didn't even *know* you could mix cream cheese with blueberries in a Danish. And who knew you could put carrots in a muffin? The most highfalutin thing I'd ever done with carrots was dip them in ranch dressing, at a cookout.

After about an hour, Will called me over to the sandwich station to give me a tutorial. He showed me the sandwich menu and gave me an overview of the fundamentals of Coterie sandwich making: Mayonnaise should go on the bread, mustard should go on the meat; if it's a vegetarian sandwich, the mustard should go on the cheese. There was a convection oven if folks wanted their sandwich hot, but that shouldn't really be encouraged because it holds up the line; it was mainly for the Reuben. Then Will got out a small spiral-bound notepad and opened it up.

"Here's the instructions. It has all the sandwiches, and it's pretty much a no-brainer. They're all pretty easy."

Easy for him to say. He knew what a Reuben was.

"You'll be making sandwiches during the lunch rush today, and I'll be out here taking orders."

I looked through the list and figured I could handle this OK. Slap some specified meat on some specified bread with some specified condiments and vegetables, and serve it up. The Reuben presented a bit of a curveball, but I figured it would just be a variation on the above, plus Thousand Island and sauerkraut, whatever that was.

I successfully made it through the morning hours, ringing

people up, refilling coffees, and serving folks croissants and muffins that I coveted mind, body, and soul. In anticipation of the lunch-time hour, Will talked me through the slicing of all the various meats, cheeses, and vegetables that needed to be replenished. The first few folks trickled in, Will took their orders and handed me the tickets, and I started making the sandwiches, spending too much time on each one, but eventually gaining my footing as the tickets lined up on the cutting board. I made roast beef and provolones on wheat; veggie cheeses on sunflower; turkey, tomato, and cucumber with vinaigrettes on sourdough; and even a few odd Reubens (and by odd, I mean strange/soggy/unrecognizable as Reubens).

Will critiqued my sandwich-making skills as we went along during the rush ("too much mayo, the turkey is swimming"; "try not to burn every Reuben"; "what is this supposed to be?"), and I started feeling more comfortable at the sandwich stand. As the early rush started dying down, Will took off his apron and went to hang it up.

"OK," he said. "I'm off."

You're what? I thought.

"You're leaving?"

"Yep, time to tee up."

Turned out Will had stayed late that day in order to break me in, but he usually came in early to bake and then left by midmorn-ing to go play golf. So he was leaving me here on my first day to handle whatever lunch stragglers came in, to preside over the small afternoon tea crowd, and to close the shop at five p.m. I would be left to my own devices, large and in charge of a café full of food and drink that I'd been craving all morning. Albacore tuna salad? All mine. Cheesy potato soup? *Es mío.* Enough cookie dough to put me to death twenty times over? ちょうだい!

A few minutes later, Will was gone, and a few minutes after that Leslie was out the door and the Chip 'n' Dale sheet cake was ready for pickup. By the end of *Car Talk* on NPR, I was alone. A few customers remained chatting at their tables, and as things quieted down I took the opportunity to leave the space behind the counter and survey the bookshelves of this, my new kingdom. There was row after row after row of science fiction, horror, classics of literature, pulp titles—a kitchen-sink collision of both sophisticated and vulgar prose on delectable display: Dickens, Dostoyevsky, Collins, King, Dick, Straub, Barker, Woolf, Hubbard—an endless supply of other worlds, other rooms, other voices, other options, both high and low. I picked a few titles off the shelf—*Floating Dragon* by Peter Straub and *Wifey* by Judy Blume—then walked over to get a *Village Voice*. I returned to the prep table behind the counter, opened the *Voice*, and started paging through it.

I immediately latched on to the Life in Hell comic strip by Matt Groening on one of the first pages. In a strange, subterranean way, I identified, immediately and profoundly, with Binky, the self-loathing, self-doubting, and anxiety-ridden rabbit gazing at me desperately from inside each panel, whispering "I am you." It was the first comic I'd seen outside of the Sunday paper or *Parade* magazine, and I marveled at how much existential dread could be contained in one quarter-page of an alternative weekly. This was no Hi and Lois or Hagar the Horrible. This comic vibrated with agitated longing, just like me.

It was the photo on the next page that made me want to run away from home and hitch a ride to Chelsea. The picture was illustrating Michael Musto's nightlife column, and it featured a go-go boy standing on a bar in a see-through Speedo receiving a sweaty dollar bill from a patron into his waistband. The sight of such a wonderfully smutty picture right there in front of me in black and white altered forever my understanding of what could be distributed into the great state of North Carolina and sold at a classy café. Something about the fact that this alluring scene was rendered in newsprint and not in glossy full-color photos made the existence of this go-go boy and his dollar-wielding friend even more real. Their world seemed closer to mine—reachable. How I wanted these worlds to converge, to manically undress, to hump in a spastic fashion. Sure, the guy in the Speedo had kind of dead eyes and probably a monstrous cocaine monkey on his back. But in another respect he was living the dream!

The sound of someone clearing his or her throat snapped me out of my tawdry reverie. I turned around to the front counter to see a small line of folks waiting to order. I whipped my head back to my *Voice* to close it, hoping nobody had seen what article I'd been lost in.

I zipped up to the counter, stretching my bangs across my forehead and hooking them around my ear once again before taking up paper and pen to take sandwich orders. I decided to collect all the new orders and then migrate over to the sandwich counter to get to work. The first few orders were pretty standard fare that posed absolutely no complications whatsoever. Then up stepped a woman in a fur coat with dyed auburn hair, her face powdered white, her lips painted crimson red, and '50s secretary glasses on her nose, through which her dark brown eyes looked at me with complete and utter bafflement.

"Yes, hello," she said in a husky voice. "I'd like an avocado jack sandwich on sunflower bread. Just sprouts and tomato."

I nodded and started writing those words on my notepad: avocado/jack, sunflower, sprouts, tomato. OK, great, I thought. Now, what's an avocado?

I had somehow not seen this particular sandwich on the list

when I'd been studying it, probably because I was too busy trying to figure out how to make a Reuben. The ugly truth: Avocados were a totally new concept to me. Sure, I'd heard the word, and if asked by Alex Trebek if it was an animal, vegetable, or mineral, I would have been able to say with absolute certainty that it was not an animal. Beyond that, I was at a loss. I was just a humble boy from a meat-and-potatoes family. I knew spinach, squash, brussels sprouts, green beans, broccoli, English peas, and butter beans. But avocados? What kind of elitist bullshit tree did they grow on?

I walked over to the sandwich table and started in on the first few orders, which mercifully just involved slapping meat on bread, adding some veggies, mayo, and mustard, and maybe salt and pepper. All the while, I was wracked with uncertainty about how exactly I was going to accomplish the construction of this mythical "avocado/jack sandwich." I couldn't very well ask this woman what it was; she was already looking at me like I was the village idiot, and I wasn't about to give her confirmation.

While I prepared the other sandwiches, I scanned the sandwich instructions for the "avocado jack" listing. I spotted it and hungrily gobbled up the step-by-step directions, written in Will's loopy handwriting:

SLICE ONE AVOCADO IN HALF AND PLACE ONE HALF OF IT ON THE BREAD. ADD JACK CHEESE AND WHATEVER VEGETABLES CUSTOMER ORDERS.

Vaguer sandwich instructions have never been written. I could feel trembling tears ready to burst out of my eye sockets and gush forth onto the cutting table in a furious cascade. Then I thought, *Hey, at least I now know that an avocado can be cut in half.*

I knelt down and opened the cooler under the counter to launch my avocado search. I moved around all the various stacks of Saran Wrapped cheeses and meats, as well as the plastic containers of sliced tomatoes, washed lettuce leaves, and sprouts. Then I saw two oval-shaped items that had the color and consistency of tree bark. I picked one up. Could this be what I was looking for?

I stood up and placed what I was now hoping against hope was an avocado on the counter. The woman stood on the other side of the cookie case talking to her friend, and as I started wondering what would happen if I just ran out of the store and never came back, I suddenly had an idea: I would take the "avocado" in hand, turn around so she sees me holding it, and see what look she gives it. Maybe she would have a flash of recognition when she saw what I had in my hand and nod at me like Obi-Wan Kenobi?

I pivoted and allowed her to see me with the rough-surfaced dark green thingamie in my hand. She looked at it briefly and then went back to her chat without giving away anything. Argh. I was feeling more like Blinky every second. Then another lightbulb flashed over my head, and I ran into the back where the larger cooler was. Maybe there would be a bag in there with a label on it saying in bright red letters "These Are Avocados, Idiot!"

I searched and searched and searched, rummaging furiously through the cooler as a choir of hell-demons floated above me singing *Carmina Burana*. I tossed aside containers of icing, sacks of tomatoes, and blocks of cheese, and, as I reached the back of the cooler, a heavenly light shone down and the hell-demons turned into angels and switched to *Messiah*. There, in the back corner of the cooler, was a sack on the shelf saying—yes, in red letters—AVOCADOS. Inside the sack was a bunch more of the tree-bark-covered egg-shaped objects that I already had sitting on the cutting board.

Mystery solved. Now all I had to do was make the damn sandwich. I returned to the prep counter and looked again at the instructions:

"Slice one avocado in half and place one half on the bread."

I took my knife and sliced the avocado open. Oh look, it has a big nut on the inside. I set aside the half with the nut and fixed my knife on the other half, which I had to "place on the bread." How to place it? Good question.

Chitter chatter filled the café, as did the now tedious sounds of NPR's *Car Talk*, whose hosts, Click and Clack, couldn't stop laughing. I knew my lady friend must be getting antsy about her sandwich, so I swallowed hard and started slicing the avocado further, cutting through the skin so that I ultimately ended up with a collection of avocado crescents, still attached to their reptilian epidermis, looking not terribly edible. I took the sunflower bread and started placing the crescents on one of the slices, attempting to arrange them in a way that suggested, maybe even encouraged, edibility. But it just didn't look right. My bangs bounced in front of my eyes, and I swiped them back over my ear with my clammy hand.

I'd hit a brick wall, completely and utterly lost, with no idea what I was doing. Maybe it'd be better just to face the facts and gracefully admit defeat. Or if not that, then at least ask for some help. I turned around to look at the lady in the fur coat and wondered how I should phrase my plea.

"Excuse me, ma'am, did you want the skins on that?"

Silence swallowed the room. Even the *Car Talk* guys shut up. The woman looked at me through narrowed eyelids.

"The skins?"

"Yes, the skins. The avocado skins."

She laughed uncomfortably and delayed her answer, waiting for me to tell her that I was joking. I held my ground, stone-faced. Because I wasn't joking.

She looked at her friend, who returned her confused gaze.

"No," she said, as if I had just asked her whether Santa Claus might help me refinance my parents' house.

I quickly nodded, extremely satisfied with her answer. "Oh, OK," I said, then pivoted to my defense: "Some people do."

After saying that, I couldn't bring myself to make eye contact with her again until I'd finished making her sandwich. I sliced the skins off the adorable little avocado crescents and discovered that I should probably spread them onto the bread like butter. I started doing that. Oh, I see, avocados are spreadable! Like butter!

"Excuse me," a lispy-voiced gentleman said from the other side of the pastry case. I turned and saw a handsome man in his mid-twenties looking at me with just a hair of impatience. He was the tablemate of a guy I'd already waited on and whose sandwiches I'd made (a veggie cheese and a Reuben). He was holding a bottled beer that he'd pulled from the beverage cooler.

"Do you have a bottle opener?"

"Sure," I said, hopping over to the register. He was tall and well-groomed, his black hair styled in the manner of a jazz-age film star, his olive complexion denoting an otherworldly sophistication that I yearned to experience firsthand, while naked, on the Riviera, in a boat, drinking crème de menthe. I opened the bottle for him after dropping and picking up the opener a few times, and handed him the bottle. Meanwhile, the lady in the fur coat huffed and puffed about her sandwich, which I'd yet to place into her greedy little hands.

"Thank you," he said, flashing the briefest of smiles. "Can I also have a glass?"

"Sure, of course," I said, sweating frantically under my vest, bangs breaking free and bouncing in front of my face. I turned to grab a glass and then thought I might offer him something else that might help him enjoy his beer more. It's called customer service.

"Would you like me to put some ice in it?" Ice, right? What could be better than enjoying a cold beer over ice in a chilled glass? So urbane, so genteel, so Continental.

The gentleman looked at me like I had just grown a nipple on my forehead.

"Ice?" he said, lisping as if his life depended on it, drawing out the "sssss" sound as if to emphasize the ssssssstupidity of the question.

"Yeah, ice. No? No ice?" I couldn't believe he didn't want ice.

He shook his head slowly and removed himself from the counter, looking slightly offended.

"Excuse me," the lady blurted out, her patience having been well and truly tested. "Can I get my sandwich now? *Without* the skins." Her friend laughed.

I nodded and returned to the sandwich table to finish up the avocado jack, feeling like I'd been shown up completely and utterly as a know-nothing hick with no taste, class, or sophistication. Who was I kidding? No one. I should probably just hang up my apron and return to Kerr Drug, where I could assist people shopping for nail polish remover, hair clips, Ogilvie Home Perm kits, and denture cream. People more my speed.

It was a good-looking sandwich that I placed in front of the fur-draped lady a few minutes later, but it was too late to matter now. I rang her up, and she handed me her money as if she were tipping a bathroom attendant, then sat down with her friend and ate her avocado/jack on sunflower, the Official Sandwich of Judgy Bitches.

That was the last of the late afternoon rush, and as I returned to my depraved *Village Voice* I was breathing heavily and my legs were tingly. I flipped the pages and gazed at them with glazed eyes. I wiped beads of sweat from my forehead. My hair was wet and dangling in front of my face like tendrils of a grapevine. After a few minutes it came to me: My blood sugar was low. The thought I had immediately after that was: *And I am in Willy Wonka's freaking chocolate factory.*

I traipsed over to the cookie case, slid it open, and grabbed the largest item I could find, one of the deluxe chocolate chip cookies. Leaning on the case, I took a big bite of it, catching stray crumbs with my hand and shoving them into my mouth as I stared off into space like a zombie devouring brains made of sugar.

Even through my insulin-fueled stupor I could feel the avocado jack lady intermittently looking at me with condescension and disdain, but I didn't care, because after this cookie I was going to go chow down on a chocolate croissant and maybe even go stick my head into a big tub of cookie dough. And during my avocado search I'd caught a glimpse of a big tub of cream cheese cake icing, so I'd be paying that a visit, too.

She could take her avocado, and she could shove it.

———

It was a trial by fire on my first day at the Elitist Sandwich Making Institute, but the humbling and humiliating experience of publicly not knowing anything about avocados or beer or sauerkraut or corned beef or what a convection oven was made me stronger. And while I was stretching my wings and learning all about the gustatory delights the Coterie had to offer, I was also getting regular exposure, via my dear sweet *Village Voice*, to culture, and by culture I mean cultcha, and by cultcha I mean pictures of hot dudes in 1-900 ads and alluring gay personals and reviews of homoerotic plays and interviews with Harvey Fierstein and articles about ACT UP and "outing" and how Mayor Koch is a total closet case. In short, I was thrown a lifeline, shown that there was a big gay wonderland out there that was mine for the taking, and that maybe, one day soon, I would be the go-go birthday boy happily unwrapping a big, thick, throbbing gift, maybe in the back of a pickup truck, maybe in a library study room, maybe in a fancy hotel room with a cock-shaped bathtub.

In the meantime, I was becoming an expert not only at Reuben preparation and avocado identification, but also at muffin making, pastry recommendations, and scanning of the bookshelves for novels with gay content. (Best find: *Prick Up Your Ears: The Biography of Joe Orton* by John Lahr.)

Within a few months I was a seasoned server of highfalutin food and beverages (no ice), with an attitude to match. I knew how to handle all comers, from the unbearable woman who came in every Saturday for two cheese straws, a bran muffin, and an Earl Gray tea and would never shut up about her son's SAT scores, to the man who told me and my coworker Jenn every week that we had "Jewish noses" and that we really should look into getting an espresso machine, to the woman who'd just been released from Dorothea Dix mental hospital and always demanded I wash my hands in full sight of her before preparing her food. During my downtime, whenever I wasn't reading the *Voice*, trolling for a good paperback, or just standing behind the counter, staring out into space, and wondering who killed Laura Palmer, I could be found chatting happily and flirting ever so slightly with the handsome surfer dudes who worked next door and came in every day for their veggie sandwiches and shop talk or breezily conversing with customers such as the gallery owner who shared my love of Anne Rice's vampire novels and Siouxsie Sioux's new bob haircut.

But my favorite customers—and by favorite I mean least favorite—were the terrible yuppie couple who always came in after the lunch rush and always, always, always ordered whatever it was we were out of. I relished waiting on them every few weeks, because for a truculent adolescent, what is more enjoyable than giving irritating people disappointing news?

In they would stroll, the gentleman wearing khakis and an immaculately combed beard, his haughty, terminally unhappy lady friend all angles and elbows between her shoulder pads and heels. They sauntered to the counter in slow motion as, say, I flipped through that week's *Voice* and noticed with delight that there was a photo of a cappuccino-brown black man's butt accompanying a review of what looked like a wonderfully unbiblical film called *Looking for Langston*. After I left my new customers waiting for a suitable amount of time, I looked up to see them staring at me with irritated eyes.

"Can I help you?" I said, knowing that in just a few short moments I would be able to tell them we were out of whatever they wanted.

"What you want, babe?" the man said to his ball and chain, and she sighed.

"What's the soup of the day?" she whined at me without looking up from the menu.

"We're out of soup." Always felt good to say that. And we *were* out of soup. I'd eaten the rest of it. It was cheesy potato, and it was good.

She huffed and puffed a few times.

"I'll just get some cheese straws."

I looked over at the cheese straw tray and saw that there were only two more of the tiny little things.

"Sure," I said, placing them on a plate and setting the plate in front of her. It was a pitiful-looking lunch.

I thought about the black butt staring up from the pages of the *Voice*. It had put me in a good mood, and before I knew it, I took a blind stab at being customer service–oriented as a curl once again bounced in front of my face, poking me in the eyeball.

"You know what I would recommend?" I said, hooking the curl back around my ear.

Both of them looked at me, suspicious of my uncharacteristic helpfulness.

"The avocados," I answered. "They're really delicious today. And I make a mean avocado jack."

The young man is not very good with a broom. At least not at the moment. He's been at it for almost an hour, and he's only covered about a third of the shop. It's five thirty, and on a normal Saturday he would be ready to lock up by now, but there he stands with the broom, just sweeping and stepping and stooping and sweeping and stepping and stooping and sweating and wiping his clammy brow and sweeping and stopping and stooping and sweating and stopping and looking around and staring into space and then doing some more sweeping and stooping.

In the back of the shop his friend and coworker Mandy, the dishwasher, is being a responsible little worker bee, spraying down the sinks one last time before gathering her things and going outside for a cigarette.

She passes by her stooping, sweeping, and sweating friend and gives him a heads-up that she's going out for a cigarette. He emits a sound by way of saying "OK," but through his unmoving lips it sounds more like "mm-guh."

Mandy generally notices things, which is more than can be said for her friend today, because he's been in that one spot for a while now and really should just move on to, say, that one table in the corner where it appears a banana nut muffin has blown itself up.

"You OK, Tim?" she asks, tilting her head quizzically.

"Yeah, 'm gay," he responds, which is what he always says when he's losing touch with reality, though usually with better pronunciation.

Mandy looks at him closely. "Just tired?"

"Myeh," he says.

"OK, I'll be outside giving myself cancer."

"Ngrate. Seesoon."

Mandy leaves, and the young man goes back to sweeping. After a few seconds he rests his woozy head on his hands, which now sit atop the broom handle. He starts swaying a little bit, back and forth, back and forth, then whoops! The broom falls to the floor and he stumbles forward, but regains his footing pretty well, like a drunk gymnast doing a sloppy floor routine. He surveys the grounds and determines that, the banana nut explosion notwithstanding, things look pretty good and he's tired and fuck it.

He trudges back to drop the broom off in the back—and by "drop off" we really mean "drop"—and then grabs his book, his Village Voice, *and his keys, and trundles up to the front door. He somehow successfully opens the door, walks through the threshold, and sits down at the cement table where Mandy is lighting up. He immediately opens up the* Voice *to the Life in Hell comic and lays his wet head down on it.*

Mandy takes a drag of her cigarette and looks at him.

"Tim?" He looks tired, or exasperated, or both, she thinks. And she couldn't really blame him: It was a brutal lunch crowd today, and it was staggered so the people just kept trickling in, minute after minute, hour after hour, making it hard for her and Tim to do the quality snacking that they usually like to get done. Then an idea hits her, and she nudges the boy's shoulder with her hand.

"Tim?" No answer from him.

"Tim?" She leans in, and all of a sudden he lifts a fist and slams it down on the table.

That was unexpected, *she thinks. "Tim," she says, "what's wrong? Tell me."*

Without lifting his head he emits a frustrated series of cries. Mandy's eyes widen as he finally lifts his head and she sees that there are no actual tears coming out of his eyes. There's just a scrunched-up red face looking agonized and lost. Well, more lost than normal.

It looks as if Mandy now sees the writing on the wall, and the writing says, "Tim has lost his mind, and I think it's because of the diabetes." As the spastic boychild pounds his fist on the table faster and harder and faster and harder and starts roaring like a girlie little lion, she stubs out her cigarette, hurries into the shop, and scuttles to the phone in the back.

She calls the boy's mother first.

"Hi, Mrs. Anderson? Hi, it's Mandy. Listen, I'm at the Coterie with Tim, and I think he might be having a low blood sugar?"

"OH NO!"

"Yeah, um, he's at the table outside, and he's really acting strange."

"OH, GOSH, MANDY, YOU HAVE TO GET HIM SOME JUICE! ORANGE JUICE! HE NEEDS ORANGE JUICE!"

Now, Mandy has talked to the boy's mother many times, and she knows that when the woman seems to be screaming she's often just talking in her normal tone of voice. Mandy very calmly holds the phone a foot away from her ear and continues listening to what the woman has to say, which is

"OK, HANG UP, I'M GOING TO CALL 911!"

Mandy puts the phone down and goes over to the fridge to get some orange juice. She fills a glass and hurries outside to give it to the patient.

"Tim, you need to drink this. Do you need me to help you?"

The boy lifts his head, looks at the juice she's placed on the table, and says, "Nah." Then he lowers his head back to the table.

The phone rings in the shop, and Mandy scurries in to pick it up. Knowing who it probably is, she once again holds the phone a country mile from her ear and listens in as the boy's mother talks at her.

"HOW IS HE? MANDY, HOW IS HE? IS HE CONSCIOUS? IS HE TALKING?"

"I just gave him some orange juice, and . . ."—Mandy looks out the front window and sees the boy sitting and looking at the glass of orange juice as if it's a zebra at the zoo—*". . . he's drinking it right now."*

"WELL, I'VE CALLED 911, AND THEY'RE ON THEIR WAY! YOU SHOULD GRAB SOME COOKIES AND TAKE THEM OUT TO HIM!"

"OK, Mrs. Anderson, I'm going to hang up now and go check on him, OK?"

"ON MY WAY OVER! I'LL BE THERE SOON!!!"

Mandy hangs up and goes back into the cooler to retrieve a big deluxe chocolate chip cookie. She hurries back out to the table, and as she approaches the door she stops in her tracks, seeing that the boy is no longer sitting dumbly at the table. There sits the glass of orange juice, untouched.

"Tim? Tim?" She walks out into the parking lot, searching left, right, and center for the young idiot. Finally she finds him slumped in the passenger seat of his fantastically unattractive car. She hears the familiar sound of him rifling through his plastic bag full of cassette tapes, which he's always doing in order to track down the one cassette he desperately needs to find. (This cassette is always at the bottom of the bag.)

"Tim?" she says as she approaches the car. She winds around to the passenger side only to see an open door, an empty seat, and no bag of cassettes. She turns around and sees the boy loping across the parking lot, zigzagging his way back to the storefront, clutching his plastic bag of cassettes in a Mongolian death grip.

Mandy walks toward him as the ambulance arrives. She waves it down and points to her friend, who has just tripped on the curb and is in the process of falling over, scattering cassettes all over the sidewalk. Let's see, what's he got? Tears for Fears, OMD, New Order, Wire, Joy Division. Good Lord, who art-directed these album covers, the Stasi?

Anyway, the paramedics get out of the ambulance and walk over to the insulin junkie, who is now sitting on the curb trying to gather his cassettes together and place them lovingly back in the grocery bag. His eyeballs linger for a few moments on The Glove's Blue Sunshine, *which, in his defense, does have an alluring cover.*

One of the paramedics sits down on the curb and tries to chat with him, but to no avail, because the boy is unable to communicate in any human language. He can only sing, which is what he proceeds to do, though the paramedic can certainly be forgiven for thinking that the young man is just dry-heaving.

The paramedic helps the boy gather his cassettes into the bag and is finally able to sweet-talk him into the ambulance so they can work their para-magic on him. The inside of the ambulance is very bright, and the boy wishes he had some sunglasses, like those savage shades that Corey Hart wore in that video for that one song. Crazy kids and their MTV.

Mandy pops her little head into the ambulance and asks if it's OK if she talks to her friend.

"Hey, Tim, how are you feeling? Are you OK? Do you remember what happened?"

The young man bursts into tears, as if Mandy, instead of checking to make sure he was OK, had hurled his bag of cassettes onto the pavement, squatted over them, and taken a whiz.

Mandy's face falls, and she's not sure what to do or how to feel, what with all the mysterious blubbering and the bright white lights of the ambulance and the fact that she can't remember if she put her cigarette out and the fact that she's never seen her friend in such a fugue state as this, even when he's wasted on Boone's Farm and quoting lines from The Golden Girls.

The screeching of tires heralds the arrival of his mother. She slams to a halt next to the ambulance, then gets out of the car and starts screaming again at poor Mandy.

"WHAT HAPPENED? WHY IS HE CRYING? CAN HE TALK? WHAT'S HIS BLOOD SUGAR?"

Wow, this woman has some volume on her. Mandy opens her mouth to answer, and nothing comes out because which question should she answer, and what is the answer to that question?

"He's going to be fine," says one of the medics sitting with the boy, with an admirably pleasant bedside manner. "His level was pretty low, but we've shot him full of glucagon, and he'll be back to himself pretty soon."

"WHY IS HE CRYING?"

"Oh, you know, when this happens, sometimes they get a little frustrated and emotional, because they can't communicate what's happening to them. It's completely normal."

Hmm. Would've been great if the medic had just said, "BECAUSE HE'S POSSESSED!" but that also would have been mean to Mama, so whatever, at least it's over now, and Mandy can finally enjoy a full cigarette.

Oh, I see she's lit one already.

CHAPTER 7

LIKE BRET MICHAELS, BUT GAYER

Coming out to your first friend—especially if she's a nice young lady with no gaydar—is a monumental occasion, so you should definitely do it at a playground after dark, just the two of you. That way it's not in any way weird or awkward.

I had graduated from high school, and in a few short months I would be leaving Raleigh for Greensboro, where I would attend Guilford College and, hopefully, allow myself to be seduced by every male professor in the Classics Department, assuming it had one. (I hadn't checked.) Once I left Raleigh I was planning on kicking down those closet doors with my gay cowboy boots (with the fringe) and venture out into the wild and hopefully very blue yonder. But before I put myself out there like that, I had to take that first step and tell my best friend Dani that she was, unbeknownst to her, a big old fag hag. I couldn't leave Raleigh without having at least opened the closet doors a crack.

It was the summer that Bret Michaels, the lead singer of hair metal band Poison, declared to the world that he was diabetic, an announcement that was greeted with a collective "Every Rose Has Its Thorn" joke. I came home one day to see him staring at me from the cover of my *Diabetes Forecast* magazine, striking a shirtless pose and wearing his trusty headband as well as a lusty expression that seemed to be saying "Talk dirty to me" or "I want action" or "Unskinny bop" or whatever. I gasped when I first saw the headline—"Bret Michaels Comes Out of the Closet." For a few short seconds there was real excitement that a popular rock star, even one as vulgar as Bret Michaels, was playing for my team, sexually. But I quickly realized what closet they were referring to. This wasn't *Homosexual Forecast* magazine, after all. The closet he was barging out of was the diabetic one. Wait, there's a *diabetic* closet?

"Argh," I'm sure I said to myself when I read the text under the headline: "'Singer talks about his life as a Type 1 diabetic.' Oh God, so what/who cares?" Sure, OK, it was nice to have a celebrity diabetic out there who was a little bit zeitgeistier than Mary Tyler Moore or Jean Smart, but honestly, what's so tough about admitting publicly that you have an irritating and sometimes dangerous metabolic disease? No, no, no, what takes real bravery is admitting publicly that you have an irritating and downright disgusting *moral* disease.

———

When I started considering the idea of maybe trying to possibly perhaps publicly declare tentatively the fact that I might could be gay, it was 1991 and there were no great gay role models to look to for encouragement, though I had my suspicions about Olympic diver Greg Louganis. Television wasn't brimming with gay characters, unless you counted Jack Tripper from *Three's Company*, which you shouldn't, because that was just a plot device. I really had no idea what reaction I would get when I started telling people, but I assumed the worst because it seemed no one could *stand* the gays, from Jesse Helms to the Old Testament God to teenage boys to the hip-hop rappers on the MTV.

In the fall of 1989 I went to see the Cowboy Junkies at the Rialto, an art house theater in Raleigh. At the time, the movie playing there was Harvey Fierstein's now-classic *Torch Song Trilogy*, a film that featured drag queens and gay romance and lewd sign language and Matthew Broderick kissing a dude in a haystack. I had read all about the movie in the *Voice* and had been dying to see it, so for about twenty minutes at the beginning of the Junkies' show it was my lucky day. When they took the stage that night, some cheeky little scamp who worked at the theater decided it would be fun to play the movie without sound as a comely backdrop to the band's beautiful, heartbreaking ballads and singer Margo Timmins's lovelorn, smoky soprano. This was somewhat inappropriate! As the band tenderly performed "Misguided Angel," a lovely ballad of star-crossed romance, and Margo sipped on a glass of wine, the screen behind them erupted in an explosion of sequins, fake eyelashes, Easter bonnets, maracas, fright wigs, and oiled-up go-go boys wearing little more than tiny Valentine's pillows in front of their jocks. It was an early scene in the movie, and it was *captivating*, to say the least, especially the go-go boys, whose bewitching mesmerism just about set my lap on fire.

The rest of the crowd was not so enchanted. At first they didn't know what to do with the spectacle, but I suppose since it was harmless drag queens prancing around nobody was really that up in arms. But a few scenes later the villagers got restless and demanding and capital-O *offended*. Harvey Fierstein's character Arnold meets a blond gentleman named Ed at the gay bar after his drag show, and they make their way back to Arnold's place to get it on. The men chat at the door of Arnold's apartment as he fumbles for his keys, though of course we the audience couldn't know what their muted voices were saying. *(I wanted to know what their muted voices were saying.)* They walk inside, and the camera shows their silhouettes against a window as their faces move closer and closer together.

"Do it! Do it! Do it! Hurry!" I said to myself as I watched the screen, eyes bulging and every muscle in my body trembling with antici . . . . . pation. The heads slowly converged, and finally they kissed, setting off an agitated rumble through the audience. After the song, Margo said a polite "Thank you" and then asked good-naturedly, "Was that song funny?"

"Turn it off!" a female voice screeched from the audience. A chorus of yelps all over the theater chirped agreement.

"You want to get rid of the movie?" Margo asked to a resounding "yes" from the audience. A minute later the projector was turned off, leaving me in the dark with no drag queens, no go-go boys, and no hot man-on-man action. All I had was the band's beautiful renditions of "Sweet Jane" and "Blue Moon Revisited" to soothe my agitated hormones. Which was fine for the time being, but eventually something's gotta give, come *on*.

So the question became: What would happen when I started broadcasting my own flashy gay movie to the masses of folks with great taste in music who just want to enjoy the band they came to watch? The answer, probably: a chorus of irritated people shrieking "Turn it off!"

—

It was term paper season, fall 1990, and what better time to coyly explore how one might incorporate homosexuality into one's official AP English studies? Our instructions were to choose from a list of movies that tackled a certain social or political issue, research the issue, and explore how the film depicts it. The list included Important Films like *Lean on Me*, *A Passage to India*, *Platoon*,

Kramer vs. Kramer, *Skokie*, and, for some reason, *Bonfire of the Vanities*. It was all "plight of inner city kids," or "colonialism," or "Vietnam," or "divorce," or "racists wanting to march in a parade" or "the tragedy of awful movie adaptations starring Melanie Griffith"—but nowhere to be found was any movie tackling a topic that really spoke to me, like "gratuitous male nudity" or "bathhouses of ancient Greece." There had to be something meaningful on this list that I could pour my jittery, starving sexuality fully into. Then, on the flyer our teacher handed out to us, I saw a TV-movie from a few years before that I remembered seeing previews for: *An Early Frost*, starring yummy Aidan Quinn as a gay man diagnosed with AIDS. Bingo.

One week later, grumpy Ms. Sutton made us publicly choose the movie we'd be writing about, and to make it fair, we drew numbers out of a hat to see who would choose first. We had twenty-eight people in the class, and I picked #27. Drat. I leaned back in my seat in an attempt at nonchalance as one student after the other went to the board to write their choice. There went *Norma Rae*, thus went *Sunday Bloody Sunday*, and thither went *Guess Who's Coming to Dinner*. I feared that someone would swoop in and take Aidan Quinn away from me, but it turned out I'd underestimated how unpopular the "gay people with AIDS" topic would be among my peers. When it was my turn to divulge my choice, I had a clear path to Aidan. I stood and wrote the movie title on the board and walked back to my seat without looking at anyone because I didn't want to see if any of my classmates realized what I'd just signed up for: two months of research and writing about gays and AIDS. In high school in 1990, that alone made you a power bottom.

I rented the movie and got to work reading article after article about AIDS, its insidious attack on the body, its tragic consequences for the gay community, and the attendant fear and loathing of gay people in the culture at large. In the movie, Aidan Quinn contracts HIV from his lover, who he finds out visited bathhouses when Aidan was out of town. For the purposes of this TV movie, it was important for Aidan himself to be guiltless, because otherwise the American audience would not side with him, owing to his being a vile gay slut going around spraying his AIDS everywhere. Instead, his lover was tasked with being the vile gay slut, and Aidan had everyone's sympathies. Sadly, he had to tell his parents Ben Gazzara and Gena Rowlands that he was gay and had AIDS in the same conversation, which was just awful. I never wanted to have to do that. Mr. Gazzara did not respond well.

"You should watch *Maurice*," Bernice, my coworker at the Coterie, said to me one day. "It might be good for your research." Bernice knew from gay folk: Her best friend was as gay as a $3 bill.

"Is it about AIDS?" I asked.

"Nah, just about gay people in England. Takes place in, like, 1900 or something."

"But why will it help me if it's not about AIDS?" I asked.

Bernice looked at me with the subtlest of knowing expressions. "Just watch it, it's good."

Bernice was on to me.

So, *Maurice* had nothing to do with AIDS. Still, it was about homosexuals, and it sounded like some sort of costume drama, and maybe it took place at some posh private English school with communal showers and hazing and games of soggy biscuit, and *I needed to see it right now.* I went to Blockbuster and tracked down the video. On the cover of the box were two young men riding horses in a misty morning scene. I swooned as I grabbed it off the shelf and walked down the aisle toward the checkout counter. Then my eyes came upon *Torch Song Trilogy* on the shelf. There was Matthew Broderick among the ensemble of actors, looking adorable with a terrible feathered hairstyle. I quickly swiped that video up as well, looking around to make sure no one was shadowing me and taking note of my swishy home entertainment choices. (I was ready with an airtight excuse: research.)

My parents were out of town that weekend, but instead of throwing a sloppy booze party like any other hot-blooded young seventeen-year-old would have, I sat home in the dark and watched gay videos. I watched *Maurice* five times, all the way to the last frame of the exit music and closing credits. Basically, the movie was the gay *A Room with a View,* and it told the story of Maurice and Clive, two students at Cambridge who fall in love but, after years of platonic concert-going, close friendship-having, and picnicking, they ultimately find their situation unmanageable. Clive marries a woman named Anne, and Maurice, after years in the wilderness during which he undergoes hypnotherapy, ends up with Clive's randy gamekeeper Alec, the end. It was a total bummer. Sure, Maurice and Alec were together and in love, but their prospects looked bleak—their relationship was illegal, after all. And Clive was living a lie with that poor Anne. It broke my heart. And I couldn't stop myself from watching it over and over, sitting on the couch, stuffing my face with sugar-free vanilla wafer after sugar-free vanilla wafer.

"Well, at least they didn't have AIDS," I said, shrugging, after watching the closing credits roll for the fifth time in two days. The gays back then had it easier in some ways, I supposed. Sure, they had to hide from society, were constantly in danger of being arrested, had to construct false lives for themselves, and probably needed to emigrate to the Continent to be able to do any solid dating. But at least they weren't collectively being eaten alive by a disease seemingly bent on their—and pretty much only their—destruction.

I finally got around to putting *Torch Song Trilogy* into the VCR on Sunday evening, and at long last got the chance to lie back on the couch and finish watching that kissing scene I'd glimpsed briefly at the Cowboy Junkies show a year earlier. Two men kissing. Romantically. In the dark. And what made it even better was the dialogue that preceded it, which included surely the most fantastic rejoinder in all of cinema. Harvey Fierstein's character Arnold tells Ed that he's a female impersonator as he unlocks the door to his apartment, then asks if that bothers him.

"Not *yet*," Ed says. Touché, Ed.

I lapped up all the gay hijinks that ensued—men shopping for clothes in the women's department, men getting it on in the back room of a gay bar, men dressed as women singing about keeping svelte by puking after every meal. Then Matthew Broderick enters the picture in the second act, and just when we're thinking that this is just the most blissfully gorgeous love story of all time, one much more likely to succeed than that of Maurice and Clive, Matthew is cruelly torn away from his frantic seventeen-year-old viewers watching at home in the dark while their parents are away from the house, in a painful scene of anti-gay violence. Killed "by kids with baseball bats," as Arnold put it to his shrewish mother. Arnold goes on to have a bittersweet happy ending, but still. Matthew Broderick—beautiful, angelic, nubile Matthew Broderick, the former Ferris Bueller—dead from a hate-filled blow to the head.

"Well, hmm. At least he didn't have AIDS?" I thought, struggling to focus on the life-affirming aspects of the two videos I'd spent my weekend drinking in.

"Yes. Maurice, Clive, Alec, Harvey, Ed, and Matthew Broderick never got AIDS." I raised my hand in the air and gave the weakest of triumphant fist pumps.

Then I turned off the television and switched on the light in the living room for the first time all weekend, returning to my term paper on AIDS-ridden Aidan Quinn as my parents' Chevy pulled into the driveway.

———

When I said "I'm gay" for the first time out loud to someone, it was exactly one week after writing it down for that same person. The person was, of course, a therapist I'd been going to, Dr. Shawn. I'd started seeing him that fall when my mom got worried that I never left the house, even on weekends, and spent the vast majority of my senior year in my room doing God knows what. (We all know what.)

"Whatever happened to Young Life?" she asked me, prompting me to roll my eyes, sigh, and return to my spiral-bound poetry notebook and lazily scribble something idiotic.

Dr. Shawn was not a warm person. But he wasn't cold, either. He just kind of sat there, taking it all in. During my first session he gave me a five-page questionnaire to fill out so that he could determine what issues I was dealing with. I took it home with me, got out a pencil to fill in the little bubbles, and started going through the questions. It was very satisfying to see the sheer number of disorders and disadvantages that I *didn't* suffer from. In one section of the questionnaire I was being asked to indicate any conditions that applied to me.

Physical abuse? *No.*

Sexual abuse? *Nada.*

Drug use? *Whenever they are offered.*

Alcohol? *Beer, PJ, Boone's Farm.*

Sexual activity? *If only.*

Then I came to a question that caused me to go red:

Sexual attraction to someone of the same sex? *Well, heh, uh, funny you should ask that particular question because* [sound of pencil breaking] *I was just wondering if this question would come up* [sound of rubber ball being slammed into wall] *and what I would say if it did and* [sound of cat howling after being stepped on] *I couldn't help but notice there's no space to, you know, explain myself below the question* [sound of books falling off a shelf] *and should I maybe just insert a little comment or maybe I could just put a check between "yes" and "no" because* [sound of toilet flushing] *I see that there's no "maybe" box and* [sound of rubber band snapping] *oh, fuck it, YES.*

I mailed the questionnaire back to Dr. Shawn, and when I went in for my next session I assumed that we would talk about absolutely nothing besides the fact that I want to shower with dudes all day, every day, forever. But he didn't even bring up the questionnaire. He just sat back, asked me about school, and nodded along as I prattled on and on about whatever tiny inconsequential thing entered my brain while I waited for him to *say something about my damn same-sex attraction issues, hurry up!*

But he never did. He just kept nodding along sagely as I blathered about being nervous about college and stressed about exams and a little worried about how much I hated my ex-girlfriend and resentful about being diabetic and just feeling antisocial these days it's no big deal. Finally—finally—I ran out of things to talk about, and there was silence in the room. I could feel Dr. Shawn's eyes on me. I knew he had to have read the questionnaire I'd filled out. He knew! Why wouldn't he just say it!

Just say it, Dr. Shawn! "You are a big ol' Nellie queen, aren't you, Tim?" Just say it!

Nothing. Silence. And at long last it occurred to me: Dr. Shawn wanted me to say it. He was deliberately letting this awkward wordless space stand and expand in order to force me to fill it with my confession.

I looked at Dr. Shawn's poker face. If I were to tell him, would he say "That's great"? "That's disgusting"? "That's hilarious"? Who knew? But let's face it, he knew already. Might as well say it.

"So I was wondering if you'd looked at that questionnaire I filled out?"

He nodded. "I did."

"So . . . yeah, I'm just wondering if you saw anything interesting in it?"

He made an expression that conveyed nothing; a facial shrug of the shoulders.

"Like, was there anything unusual that you saw?"

After a few more excruciating seconds of silence, Dr. Shawn finally spoke.

"Was there anything in particular you wanted to talk about?"

"I, uh, well, just . . . was wondering . . . if you saw . . . that part where . . . the question about . . . sexual attraction."

He nodded. "Yes, I saw that."

"Well, what did you think of my answer?"

A few silent seconds went by. "What do *you* think about your answer?"

Few more seconds. "I think . . . I don't know. What do *you* think?"

I sat there wishing there was a third person in the room— maybe a drag queen in a mink coat and bloodred high heels to whom I could turn and say, "What do *you* think, Sassy?"

It was clear I wasn't going to get anything out of him before offering myself up on a silver platter with an apple in my mouth.

When I'd dreamed about how this particular session would go, it had gone something like:

[Tim walks into Dr. Shawn's dimly lit office, following a trail of rose petals to his usual seat in the corner. The room is lit only by a few candles and a lava lamp on the coffee table. Dr. Shawn, standing there in a wifebeater and sensible slacks, greets him.]

Tim: Dr. Shawn, what on earth is going o . . . ?

[Dr. Shawn dashes up to Tim and presses his index finger against his lips.]

Dr. Shawn: Don't speak.

[Dr. Shawn turns to the wall, touches his nose, and a heart-shaped bed with bloodred satin sheets descends to the floor. Dr. Shawn crawls onto the mattress, turns, and beckons Tim to the bed with his big toe. Tim slides into the sheets next to him.]

Dr. Shawn: Now, let's talk about that questionnaire you filled out last week . . .

[And scene.]

This obviously made perfect sense and would have been a completely healthy outcome for the both of us. Sure, Dr. Shawn was an only mildly attractive married middle-aged man who in any other circumstance would have never entered my daydreams dressed in anything more revealing than a turtleneck. But he was a man. A full-grown man. And now he was the only man in the world to know my deep dark secret, which was kind of sexy.

There was no seduction, in any case. Just me sitting there in a painfully quiet and fully lit room, forcing myself to say the word "gay" in reference to myself out loud and in front of this man of mystery sitting before me. He could have been thinking about how disgusting homosexuality is; he could have been thinking about pepperoni pizza. I didn't know. And he wasn't telling.

I relented and gave it up.

"I think I'm gay."

He nodded. "And what do you think about that?"

What *did* I think about it?

"It's . . . annoying."

He nodded. "I can imagine it is."

"And . . . irritating."

"Yes."

"And . . . frustrating."

"Well," Dr. Shawn began, "it is right now, I'm sure. But you're young. Everything's annoying and irritating and frustrating."

I walked out of his office that day completely naked—sadly, only in the metaphorical sense. I'd finally, after much quiet nudging, pulled off all my clothes, flung them on the carpet, then just sat there and let a silent man look at me and wait for me to tell him how I felt about being naked.

I felt a draft.

———

So it was onward to the friend confessional. The night began, as so many great and meaningful nights do, in a pool hall. Dani and I had gone to one of our regular haunts, the bowling alley on Hillsborough

Street downtown, which had a quiet room near the snack bar with two pool tables that no one ever used, as well as a chalkboard on the wall that invariably featured charming smut written by some guttersnipe who'd wandered in off the street. (Sample: YO MOMMA PUSSY SMELL.)

Journey's greatest hits were howling out of the bowling alley's speakers as Dani proceeded to beat me senseless in pool, as was her wont. I'd made a plan that at some point in the evening I was going to tell her the terrible truth, and as the defeats stacked up I began to get twitchy and worried about actually going through with it. It's hard to just drop something like that into normal pool conversation.

> *"Nice shot, Dani! Did I ever tell you I want the drummer from INXS to beat me with his drumsticks?"*
> *"Remind me, Dani, am I stripes or solids? Also, I kinda wanna tongue-kiss the lead singer of Depeche Mode, Woody from Cheers, and all of the Beastie Boys."*
> *"Another solid victory, Dani, well done. You know what would taste good about right now? Matt Dillon's cock."*

A change of venue was in order. Because who can come out of the closet to his best friend while a chalkboard with the message BIG OLE FAT ASS PUSSY hangs on the wall?

"Hey, you wanna go to the park?" I suggested after she beat me again. "We could get some snacks and go swinging."

"Yeah, OK," she said. "I'm bored with beating you anyway. Let's go."

So we headed over to the playground at Shelley Lake to swing, smoke some cigarettes, and tell each other we were gay. I pulled in to the empty parking lot, found a space, and shut off the car. We walked down to the playground and sat ourselves on two swings.

Swinging, in our case, usually led to singing, and it didn't take long for Dani to launch into one of her favorites by Janis Joplin.

It was the one about freedom being just another word for nothing left to lose, and I joined in with her, thinking, "Janis, honey, you really are singing my tune tonight." Dani and I swung higher and higher as we sang, and as the song ascended out of my vocal range it seemed like the moment had arrived. I had to stop singing and tell her.

I halted our gorgeous duet and left her all alone to finish off the song. When she realized that I was no longer singing, her *la-la*s began to drift off until the clinking of the swing-set chains was the only sound left in the air.

"Uh, so, I wanted to tell you something," I said.

Dani had been talkative that night, and it had been a challenge to find an "in" for my horrifying declaration. I needed to get in there before she started a new song, especially if it was the jingle for Dark and Lovely hair products, because I would *not* be able to not sing along to that; it just wasn't in my constitution. But I'd managed to force my introductory phrase out of my mouth and now either had to make something up real quick that could be considered newsworthy enough to justify such an opening or tell her the truth. Which would it be?

"Uh, OK," she said, hopping off the swing. We walked over to the sandbox and sat on the wooden rim. She took out two cigarettes, handed one to me, and we lit them.

"What's up?" She looked a little nervous.

"Oh, I don't know, there was just something that I've been meaning to tell you."

She looked away from me as she exhaled a plume of smoke.

"I'm gay."

Dani jerked her head around. Her eyes were wide with shock. "Oh!"

"Are you surprised? I mean, did you know?"

"No! I mean, yes! I mean, no I didn't know, yes I'm surprised."

"Really? Is it weird? Does it bother you?"

"Oh, no. I mean, no. I mean, yeah, it's weird because . . ."

Because why, Dani?

"Uh, well," she stammered, "I thought you were going to say something . . . very different."

"What?"

"It's embarrassing. I thought you were going to tell me you're in love with me."

"Hmm. Quite the opposite."

"Pretty much, yeah. Still, you know"—she slipped her hand quickly across her brow—"*phew.*"

We sat and smoked for a few minutes. I shifted uncomfortably, wondering what Dani was thinking, really. Perhaps she was visualizing me having sex with another dude and trying to figure out how that worked. She might be expecting me to start critiquing her flannel shirts a little more pointedly or showing up to our next outing dressed as a Sweet Transvestite.

This was going to take some getting used to, the whole allowing-someone-else-into-my-previously-secret-life thing. I was standing on a stage with a brutal spotlight on me after announcing myself as a great stage performer, but I had no idea what type of performance I was supposed to give. A Shakespearean soliloquy? A PowerPoint presentation? Will simple jazz hands suffice?

"Wait," Dani said, clearly having arrived at a point of significant import that my recent confession had set in stark relief. "Does this mean I can't tell gay jokes anymore?"

"Oh, of course not!"

"Oh, good. Wait, of course I *can't* or of course I *can*?"

"You can tell gay jokes. As long as they're not about me."

"Awesome. Because did you hear about the gay electron?"

"No."

"Went around blowing fuses."

That was a pretty good one.

Our diabetic hero is quite the dancer. By that I mean that he likes to dance, not that he looks good while doing it.

He's also a mischievous little thing. His parents are out of town this weekend, so naturally he invited a bunch of miscreants over to listen to awful music, smoke weed, drink cheap beer and Boone's Farm, and dance like the developmentally disabled. It was embarrassing to watch.

Thankfully for him some of these miscreants are responsible and know to clean up after themselves in the morning before taking off. Dani is right now doing a bang-up job of washing all the dishes, and Julie is doing the more demanding and, perhaps, more rewarding chore of clearing away the seventy-two empty Milwaukee's Best Light beer cans strewn throughout the house. This is no small task. It was a bacchanal last night, and folks were just hobbling around wherever they damn well pleased: in the rooms upstairs, out on the deck, in the bathroom, on the steps, in the bathtub, on the bathroom floor, everywhere. And now Julie is in the middle of an Easter egg hunt, except instead of colored eggs she's searching for cans of really gross beer, often half-drunk and leaking into the carpet.

Our hero is in the shower trying to wash beer out of his curly bangs while singing his secret favorite song, "Alone" by Heart. It is hard for him to do both of these things at once. He's struggling with the lyrics, which is very unlike him.

"I hear the picking of the clomp, I'm lying, dear, the roof's in fark . . ." he sings. "I wonder where the stars tonight, no ants are on the telephone."

He usually sings this song impeccably, with full fake vibrato, but not today. It's a powerful tale of longing, but he's just mangling it. Yeah, we know what's going on. He's sniffing the soap, and, wow, he just licked it. Now he's digging his front teeth into it and examining the imprint he's made. OK, game on.

Julie is taking a break from her beer can quest and is now drying the dishes that Dani has just washed, both of them enjoying the god-awful serenade coming from the bathroom just down the hall.

"He's got an amazing voice on him," Dani has just said. "It's angelic."

Yes, like an elderly, sick Shirley Temple.

After a few minutes the singing drifts off, and a merciful silence takes its place. Suddenly the girls hear a big thud.

"What the fuck?" Julie says. Dani turns off the faucet, and they hurry down the hall.

"Tim? Are you OK?" Dani says, knocking on the door. "Tim?"

The girls look at each other. "Shit," they both say.

"I'll go in," Dani says bravely, evoking the great alien-killer Sigourney Weaver. She opens the door into the small, steam-filled bathroom. "Tim?" There's no answer.

Dani's face tightens into an expression of dread as she realizes she's going to have to open the shower curtain and see what's inside. Our hearts go out to her. We are all terrified.

SWISH goes the shower curtain as she opens it. And there's our hero. Naked, wet, and shaking.

"Yep, he's having a reaction," Dani says back to Julie.

"Should we call an ambulance?" Julie says, marveling at how pale their friend's butt is.

"No, I think we can handle this. Can you get some juice or something from the fridge?" As Julie leaves to search for sugar, Dani kneels

down to her friend as he tries to peel himself off the tile. She leans in and takes his head in her hands so that he won't bang it.

"Tim, Julie's getting you some juice, just hang tight, OK?"

Our hero is displaying no apparent self-consciousness about being naked in front of his friend, which is amazing, because look at him. He's like a nude albino ghost.

"Here you go," Julie says, handing Dani a tall cup of juice. Dani takes it and lifts it to her friend's face, struggling to keep his head steady so that the juice will successfully go into his mouth. Her friend isn't cooperating.

"Tim. Tim. Tim! You've got to drink this." As Dani speaks, Julie reaches over her and into the shower stall to turn off the water that has now soaked the poor girl.

The stubborn young lad finally opens his mouth and allows his friend to pour some juice in. He takes to it and awkwardly starts using his tongue to try to lap up more.

After a few minutes, he is able to use human language. Well, at least one word.

"Sorry," he says. It's always the first word out of his mouth when he comes to. And he should be. No one should have to see what we are seeing. He then irritably moves his head away from the cup, having had all he wants.

But Dani knows he's not out of the woods yet. He's got to have more or he could slip back into the danger zone. Thankfully she's been through this before. And even if she hadn't, she's seen Steel Magnolias. *All she ever needed to know about dealing with a grumpy diabetic she learned from Sally Field.*

"Shelby," Dani says to him in an admonishing tone. He looks at her blankly, still stubbornly holding his head out of reach of the cup. She looks back at him as if to say, "That's right, we're performing this scene whether you like it or not."

"Drink your juice, Shelby."

He scrunches up his face, looking nothing like Julia Roberts.

"Cooperate, please. Drink the juice!"

"Honey, drink, please!" Julie chimes in, channeling Dolly Parton.

"Drink the juice!"

"You need the juice!"

"Drink it!"

Dani takes hold of his face and begins forcibly pouring the OJ into his wet little mouth as he struggles against her. Some of the juice makes it in, though the dribbling is considerable. Finally the naked boy relents and, sitting on the floor of the shower stall looking like an alien amphibian, opens his mouth and allows his friend to pour more juice in.

A few minutes later he's once again a self-aware human. He looks down at his naked white body, which is splotched with pink from the hot water of the shower. Like Adam and Eve before him, he is deeply embarrassed—the very personification of the colors Shelby chose for her hilarious wedding: blush and bashful.

CHAPTER 8
MEETING WITH THE MOON GODDESS

We all have wild imaginings of the sexual adventures that await us when we go away to college and completely reinvent ourselves as seductive, hot-lipped Casanovas. This is what all humans want from college. And I was nothing if not flailingly, painfully human. So when I prepared to move away to Greensboro for my freshman year at a small liberal arts school called Guilford College, I got down on my knees and prayed to my lord and savior, Morrissey, to please, please, please let me get what I want.

I was still gun-shy about spilling the beans about myself after telling Dani—my big coming-out party ended that night at Shelley Lake Park. Still taking baby steps, I wasn't ready to bust open the closet doors—rather, I was just busying myself rearranging the clothes in the closet, alphabetizing my cassette tapes, color-coding the polyester slacks, arranging the vests by degree of paisleyness, and intermittently pulling out a porno mag to do some reading.

In preparation for the big life change, I made a bold decision: I would cut my trademark naturally curly bangs. Or rather, my hair-stylist Debbie made a bold decision: She would cut off my trademark naturally curly bangs. I'd gone in and asked her to shave my head short all over, but leave the bangs. I was ready for a change, sure, but I still needed my hair to hang in my face, for God's sake, come *on*.

"You sure you don't want me to do anything with these?" she said, pointing at my bangs with barely disguised disdain. She'd always hated them and had been dying to get rid of them for as long as I'd been going to her.

When she asked, I made a split-second decision to give her permission to give them a slight tweak. A minor modification. A tiny clip.

"Yeah," I said, "why don't you just trim them a little, clean them up?"

She didn't have to be told twice. She barely had to be told once. She clipped the rest of my hair with a number-two guard, then, with a little too much enthusiasm, she set to work on the bangs, her holy grail. As she completed this last bit of work, she stood in front of me, blocking my view of myself in the mirror. I should not have allowed her to do this.

When she stood aside after applying some mousse, there was my sad face in the mirror staring back at me. My hair was shaven close all over, and dangling down in front, just above my eyeballs, were just three slender tendrils of hair, each about the thickness of a stick of incense. There was no getting around it: I looked retarded.

"OK?" she asked.

"Um, wow, you cut a lot."

"You wanted me to clean them up, right?"

I should have been more specific. As she busied herself with brushing my neck and shoulders off and sweeping all the hair off the floor, I sat there in disbelief. What was I to do? This was the kind of haircut one got before going away to clown college or mime school. How can I expect to be taken seriously with this hairstyle? Heaving a slow, silent sigh, I closed my eyes and gave Debbie permission to snip those last three coils, the only remnants of my former hairstyle.

"You sure?" she said, as if all was going according to plan.

Eyes still closed, I nodded nervously. "Just, yes, do it. Please."

Snip.

(Shit.)

Snip.

(Shit.)

Snip.

I opened my eyes. Wow. There was my forehead. I hadn't seen it in forever. And my eyes. So bloodshot, so sunken. There was no hiding behind this haircut. It allowed for no dodging, no weaving, no ducking, no diving. *God*, I thought. *I look like I haven't slept in years.*

I paid Debbie and left, feeling nude as a newborn eighteen-year-old baby. When I got to my Plymouth, I dove in and searched for a plaid golf hat that I knew was in there somewhere. I finally found it in a nook under the seat, pulled it out, and covered my head with it.

Driving home, I intermittently looked at myself in the rearview mirror, lifting the hat off a few times to make sure my hair was still gone.

I would never trust a hairstylist again.

———

I'd chosen Guilford because I was convinced I needed to go to a small school. There would be fewer students in each class, probably more one-on-one interaction with teachers, and, most importantly, a smaller number of people to know that I was gay. I wanted to start small, and this school of a mere 1,600 students seemed perfect. It had a charming little campus with lots of old brick buildings, it seemed to attract young men unafraid to wear earrings in their left ear (which I erroneously believed signified all), and it didn't have a Greek system or a prominent sports program. But my choice of Guilford was based upon one overarching—and frustratingly faulty—assumption. Namely, that the city of Greensboro was ninety-nine percent gay.

Greensboro was home to UNC-Greensboro, aka "UNC-G," aka, to most of the kids in my high school, "UNC-Gay," thanks to the university's notable art and music programs. So, the word on the street was that UNC-G allegedly attracted a lot of gay folk, and this is what was constantly in the back of my head as I flipped through various college brochures. But I didn't want to go to UNC-G. This scholastic snob thought that was for flunkies. But in my magical thinking, if UNC-G was a homosexual haven, then Guilford also must be, because it was in Greensboro, too. Because it was just down the road. Yep, that logic was airtight. I could definitely see myself attending this idyllic little college where the majority of dudes handsomely practiced the love that dare not speak its name, constantly standing shirtless in their drum circles on the quad between classes and manfully reciting Shakespearean sonnets declaring that love is not time's fool.

UNC-G did have quite a gay student body, that much was true. Sadly, Guilford College was a good twenty-minute drive down Friendly Avenue, on the opposite end of town. A side of town that had far fewer folks sporting pink triangles on their backpacks. But on the plus side it did have a very manageable student body population, so it was my intention to, in the most unobtrusive way possible, find the approximately two percent of these student bodies who were gay, bi-curious, sexually confused, aroused sometimes in the locker room, or had one time accidentally kissed a tranny. How was I supposed to find these people? Well, maybe my roommate would be of some assistance?

On my housing application I had hinted that I would prefer that they stick me with someone who would not be averse to seeing hot nude and Speedo-clad lunkheads hopping out of my bed in the mornings and making me coffee. I got Jeff from New Jersey.

Jeff was a meek, sickly, painfully shy guy from Princeton who had been driven, kicking and screaming, by his parents to North Carolina to get a good Southern education. He never left the room when he wasn't in class, if he went to class. When he was in the room, he spent all of his time at his desk talking on the phone to a high school friend back in Princeton and drawing comic book characters on his sketchpad. His favorites were Pogo, Calvin and Hobbes, and the Little Mermaid. He had a full color wall-size poster of little Ariel on his side of the room, which I'd lobbied against unsuccessfully.

His drawings, especially of Calvin and Hobbes, were dead ringers for the original characters. I knew because I would look through all of them while he was in class or in the shower or at dinner, and they gave me quite an insight into his unique take on the world. Here was one of Calvin being dropped off at school—the College of North Carolina, in this particular picture—holding on to the door of the family station wagon for dear life as his mother, pulling and tearing at his legs, tried in vain to disconnect him. Here was a sad scene of separation in which Calvin, screaming and cry-ing, was saying good-bye to Hobbes, who, in this drawing, had been renamed New Jersey. And here was a very touching/troubling one of Calvin and his mother at a nice restaurant, with Calvin reaching for the check and patting his mother's hand. Dear God.

His crippling Oedipus complex notwithstanding, Jeff was very approachable, and, though he was immensely antisocial, he had a friendly demeanor and a soft countenance. We started getting to know each other after both of our families had left us in peace. I tested the waters by disclosing my diabetes affliction and its implications for his life.

"I'll keep some candy bars or whatever in this drawer, OK? So if I get all twitchy or something, or if I'm unresponsive or really sweaty or stupid or flailing around, just force me to eat something from the drawer."

He looked as if he wasn't sure he was up to this responsibility.

"Just, like, point it out to you?" he asked.

"Yeah, or, you know, if I'm not responding, just unwrap it, pull off a piece, and force it into my mouth. Just, you know, shove it in. My reflexes will kick in, and I'll just start chewing. Just, you know, don't shove it all the way down my throat."

He nodded his head as if to say, "I can't handle any of this, please don't make me."

"Or, better yet," I said, sensing his discomfort, "you know what? I'll get some tubes of cake icing, so you don't even have to worry about choking me. That way you can just put the tube up to my mouth and squirt it in."

This conversation was more homoerotic than I was intending, and way more homoerotic than he was prepared to deal with. And I hadn't even brought up the gay thing yet.

We sat in an awkward silence for a few seconds until I finally put us out of our misery by saying, "It probably won't happen, don't worry."

After a few weeks of witnessing his utter misery at being away from home—his nightly phone conversations with his mom, his best friend, one of his brothers, or, if absolutely necessary, his dad—I asked him about his relationship with his mother one day while I sat on the edge of my bed and he sat penciling a new drawing of Calvin beating his head against a brick wall labeled "Work Study." I asked in a roundabout manner, so as not to let on that I was sitting in judgment or that I'd rifled through his drawings.

"So, do you miss your mother?"

He gave me a sheepish grin, and his freckles started to glow.

"Yeah, don't you?" was his answer.

"Sure," I said. "Well, not *your* mother. *My* mother. And my dad and my cat."

He smiled and nodded.

"You don't like it here, do you?" I asked.

"No," he said without missing a beat. "I hate it, actually."

"Where would you rather be?" I said, bending forward, hands and index fingers poised Oprah-like in a triangle at my nose.

"I wanted to go to school in New Jersey, but my parents thought it would be better for me to get away from home."

"Um-hmm. So, what are you going to do?" Might you want to move out and allow me to put up the rest of my Siouxsie and the Banshees and Cocteau Twins posters? You know I have five more.

"Well, I don't want to stay here. I think I might transfer out after this semester."

"But, do you really want to spend the rest of your life in New Jersey? Don't you want to see more of the world, like Ohio or North Dakota?"

"Not really," he replied. "What I really want is no different from what everyone else wants: the house in the suburbs with the white picket fence, the dog, the big backyard, the station wagon."

So he was just an old-fashioned kind of guy. It was kind of cool in a way. Harmless and sweet.

"Yep, just me and my mother," he finished, staring off into the distance.

I felt, for the first time ever, like the most well-adjusted person in the room.

So, my roommate was going to be no help in assisting me out of my dreary sexless wasteland of a love life. Fine. And he would probably not be able to keep me from slipping into a diabetic coma in the middle of the night, either. Sure, OK. For the latter problem I would just make sure to go to sleep every night with a row of Twinkie packets under my pillow. For the former problem, hmm, maybe I should check out the LGBT group?

If there was a conglomeration of stable, easy going, and blissfully happy souls on a college campus in 1991, it was surely not the lesbian, gay, bisexual, and transgender group at Guilford College that met once a week to catalog their disappointments and cry on one another's shoulders. The meetings were under-attended stone-cold-bummer festivals. Jam-packed glitter ball party-bomb free-for-all hedonistic bacchanals were more what I was after, with games like Gay Charades, Gay Naked Twister, Gay Strip Poker, and Pin the Tail on the Smooth Bleached-Blond Men's Underwear Model. I needed a safe yet lively space that would allow me to lose all my inhibitions, shed my desperate diffidence, and maybe make some barely dressed new friends, who would travel with me down my own yellow brick road to the Emerald City where we could cut loose at invite-only tickle parties with the Wonderful Wizard of Oz's harem of hairless boy toys.

At the LGBT meetings we never even played a quick game of "Gay or Just European?" I had hoped that the folks in the LGBT group would push me out the closet doors with their strong, large hands, not reinforce my own neuroses about how awful our plight was and what a tough, non-yellow-brick road we'd be traveling down in life, especially us ugly ones, because I'm pretty sure we all thought that most of us were hideous. It was basically a small group of morose, socially awkward souls who, truth be told, I had little desire to see naked. Sad-eyed, pale, and unkempt, most of them looked as if they had spent their entire adolescences hiding in their rooms with the lights out reading Michel Foucault in their Jedi robes. In short, they reminded me too much of myself (though, full disclosure, I'd never been able to make my way through even one chapter of a Foucault book), and God knows I didn't have any patience for any more of *my* kind of low-rent nonsense. I was craving slutty sophistication, classy coital catharsis: blow jobs on yachts, rim jobs on private planes, taint rubs in penthouse hot tubs with chocolate fondue fountains at every corner. This LGBT was not delivering any of this, not even the fondue. (I was under the impression all gay gatherings would have fondue.)

The leader of the group was a sad-faced boy named MJ, a bisexual who lived just a few doors down from me in Milner Hall. He had an angular haircut—severe bangs in the front, playfully jagged cuts on the sides, a few curly tassels in the back—a coiffure that overall seemed a reverential shout-out to eighties glory days long since passed. MJ had a nerdy, deceptively friendly, boyish face; he always seemed on the verge of a smile, but once it arrived his smile could only be described as . . . sarcastic. Like, he wasn't really smiling at you, he was just going through the motions of smiling at you so you would piss off and leave him alone. This what-are-you-looking-at defensiveness of his ensured that I kept my trap shut good and tight during the weekly meetings. Still hypersensitive about bringing attention upon myself, I was having a hard time saying the words "I'm gay" out loud and had greatly overestimated my ability to say it even in a room full of others of the same persuasion. So, though I attended the meetings every week, I would try my best to blend in with the furniture while listening to other people jibber-jabber endlessly about some depressing thing or other:

skinny, pimply, bespectacled Daniel lamenting how he doesn't fit the muscle-bound gay ideal; jowly Jarvis talking about how nervous he was about telling his parents the truth about himself; affable Alyson wondering why she should come out on Coming Out Day if she didn't even have a girlfriend; and glum MJ bringing things in for a landing by complaining about some homophobic slight or other that he had suffered in the past week, like being told to turn down his Pet Shop Boys, for the love of God, by our RA. (MJ was a big fan of their second album, and the entire dorm knew it.)

Not that I would have been any better, if I'd had the balls to even speak up. Had I done so, I probably would have started things with a dramatic "Why am I so alone?" and then just started weeping. But I was a complete and utter coward, so I decided I would not say anything until called upon to do so, and even then only with a gun to my head. I planned to just sit there until someone hot walked into the room, sat down next to me, popped open the first few buttons of his Calvin Klein top, gripped my knee with his strong hand, and, leaning in, whispered into my trembling ear, "Tell them, Tim. I'll be right here, with my shirt off."

That said, there were some evenings when a ray of light shone through the grim proceedings, like when the Guilford gay group cohosted a party with UNC-G's gay group, an event that brought in some new folks from the other side of town, thus joining country mice with city mice. The party was taking place at an on-campus student house called the Pope House, where the most visible gay boy on campus lived. His name was Matthew, and he was a full-time homosexualist: He had bleached-blond hair and never left the house without some queer-themed T-shirt on or other. It was ACT UP one day and a screen print of two hot dudes kissing the next. He never really hung out on the Guilford campus, spending most of his time with the townie queers. And he definitely didn't go to the LGBT meetings because, hello, he already had a life. But he was apparently happy to host a meet-up at Pope House before everyone adjourned to the bars.

I didn't have any friends at Guilford yet, so I went to this party by myself. I only had to hang out in the bushes for about a half hour before deciding that enough people had shown up there to make it safe for me to slip in without causing a scene. A few folks were standing in the doorway, so thankfully I didn't even need to knock, I just squeezed through them as they talked absently, not noticing me. The outer rim of Pope House's first floor was flecked with folks conversing and drinking, some of whom I'd seen around campus. I went through and slouched down into the first seat I could find, which ended up being in the living room, smack in the center of the house. I tried to look like I belonged there, moving my head to the music, smiling, and picking up snacks from a tray on the coffee table and nervously nibbling. Matthew walked through looking annoyed, searching for someone or something that had displeased him, and caught sight of me, a mysterious stranger in his house eating his snacks like he owned the place.

"Hi," he said. "You go to Guilford?"

"Yes, I . . . Milner, you know, over there, I do, uh-huh. From Raleigh."

He nodded and furrowed his brow slightly, unused as he was to the exciting new English syntax I was making up as I went along. I was ready to let him know my favorite bands and foods and career plans, should he ask.

"Huh," he said. "Well, welcome!" And with that he was off to solve some party problem or other. I figured I would just wait until later to tell him that my favorite movie was *Blade Runner* and I planned on being either a stenographer or Greg Louganis's personal assistant.

At that moment a new pack of partygoers arrived amid a flurry of kisses, declarations of "Haaaaaaay," and impromptu flash dances. I figured the gaggle of gaywads twirling around the hallway must be from UNC-G. They were way too uncouth and gay-positive for Guilford. As a few of them made their way into the living room, I noticed a girl I'd seen at one of the Guilford LGBT meetings. She'd been a guest speaker from the UNC-G group and had a remarkably friendly face for a lesbian. She also had the most preposterous hairstyle I'd ever seen at that point in my life. (It would be another eight years before I made it to Tokyo.) On one side it was shaved close to the head, with a bit of puff starting about an inch above the ear, but this puff grew as she turned her head, traveling diagonally down in the back as the hair got longer and curlier, until on the other side of her head it was a full-fledged bob. I had to give her points for originality and chutzpah. Her absurd coiffure, coupled with her chubby frame and overall friendly demeanor, made me think to myself *Now this is a person I can surely talk to.* Because all fat people are jolly.

All fat people are *not* jolly. She lit a cigarette and sat down in the chair next to me, moving her head in rhythm with the beat of the obnoxious rave music that was playing on the stereo. (She had great rhythm for a lesbian, too.) Seeing her responding to the music so groovily made me listen a little bit closer to what was playing, and what was playing was a house anthem whose lyrics went something like this:

"Fi- fi- finger. (Ah!) FingerFUCK. Fi- fi- finger. (Ah!) Finger-FUCK."

Color me shocked. I was, I'd always thought, no prude. I prided myself on my broad palate for the degenerate arts. I considered the Buzzcocks' "Orgasm Addict" a pure pop classic. I happily sang along to The Sugarcubes song "F**king in Rhythm and Sorrow" while riding around in my Plymouth in high school. Bongwater's *The Power of Pussy* was one of my current favorite albums. I only dry-heaved three times while watching *Pink Flamingos*. But this was . . . this was . . . just so shameless and gross. It was one gloriously offensive word sung over and over and over. It had nothing going for it but sheer lowest-common-denominator smut.

"I'm sorry," I said, turning to my new best friend with the idiotic hairmop, "is she saying . . . *fingerf*ck?*"

She stopped moving her head to the music, looked at me with an affronted expression as if I had just asked her if gravity was provable, and said, "Uh, *yeah.*"

"Put your p-p-p-p-put your finger p-put your finger in the hole."

I nodded, still not believing my ears. She looked as if she couldn't believe hers either. "Have you not heard this at the clubs?" She sneered with her lesbian lips. "It's pretty much all over the place."

"Oh, um, no, not at the places I've been going." The places I'd been going were, in order of highest to lowest frequency: my bedroom, class, the cafeteria, the library, the computer lab, the men's showers at my dorm, and the LGBT Gatherings of Doom and Sadness. And no, I hadn't heard "Fingerf*ck" at any of those venues.

It was 1991, of course, the year that rave broke big in the US, and it came to Greensboro in a big way. All the kids were falling over themselves to be first in line at the next all-night ecstasy orgy sponsored by glow sticks, pacifiers, and dirty 'n' degenerate electroshock tunes on the turntable. But I didn't know any of this yet. I hadn't gone to my first rave, though I was weeks away from it. I was an innocent babe in the woods who didn't know that it was even legal to name a song "Fingerf*ck."

Thoroughly disgusted with me, my ex-new best friend stood up and lip-synced as she danced away and rejoined her friends to tell them that this weird square she'd just met hadn't ever heard of their favorite song to dance to while souped up on crazy drugs and giving each other inner thigh massages. So perhaps I should go to one of these raves. Maybe fatuous, repetitive, epileptic ear-rape was what was really missing from my life. Apparently it's what all the gay boys like. If you can't beat 'em, fingerf*ck 'em, amiright?

So a few weeks later I went with a few folks from the Guilford radio station to a rave party downtown. I'd just joined WQFS as a new DJ, getting my own radio show in the highly coveted two-to-five a.m. slot on Saturday mornings. I tended to hear some of the scuttlebutt about what folks were up to for the weekend. When I heard from another DJ, Becky, that there was a rave party in the offing, I jumped at the chance and invited myself along on the field trip into town.

Becky and I walked over to the dorm where we were to be picked up by whoever she knew who had a car, and on the way I took the opportunity to do some reconnaissance.

"So, have you been to a rave before?"

"Kind of," she said. "I went to this one club night at this bar, and it seems like it started turning into a rave the later it got. You know, lots of laser beams and spontaneous massages and children's clothing. Not sure what this one's going to be like."

"Have you heard of the song 'Fingerf*ck'?" I ventured.

"Oh yeah, that song is retarded. But, you know, hilarious. Kind of like raves in general."

We strolled in and ordered nonalcoholic beverages because none of us were of age. It didn't take long for me to get bored, but then miraculously, a song came on that I recognized: Blur's "There's No Other Way." Sure, it was a severely chopped-up and reassembled rave remix, but beggars can't be choosers, so we the WQFS DJs entered the dance floor and started shaking. It wasn't long before

I felt someone touching me on the neck and shoulders. I turned around and saw that it was a young lady vampire with short bleached-blonde hair, alabaster white skin, a black lace corset, fishnet tights, a spiderweb drawn at her left temple, and fuck-me pumps. How was she dancing in those? I smiled at her, and she moved her hands to my chest, squeezing and massaging my admittedly smoking hot pectorals. Was I being seduced? Already? By this undead lady? I really wanted to ask that she take a breath and perhaps give her boyfriend Lestat a chance to charm my pants off, but I was enjoying the attention too much. She eventually moved on to some other chump, as folks in the capricious throes of ecstasy-fueled dance mania are wont to do, and after a few endless rave jams about sex and orifices and breasts and dicks and other indecent vocabulary words, I moved to the sidelines to watch others dance stupidly.

Becky and the WQFS folks scattered in different directions, and I quickly lost track of them. A new song was coming on, and it was a slow burner that some folks weren't sure they could dance to, so the floor started clearing off. But one guy appeared to know the song, whose only lyrics seemed to be "Make me cum." He toddled onto the dance floor and started moving, beguilingly. In the next few minutes I would get an eyeful of him and another strapping young buck "dancing" together, a tableau that would convince me that I was gazing on the immaculate image of my two future husbands. Because I was ready to propose to both of them.

Bachelor #1 had a backward black baseball cap on, turned at a slight angle. He wore no shirt, just a criminally tight black pinstriped vest against which his rock-solid upper body muscles pressed adamantly. His black jeans were also tight, his junk also adamant. His dancing style was minimalist. There wasn't any flailing about or "fag clapping." He just stepped around swaying rhythmically, occasionally wiggling a little in the manner of the *Twin Peaks* dwarf, one of his arms raised with his hand clenched in a seductive fist. His lips were curled into an "I'm too sexy" smirk of the first order, one that said, "Yes, I know you're watching me, keep doing it, because just you wait."

Bachelor #2 was the show-off. Not even bothering with a shirt, he prowled the dance floor like a Nellie panther, circling #1 with a glint in his eye. He wore tight blue jeans and Doc Martens and had a tattoo of a cross on his back, which was both sexy and wholly inappropriate, seeing as what he was about to get up to. He honed in on #1 closer and closer until their bodies touched, sending an electric shock through my body: #2, approaching from behind, placed his hand on #1's shoulder and the two started moving in tandem. All of a sudden I never wanted to watch anything else ever, just this, just these two, becoming best friends forever, in front of all of us. I'd never actually seen a porno movie, but I was sure that this was what the first five minutes of one looked like.

I stood at the side of the dance floor, transfixed. And before my eyes things got real. The two young men were now moving as one body, pressed tightly against each other, brazenly simulating the act that I believe the Bible refers to as "an abomination." "Thou shalt not lie with mankind, as with womankind," Leviticus says. From where I was standing, though, there was no "lying with mankind" going on; it looked more like "one mankind plowing another mankind from behind, rewind."

I was beside myself with yearning. How could I make this type of thing happen for myself? These gentlemen did it wordlessly, on the dance floor, while the most unromantic song played on the turntable. What are the chances? I'd always thought that I would meet my first lover in a record store when we both reached for the same Smiths bootleg album at the same time and proceeded to fight/flirt over it by quoting Morrissey lyrics. ("No, *you* just haven't earned it yet, baby.") But it seemed like in that scenario it would take too long to get to the part where you're bumping and grinding half naked under a strobe light. I want to get to that part, like *now*.

The boys finished their dance and escorted each other to another room in the club to discuss literary theory and jerk each other off. How does one continue one's night of innocent dancing after a display like that? Nothing, and I mean nothing, could measure up. I'd lost track of my WQFS mates, which comforted me a little because at least they probably hadn't seen me salivating on the sidelines of an impromptu almost-live-gay-sex show. As my tawdry fugue state dissipated and I slowly came back to myself, I couldn't help but wonder: Where was I? How did I get here? What was my name? Who are all these people? And what on earth is this god-awful song blaring from the speaker that this tiny Asian girl in black lingerie is dancing to?

———

Needless to say, I started going to raves a lot. I kept close tabs on Becky and Co.'s plans and piggybacked on them whenever possible. Meanwhile, over the Christmas holiday I figured I should probably continue my sheepish, thoroughly abashed coming out and tell a few more friends. I was still so afraid of saying the words out loud—I hadn't said "gay" about myself since I'd told Dani the previous summer. And since I'd been at Guilford I appeared to be moving backward, stepping farther back into the closet. Things hadn't been going according to plan—I'd assumed that once you started saying "I'm gay" that it would just start an unstoppable avalanche of "I'm gay"s until everyone knew, everything was fine, and folks started pre-empting you before you even had a chance to make your proud declaration.

"Oh, by the way, I'm ga—"

"I *know!*"

Thing is, I was still afraid of the word. Saying the phrase while standing in front of the mirror—"I'm gay"—it just never sounded as nonchalant as I wanted it to sound. It's such a simple, basic sentence, but, for some reason, very hard to say about yourself.

"That's gay"—so easy.

"I'm gay"—terrifying.

Still, I forced the words out of my mouth a few more times during the break, telling my friends Mandy and Neal one night and my sister another night. I was still having trouble just blurting it out—the lighting had to be just right (almost total darkness), and we had to be far, far away from any prying human ears. But I did it. I communicated my gayness. Sure, Neal actually guessed before I even said anything, and my sister almost had to literally pull it out of me by inviting her lesbian friends from college out with us and using them as truth magnets. Still, my mouth formed the words "I'm gay," and it felt less horrifying each time.

When I returned to Guilford for the spring semester, I had a little less weight on my shoulders, which made dancing at raves even easier. And there was an exciting addition to the LGBT group: A young man named Trevor started showing up. He was just back from a semester abroad in England, and he was a truly crush-worthy specimen: rail thin, messed-up teeth, greasy hair, oversized clothes, and terrible posture. He also had the most brilliant ice-blue eyes I'd ever seen. One could swim for miles in the puddles of his irises, if one were trying to be poetic. And his deep, resonant voice felt as sturdy as a sycamore tree, under which you could lay cooling yourself after your twenty laps in his irises. He was who I would have been talking to my girlfriends about all day and all night as we sat up and did one another's hair, if I had had any girlfriends at Guilford with whom I was comfortable chatting about boys. Instead, I just dreamily chatted to myself about Trevor, while shaving my head by myself in my dorm room as Jeff talked on the phone with his mom.

Trevor lived right down the hall from me in the Milner dorm, so we would sometimes run into each other coming to and from the showers. I would, say, walk out of my room with my towel around my waist, see him walk toward me, and then loosen my towel so that it fell farther south, just enough to be awkward. He, meanwhile, would have three towels on, one around his waist, one over his shoulders, and one on his head like he was Rizzo from *Grease* or something. I never ever saw him with fewer towels on. Nanook of the North was less fully clothed. He was obviously shy and awkward around other semi-naked men, so I made it as obvious as possible in other locations that I had a thing for him: staring at him in the cafeteria and trying to catch his eye between stanzas of Chaucer; trying my damnedest to get to the mail room in time to catch him looking through his mail and corner him into having a conversation about, I don't know, Echo and the Bunnymen?; walking slowly when I knew he was behind me in the hall so that he'd have to overtake me (he never overtook me). When would Trevor just give up these unnecessary games, let go, and surrender to love? Maybe if I made him a mixtape.

I spent a few hours one Saturday afternoon in the WQFS listening room and put together the sickest collection of post-punk, New Wave, shoegaze, and dream pop nuggets of wonder I could possibly have been expected to assemble. I then made a copy of the collection so I'd have one for myself, then, after confirming with Becky that I would be hitching a ride with her and her friends later to some rave or other downtown, I left and went to dinner in the cafeteria, where I sat by myself reading Anne Rice's *The Witching Hour*. I knew Trevor liked Anne Rice—had heard him speaking admiringly of her vampire books. And there he was, sitting with a few other LGBT folks I knew. I'd just go say hi.

"Hey, Trevor," I said, tucking the book under my arm to call attention to it. "What are you up to?"

"Oh," he said, "just, you know, eating."

"Big plans tonight?"

"No, I don't think so. Just probably going to chill out. There's a thing I was going to go to; not sure if I will."

"OK, well, I'll see you later." And I went back to Milner, planning on knocking on his door later, mixtape in hand.

I knocked on his door about an hour later, and after about ten silent seconds, he opened the door.

"Hey! Um, hope it's not a bad time!"

"No, no," he said, trying to smile and look like I wasn't bothering him.

"I made you a mixtape!" I yelped, holding it up.

"Oh," he said. "Thanks, that's . . . great." He took it from me and started looking at the track list.

"Yeah, I was at the radio station and was making some mixes for myself so I went ahead and made an extra one 'cause I know we like a lot of the same music and, you know, and, I figured, and, eh, why not? And, yeah. And. You know. I put some Kate Bush on there!"

"Thanks a lot," he said. "You want to come in? I'll put it on."

"Sure!"

I went in and sat down in a chair he gestured me toward. He stuck the cassette in, and the first strains of synthesizer from "In the Space Capsule (The Love Theme)" from *Flash Gordon* by

Queen, suckled our eardrums. It soon segued into tracks by the Bunnymen, This Mortal Coil, The Damned, Wire, Lush, and Slowdive. When "Crushed" by the Cocteau Twins started spangling all over the place, he would be mine.

We chatted a little bit about bands and classes and various things, and I kept waiting for the air between us to electrify. Our mutual chemistry should be making itself known any minute now.

"Oh, crap," he said, looking at his watch. "I'm supposed to go to this moon thing. I told my friend I would go."

"Moon thing?"

"Yeah, it's this full moon ceremony that's going on out in that field by the tennis courts."

"Full moon ceremony? Like witches and such?"

"I think they prefer the term *wiccans*," he said. "But no, I don't think they're all practitioners."

"Oh, OK, well . . ."

"You could come, probably," he offered.

"Oh, well, I, uh . . . don't know if I'm dressed properly."

"Eh, it's casual. Plus, you know, dark."

So I took him up on his halfhearted offer and walked with him outside. As we passed from the Milner dorm hallway out into the darkness, I couldn't tell for sure if I should be thinking about this as a romantic excursion with erotic possibilities or simply something that was happening because he'd found himself in the unfortunate position of having an unexpected guest come to his room just before he was supposed to go somewhere and he couldn't think of a good solid reason not to invite that random guest along.

We got down to the field and Trevor greeted his girlfriends, introducing me to a few of them briefly. There wasn't much time for chitchat, though, as the hour of the ceremony was soon upon us. We were instructed by the nice lady presiding over the assembly to gather together and form a circle. There were about twenty-five of us, so we made a large-ish ring in the dark as the light from the full moon shone on our pale, pale faces. I was sure to stay close to Trevor so I wouldn't be flanked by two perfect strangers on each side. Our moon mistress, a friendly-faced, frizzy-haired woman dressed in jeans and a cardigan, asked that we all hold hands, then addressed us and our overlordess.

"Lady Moon, bright and serene,
Shining with the bounty of the Mother,
Look down on us, your Children of the Earth.
Come, light of the Goddess,
Fill us with your power.
Impart to us your light and blessing.
Your love and grace surround us."

I was pretty sure at this point that this ceremony would probably be number one on the list of Things I Could Be Up to at This Moment That Would Horrify My Poor Mother. Worse than Jerking It in My Dorm Room to Pictures of Dudes, worse than Losing the Bible She Gave Me Before I Left for College, but maybe just this side of Dancing in Rainbow Speedos on a Float in a Gay Pride Parade.

Thankfully for my mother, I wasn't listening too closely, thrilled as I was to be holding a gay boy's hand for the first time. Trevor's and my hands were lopsidedly locked in a dispassionate embrace, my hand clinging to his as if its life and the life of its fingers depended on it, his returning the sentiment with what can best be described as raging apathy. His indifference to me was palpable. It was as plain as the nose on the man in the moon's face, which shone so brightly down upon us. But I ignored this instinctive knowledge I had already absorbed into my brain and focused on the facts: I am holding a man's hand. A man is holding my hand. And this man, I'd been told, liked other men. We're practically engaged! Sure, we were instructed to hold hands, but that didn't change the fact that we were, in front of everyone here, engaged in a brazen display of unbridled inter-digitation. Filthy.

Apparently the moon's energy had been summoned with this opening incantation.

"Her energy is among us," our mistress intoned. "Now we must direct it, use it, release it. We must give thanks."

Thank you, Goddess, for finally finding a man to hold my hand. Next time, maybe find a man who doesn't act like you paid him to do it?

"Power blessed to me by the Goddess,
rise in me for healing,
to replenish and renew my being.
Power blessed to me by the Goddess,
Surround me with strength.
By the power of the Goddess,
So mote it be."

So mote it indeed.

"Now, let us all enhance the energy around us by giving thanks back. Laurel, would you like to start? Just gently squeeze the hand of the next person when you are finished, as we go around."

Oh, *Lord.* We were now going to be forced to give thanks to the Goddess in front of everyone. I didn't even like saying the prayer at the dinner table in front of my family.

"Thank you, Goddess, for bringing us here tonight, for bestowing upon us the energy we can use to make our lives and other lives better."

The next person in the circle also gave thanks to the Goddess for some vague thing or other. I don't know, I couldn't listen because I was too focused on what on earth I was going to give thanks for. My persistent, relentless virginity? My great WQFS time slot? The advances being made in sugar-free candy technology? (Advances were *not* being made.)

Down the circle we went until we got to Trevor. "Just want to give thanks for friends and for beautiful nights like tonight."

Simple, elegant. Well played, Trevor. Next up: me.

I can't recall with precision what I emerged with, but I think it went something like: "I'd just like to thay sanks for the company of everyone and for all the people and the things. So, thanks." (Silent staring at/squeezing the hand of the next person to encourage her to hurry up and start giving thanks and get the moon's judgmental eyes off me.)

This was not my best moment in public speaking, though it was perhaps an improvement over the time in high school that I got in front of my speech class and taught the students how to fold a dollar bill into the shape of a bowtie:

"And then you fold it this way. Then this way. Then fold that over this way. Then fold the four corners like this. Then do this. Then this, aaaaaaand voilà! Bowtie!"

The thanks continued around the circle until we once again reached the mistress of ceremonies.

"Now, let us close this rite with an address to she whom we are here to celebrate.

"Goddess and Spirits,
You have heard our voices,
and our Craft has been completed.
Depart with our thanks and our love.
By the power of the Goddess and Spirits,
This Circle is undone but not broken,
So mote it be."

And so mote it was. All of our hands dropped to our sides, none so rapidly, it seemed to me, as Trevor's. His feelings toward me were making him anxious. (Those feelings: disinterest, discomfort, and whatever the opposite of lovelorn is.)

"Well, that was fun," I said to him.

"Yeah," he said. "There were quite a few people here; I was surprised."

I struggled to think of something to say to keep the conversation going, but my brain was unable to recall words and basic grammatical sentence structure because of the massive amounts of Moon Goddess energy swirling in the air around us.

"Well," he said, "I'll see you later; I'm supposed to go get some coffee with my friends, so . . ." As he talked he was actually backing away from me.

"Oh, sure, I'm going to head back. Enjoy the mixtape!"

"Oh yeah, thanks a lot for that. I'll see you later."

He walked away to rejoin his girlfriends, and I stood there looking up at the moon. *Oh, Moonman,* I thought, not even bothering to address the Goddess, seeing as how she'd let me down utterly, *I didn't even like him that much.* I didn't, really. But the fact that he didn't like *me,* that he obviously was not interested *at all, in the slightest, probably not even for cash*—that was unacceptable.

I put my hands in my pockets and started walking back to my dorm. My fingers found an old Tootsie Roll in one of the pockets, a leftover bullet in my perpetual battle against Low Blood Sugar Madness. Even though my blood sugar wasn't in the least bit low— it was probably on the high side, in fact, thanks to the excitement of being on a fake date with an uninterested unsuitor—I unwrapped it and put it in my dry mouth.

A tiny indiscretion, certainly, compared to what I *wanted* to put there.

Oh, how our little boy has grown up. Once he was just a little child twirling about blissfully in his room pretending to be God knows what—a sassy waitress, a pilot, a Stormtrooper. Now look at him: He's sitting in there in that DJ booth at his college radio station like a real adult, just stone cold pumpin' out the bangin' jams, or whatever the culturally disabled youth of the nineties say.

Let's survey his kingdom: He's got one song playing on a CD player in front of him with a second CD player cued up to the next song on his list, plus two LPs on the turntables beside him, with their respective needles positioned by him at the beginning of each desired track so that when he presses the power button on each one the song will start and his seamless music event will continue uninterrupted. He has placed each album sleeve behind its respective turntable so he can keep straight which one corresponds to which album and song. He's got this operation down.

Of course, there are any number of things that can go wrong for our DJ—he presses the wrong button and his microphone is shut off during an address, he presses the wrong button and his microphone is on so that people can *hear him beating his pencil to the beat while a song is playing, he accidentally brushes his arm against something and things come crashing down—a stack of CDs, an album sleeve, an open soda bottle, his aura of basic competence. Will any of these things be happening today? Would we be here otherwise?*

He of course is forced by station rules to play some songs from albums that have just been released, so he's constantly having to interrupt his stream of celestial post-punk classics with stuff from obscure, kind of grungy American bands with names like Nirvana and Pearl Jam. God, what an awful, unattractive racket they make, our DJ thinks. We agree wholeheartedly with him. These bands are going nowhere fast.

He's sitting in for a fellow DJ who is sick. It's an afternoon show, and, because he's not used to doing a show during normal waking hours, he's quite nervous about performing his DJ duties when people are actually listening and, more importantly, while the station manager sits in an office down the hall, listening to his show. So far he's been acquitting himself nicely. Look at him now, for instance, sitting before us and leaning into the microphone to address his audience as the song comes to an end, tell them what they've just heard, and coax them into staying with him for the next hour because he's got some smashing music coming up from Brian Eno, the Darling Buds, and Altered Images. What a silky smooth radio voice he has.

It's true, though: He's talking awfully slowly. Granted, there's a fine line between the laid-back, mellow delivery he's obviously going for and an address . . . that . . . involves . . . way . . . too . . . many . . . . pauses. As if to illustrate my point, he takes a deep breath between the words "Altered" and "Images" before turning to one of the public service announcements all DJs are required to read once every half hour. Usually it's hard for him to read these with a straight face, it being way too challenging to utter the words "sexually transmitted disease" without being a little bit of a scold (and, in his case, a little bit jealous). It is always his delivery of these PSAs that lets his audience know if he's bringing his A game or not.

"OK, folks, it's PMS time," he says into the microphone. Unclear if it was a joke or an accident.

"What do sex . . . tattoos . . . body piercings . . . toothbrushes . . . and contact sports have in common, hmmm?" he asks, squinting and struggling to decipher the jumble of words on the index card. "The answer is . . . all of these things can put college students at risk for . . ."

At this moment there is an interminable pause for . . . dramatic effect? Brechtian distance? The fuck of it?

". . . hepatitis B, a serious disease that can lead to . . ." He drops his notecard onto the control board, and for the next few seconds his late-afternoon audience is treated to the sounds of his teeth chattering while he tries to pick it up with his soggy fingertips, which are now dripping wet from wiping at his sweaty forehead. Ah, he's got it now. And just in time, because Tracy the station manager is standing outside the DJ room looking concerned that one of her DJs is doing a show while stupid drunk.

". . . chronic, even life-threatening liver disease." Now he's thinking to himself: "Liver"—is that even a word? Indeed, he pronounced it with a terribly hard "v" sound, as if he were moving his lips for the first time after waking from a coma. He slaps himself.

"The majority of people infected with hepatitis B are young adults, and there is no cure." Seeing that he's made it through a sentence without any weird pauses or exaggerated mispronunciations, Tracy backs away and returns to her office at the end of the hall.

"A safe and effective vaccine can prevent hepatitis B. Health officials . . . recommend that . . . all students get vaccinated." He wipes his forehead again and starts staring at the sweat beads accumulating on his forearm and rolling into his elbow pit. So weird, you don't usually think of your forearms sweating. But they do, he's finding out. And he's apparently determined to think about for a minute. A long silence follows, during which Tracy, who has just sat down in her office, stands back up.

"For more information," he finally says, cutting through the dead air, "call this number and ask for someone." He ad libbed that last part as he put the wet notecard back in the recipe box all the PSAs are kept in.

"OK, fraggles," he said, losing all sense of college radio decorum, "up next . . . is the most . . . beautiful . . . song . . . you've . . . ever heard."

At this, by the grace of God, he stops talking and presses the correct but-ton on turntable #1, which is cued up to play some art-faggy nonsense by the Cocteau Twins called "Feet-Like Fins."

He switches off his microphone as the ethereal guitars on the track begin filling the room, a small gesture of aptitude we didn't expect from him at this point.

The song plays, and he just sits in his chair. He stares ahead at the two CD players in front of him, probably wondering what on earth those two things are. Are they the same thing? Should he be doing something with them? Are they from the future? Why does his hand look so weird, and why is the area between his thumb and forefinger so wet?

The song slowly builds to the dramatic crescendo that he's been waiting for. There go the cymbals heralding the opening of the heavens into an aural orgy of cosmic coitus. Then there is the sound of a needle scratching against the record, followed by the silence of the grave. Have we all just died?

No, he realizes, the record sleeve that was leaning against the wall behind the turntable fell forward onto the playing record, sending the needle across the vinyl and then off it entirely.

Ever slow on the uptake, it takes a few moments for our DJ to realize what's happened. He gingerly lifts the sleeve off the turntable and leans it back against the wall, then turns to his microphone to address his public and offer an apology for this appalling act of gravity. Whoops, he's forgotten to put on the headphones.

"Whoa . . . hello . . . think we . . . had . . . a . . . accident," he struggles to say. Oh, and look, there's Tracy at the door.

"Tim!" she says. He turns to her with his dead glassy eyes. "You're not coming through. It's dead air."

He turns back to his microphone and instinctively knows what she's saying because, though he didn't understand a word of what was coming out of her mouth, she was pointing at her ear, shaking her head, and giving the universal facial expression that means "I can't hear a fucking word you're saying."

He turns his microphone back on and, realizing his headphones have slipped off his increasingly soggy head and are now dangling from his wet neck, slips them back over his ears and breathes into the mic. He hears himself. We are back on the air.

"Ooooooookay, sorry, everyone. Technical diffi . . . [deep breath] culties. Here's another . . ." Another song, presumably. Surely not another technical difficulty. He shuts off his microphone and presses the start button on turntable #2, which is cued up to play, appropriately enough, "Really Stupid" by The Primitives. If only he'd cued it up correctly. He hadn't placed the needle precisely at the very beginning of the track, so when the song starts playing, the guitars go "whiiiiiiirrrrRRRRRRRRRRRRAH" as the record spins to its requisite 45rpm speed. So he DID mean another technical difficulty. Well done, sir.

Tracy looks at him as he searches through his army bag of books, random pieces of paper, and trash. He pulls out a king-sized Snickers bar, rips it open, and slides its massive shaft into his open mouth, taking at least half of it in in one go. I feel like I'm watching something I shouldn't be. Tracy clearly does, too.

"Tim, are you OK?" she says as he takes his massive bite of Snickers and starts chomping. "Do you need something? Want me to take over for you while you . . . eat?"

He shakes his head. "No . . . sorry . . . I . . . fine . . . inaminute."

"Do you have anything else cued up?"

He nods. But he doesn't have anything else cued up. Or at least, he has no memory of cueing anything up. But he definitely knows what he wants to play next. He just has to locate it, somewhere in the room among the stacks of CDs and records he'd brought in from the station library.

He'll cue something up right after he finishes off the strawberry Pop-Tart he's currently fishing out of his bag. But wait, "Really Stupid" is getting ready to finish its short two-minute thirty-one-second running time. There's no song on deck. Iceberg straight ahead.

Next technical difficulty in 5, 4, 3, 2 . . .

CHAPTER 9
HEAVEN KNOWS I'M MISERABLE NOW

I think it was in the summer of 1993, when I was bent double on the side of I-40 hurling my guts out onto the side of the road at four in the morning while also blubbering like a little baby, that I realized I was losing my sense of humor about myself.

I wasn't puking up alcohol. I'd gone to a July 4 party the previous evening, sure, but I'd only had one beer, and I'd ended up back at my shitty basement apartment at University Gardens in Chapel Hill at a pretty early hour.

No, I was throwing up the way you do when you've had one beer, smoked a bunch of weed, stayed up all night punching the wall, battling a cave cricket invader, and silently screaming until you look like you've been clubbed by a lumberjack, and also you hate yourself. And because this loathing can be best expressed either (1) through interpretive dance or (2) by vomiting up bile, you choose the second option because your cat is sleeping on your leotard.

I was supposed to hang out with the family in Raleigh that day, and so decided to go ahead and get on the road early that morning since I obviously wasn't going to be getting any sleep. I'd already almost puked a few times by the time I left my apartment. This was not unusual. Over the past year I'd developed a new malady: Every so often, I was seized with the nervous urge to throw

217

up. Not a figurative urge to throw up, but the actual urge to shoot whatever's in my stomach onto the wall. It was awkward at parties. Because sometimes it would just happen out of the blue, and, though I eventually was able to control the churning of my stomach and keep the vomit from leaping past my throat, I could never hide the moronic facial expression you get when you are about to hurl. I'd pretend I was going to sneeze and had to cover my mouth, or I'd pretend that I was silently coughing. I got by. And I was nothing if not a perfect gentleman when I vomited. If I was at someone's house, I excused myself and went to the restroom. If the restroom was occupied, I ran outside and puked in the bushes.

So I'd gotten into my car, blasted some Blondie, and steered my jittery, clammy self onto the interstate for the quick ride to Raleigh. But sometimes vomit, like a deep dark secret or a tumor, just needs to come out. I had just passed Exit 274 when I realized that I was about to hurl whether I liked it or not. My guts twisted and churned and sent gallons of vomit up into my head, but I wasn't going to just puke onto my steering wheel, no. I wasn't some commoner. I would pull off the side of the road first. So, as snotty vomit trickled out of my nostrils, I veered off the interstate, stopped the car, stepped out, bent over, and spewed a hurricane of wretched liquid onto the shoulder.

It was when I was wiping some of this delightful mixture from my eyelashes and eyebrows and out of my ears that I realized a police officer had pulled up behind me. I could see the reflection of his lights in the surrounding trees and in the pale, diseased-looking puddle of filth I'd just left on the gravel.

It's at times like these that you might pause briefly to reflect upon the remarkable journey you've taken to get to the position you are in right now.

I'd left Guilford College after one year, deciding that, instead of needing a tiny school with a minuscule gay population, I needed the opposite of this: a giant school with a slightly less minuscule gay population. Much better odds. (Or worse, one or the other.) So I applied to UNC–Chapel Hill as a sophomore transfer student and was accepted. That summer I reconnected with Jennifer, the then parabola-haired friend from high school I'd met at the legendary PJ party four years before. She was quitting UNC-Wilmington to work and save money, and we decided we should move to Chapel Hill together. I definitely didn't want to subject myself to another roommate lottery, and she knew how to handle my low blood sugar attacks, so it was a perfect arrangement. There was just one minor thing she didn't know that I thought perhaps I should tell her. But as we all know by now, Libran gays don't come out of the closet—they are pulled.

I was back at home living with Mom and Dad for the summer, and Jennifer had come by one night so we could catch up. During the briefest of lulls in our conversation, completely out of the blue, she made a confession.

"I'm gay," she said, looking deep into my eyes the way only a lesbian can.

"I am, too." I smiled, excited because, wow, what a coincidence.

"Really?" she said. "You are, really?"

"Yep." I nodded. "As a chaise lounge."

"Oh, I'm so glad you told me," she said, taking me by the hand in the way that lesbians usually didn't. "Oh, and by the way, I'm not gay."

"Wait, what?"

"Yeah, I'm not actually gay. I mean, well, I was once, at a party in Wilmington, briefly. But it didn't stick."

"Wait, so you were just . . . baiting me?"

"Oh, Tim, how else was I going to get you to tell me? You're a total Libra."

She had a good point. And I like a crafty bitch. So that was that. We decided that night that we would move to Chapel Hill and she would help me be gay. Because a boy can't be expected to do that on his own.

"So . . . ," she continued, "shall we go to Legends?"

Why yes, we should. Legends, in downtown Raleigh, was one of the city's only gay bars. I'd never been there—indeed, I had never been to an actual gay bar, only to rave parties where dudes occasionally played slap-and-tickle on the dance floor while I sat on the sidelines, stubbornly and stupidly afraid to let my freaky gay flag fly—and was eager to see what it was like. Would there be a merry-go-round? A kissing booth? A lifeguard parade? Of course not. It was a Monday night.

So we got in Jennifer's Chrysler and headed downtown, with me giving her street-by-street directions on how to get there because I of course had them memorized.

"Turn right on here and then go straight."

"No," Jennifer scolded. "Go *forward*."

Yes, go forward. Go straight and you end up at Applebee's, probably.

We parked and sauntered past the pornography store and into the cozy embrace of baby's first gay bar. The place was empty except for a young twenty-something in a suit, sitting and chatting with a similarly dressed elderly man.

The bartender, a fit gentleman in a tight T-shirt and cheeks hollowed out by Michelangelo himself, smiled at us young whippersnappers, looked at our IDs, and said, "So, a round of Shirley Temples, kids?"

We agreed with his suggestion and decamped to a tall bar table in the corner of the room, where we could talk while enjoying a great view of one of the television screens suspended from the ceiling that was currently playing a video of an erotic massage being given to one hot hairless stud by another hot hairless stud. Though I'd seen my share of hot gay pornographic pictures in my time as a shoplifter of them, I'd never seen an actual porno. This one seemed like a pretty good place to start. Sadly, because of obscenity laws, this film was censored all to hell. We got plenty of close-ups of tight buns in Speedos, oiled-up torsos being worked over by big, strong hands, and snarls of affection/appreciation by both parties, but there was no big reveal of what the people really wanted to see: the junk.

"Tim? Hello!"

"Oh, I'm sorry, what?" I was a million miles away, over there, where the junk was hiding.

"I said do you know of any gay bars in Chapel Hill?"

"Hmm. No, I've heard there are gay people dropping from the trees and such. But I don't know if there's a bar." Now can I just get back to watching the teevee?

Jennifer excused herself to go to the restroom. I looked over to the bar and saw that the young man was gone. His erstwhile elderly companion was looking my way and intermittently staring up at the television above the bar that was playing the same film. I looked back at the dirty video, then in the direction of the restrooms for any sign of Jennifer.

I turned my head back, and there he was standing next to my table. He looked at me and up at the screen, then back to me.

"He's pretty good, huh?" he said.

"Yeah, definitely," I said, assuming he meant the masseur, whose skills were undeniable.

"Yeah," he replied, looking back up at the screen. Then he mumbled something I couldn't make out.

"Yeah," I said, because what else was I going to say?

"Hey," Jennifer said as she sat back down. "Who's your friend?"

"Oh, um, I don't know, actually."

"Hi," she said, reaching out her hand to the man. "I'm Jennifer, and this is my boyfriend Tim."

He took her hand weakly and nodded, then slunk away. For a tiny, terrible moment, my heart broke for him. Because old men on the make need love, too, God knows. But did they have to get it from me?

I realized something else that night, besides the possibility that I would end up at age eighty out at a bar on a Monday, looking for love in all the wrong places when I should be at home playing canasta with my husband: Having a wingwoman to help me navigate these tricky gay waters was an absolute necessity. If I hadn't had Jennifer there to bail me out, I would have probably ended up eloping with this old man to Vegas simply because I didn't want to hurt his feelings and because no one else had asked.

And if Jennifer could help me avoid unwanted suitors like that poor man, perhaps she could also assist me in securing some hot rod or other to get me laid?

I spent the summer trying to walk homosexually upright now that I was partially out of the closet. I spent a lot of time at the Fallout Shelter in Raleigh, which held an Indie/Industrial/Goth Night on Mondays that brought in a mixed crowd of young miscreants eager to get their rocks off to a bunch of erotic, hollow-cheeked clatter. I went there religiously with Jennifer, Mandy, and her boyfriend, Allen, all summer.

Every Monday a parade of pierced, suspender-clad eyeliner junkies descended upon West Street downtown to see, be seen, show off their tattoos, and have a pose-athon. The vast majority of us weren't old enough to drink, so to fill up the empty spaces that most folks usually fill with alcohol, we danced, watched each other dance, smoked, watched each other smoke, talked about how dumb everyone was, and snuck hits of weed.

When not engaging in important social jibber-jabber, I spent most of my time leaning against the wall by the dance floor looking around for eligible undead bachelors who might be convinced to take me back to their vampire lairs and show me their hard, throbbing coffins. Maybe that one with the Morrissey coif dancing nearby with his shirt off and his sinewy muscles undulating ecstatically under the black lights?

I watched him for a while, and by the end of "Beers, Steers, and Queers" I was having to wipe saliva from the corners of my lips. This boy was making love to that dance floor like a pro. And there he stood—or, rather, partially stood, since he was bent in half touching his toes, sweat glistening off his back and shoulders, sequinning all over his Chinese tattoos—daring me not to walk right up to him when he stood back up as the next song blasted out of the speakers and shout into his ear,

"Hi, um, you're a really good dancer!"

"Oh, thanks!" he shouted back, smiling. I had my hand on his soaking wet shoulder.

"Uh," I continued, still shouting into his ear, "do you date guys?"

He shook his head and shouted back, "NO. I'M REALLY FLATTERED, BUT . . . NO."

I nodded and said, "THAT'S COOL." Disappointing, but hey, at least he didn't deck me. And I was proud that I'd had the nerve to seek him out and get quick confirmation that there was no way in hell I'd be getting to see his mausoleum.

I looked over and saw Allen chatting to a cute boy on the other side of the dance floor so, wasting no time, I slunk over to where they were intermittently dancing, slapped Allen on the back, and did the "what's up" head nod, flashing the cute boy the quickest and most tantalizing of glances.

"Temple of Love" by The Sisters of Mercy began pumping out of the speakers, and it sent us three into a frenzy of hopping about in a dance-like flailing of limbs. I took the opportunity of this very long song to check out Allen's friend. He was pale as the dickens, with sleepy eyes and a lopsided smile, and I was already in love with his hilarious, jerky dancing.

"Who's your friend?" I screamed into Allen's ear after the song finished and "Personal Jesus" erupted from the speakers.

"WHY, DO YOU THINK HE'S CUTE?"

"SURE," I said. "HELP ME OUT?"

I continued dancing to Depeche Mode as Allen consulted with his adorable friend. They had a little back and forth for a minute, and then Allen leaned over to me.

"He says you're cute, but he doesn't want to get involved with a newbie."

"A WHAT?"

"SOMEONE WHO'S NEVER DATED A GUY BEFORE."

"YOU TOLD HIM I'VE NEVER DATED A GUY?"

"YEAH, I DID, SORRY."

Ugh, really? I thought. *Not wanting to take home a desperate virgin? That's a thing?* Either that or he was just being polite. Jesus. Strike two.

I looked over at the bar, where the small number of actual adults old enough to drink congregated. Maybe there would be a dusty old professor of English among them who would take me home and read to me.

I sauntered to the bar to check out the merchandise, and to my amazement saw a guy nursing a beer whom I'd had a crush on when I was in high school. He ran a gift shop in North Hills Mall that I used to go to so I could browse through the posters and also gawk at him. He was perfect for me: ten years older, tall, rugged, handsome, great arms, and completely out of my league.

I'd never seen him dressed in anything but black jeans and a tight black T-shirt. He must have had dozens of the same ensemble. *It suited him,* I thought as I squeezed in beside him at the bar. Concerned about looking too bright-eyed, dopy, and virginal, I set my face with a mature, bored expression, and gazed over at him, full of what I hoped was enticing German ennui. He looked over at me. I said "Hey," but didn't smile because to smile was to buy into the lie that men are anything but trails of misery and deception, as young Werther might have put it if he were here with me at the bar watching epileptics shake it to the Lords of Acid.

"Hi," he said, sounding even more bored than me. He then reached out his arm behind me. I turned my head and closed my eyes, positive that at any moment I would feel his strong grip on my shoulder. A second later I opened them and saw that he was pulling his arm back, and his hand was holding a beer. Oh. I was standing in front of his beer. That's what was happening there.

The man in black left the bar and strolled over to one of the pillars by the dance floor, taking his beer with him. Bye, man in black. Bye, beer.

Strike three.

Desperation, the new fragrance by Tim Anderson. Makes you smell undateable, apparently.

A few months later Jennifer and I were ensconced in Chapel Hill, slumming it in an exquisite basement apartment on Pritchard Avenue Extension. It smelled like centuries-old mold, was extremely poorly lit, had brown carpet that camouflaged the numerous jumping cave crickets that had probably lived there for generations, and was conveniently located next door to a married couple who clearly needed counseling, judging by the number of plates and coffee mugs being hurled against their kitchen/my bedroom wall. Most important, it was cheap as dirt and close to campus, exactly the type of glamorous abode any blossoming young gay boy would wish to plant his vanity mirror in, if only he could afford a vanity mirror and didn't constantly dread seeing his own reflection.

Known by its fans as "the Southern part of heaven," Chapel Hill was allegedly North Carolina's liberal oasis, a place the depraved and deprived could converge upon to let their freak flags fly. Were you a young boy who liked to wear your girlfriend's skirts? Were you a skinhead in impossibly tight jeans who loved nothing more than to hang out constantly in front of a hipster pizza parlor? Did you love tuneless indie music and change your hair color according to the hue of your mood ring? Well, then, apparently Chapel Hill was the place for you, if the words of North Carolina Senator Jesse Helms were anything to go by. Once asked what he thought about the prospect of building a new state zoo, Helms said, "Why do we need a zoo when we could just put up a fence around Chapel Hill?" OK, that was a pretty good one.

Chapel Hill was, at the time, the next big thing. It was 1992, Seattle was old news, and the Chapel Hill music scene was blowing up with nationally and internationally revered bands like Superchunk, Archers of Loaf, Flat Duo Jets, and Polvo, bringing unwashed young corduroy enthusiasts from all over the country to the hallowed ground of Franklin Street to see and be seen at local venues like the Cat's Cradle, Local 506, the Hard Back Café, and The Cave. You couldn't swing a guitar string on the street without lassoing at least one bassist, one drummer, and a few thrift-shop mamas wanting to be rock stars.

Jennifer and I didn't want to be rock stars. I played the violin but hadn't picked it up in a few years, and Jennifer was tone deaf. (Ask her to sing "Lovesong" by The Cure for you sometime.) But we weren't opposed to being close to those who wished to be rock stars. After a few months of waiting tables at a cocaine den with a truly horrendous record of health code violations called Colonel Chutney's, Jennifer managed to get a job at Pepper's Pizza, ground zero of Chapel Hill cool. Every employee there, to our naïve eyes, was in the top tier of the city's social life, and if we could just touch the hems of their secondhand garments, we were bound to find out where all the best parties were. And maybe they would know if there'd be any gay people there.

Each Pepper's employee had some sort of cosmetic handicap that prevented him or her from getting a job in the real world: pink unwashed hair, tattooed faces, heroin eyes, bull-ring piercings, scabies, etc. It was a wonderland of hipster funk, and we wanted all up in it. So it was quite a coup when Jennifer, who had no outwardly visible signs of her potential as a dirty hipster unless she wore a shirt low-cut enough to show the peace sign tattoo on her left breast, landed a job in the kitchen. She set to work with gusto, and within no time she was as surly as the best of them.

My first item of business was to try to find some damn gay friends. Immediately upon arriving in town, before even registering for classes, I called the office of the campus gay group, B-GLAD, the Bisexuals, Gays, Lesbians, and Allies for Diversity, because you gotta start somewhere, may as well take the easy route and grab the low-hanging fruits, no? No one picked up the phone, so I left a message.

"Hi, hello, um, hey, this is, uh, my name is Tim and I'm tall and slim. Ha ha, just kidding. Anyway, just calling to find out about your group and stuff and, you know, just moved here and want to see what you guys are about so if you could give me a call . . ."

A few days later I got a call from the president of the organization, a gentleman named Doug whose pants were, apparently, impossible to charm off.

"Thanks for calling me back!" I said, genuinely surprised. "I wasn't sure if maybe I got my phone number right or if maybe I didn't press pound."

"Uh, yeah, so I got your message. What exactly is it you wanted to know?"

"Oh, just, you know, stuff about what your organization does." Specifically, I left unmentioned, whether there were any Speedo-sponsored ice cream socials planned.

"Well, we meet once a week to discuss strategy for outreach and to plan activities. You can come to a meeting if you want."

"Great. And how big is the group?"

"Oh, I don't know. Small but growing. Does it matter?"

*Defen*sive. OK. "Oh, no, I'm just, you know, curious."

"Yeah, well, there's a trivia night coming up. You can come to that if you want."

"Sure, OK, well, that sounds like fun." That did *not* sound like fun. "Thanks for your time, I'll hopefully get a chance to meet you guys soon."

He hung up without saying good-bye, and I got off the phone feeling whatever the opposite of wooed is. For an organization called B-GLAD, their spokesman was awfully glum.

Soon after that I went down to the liberal commie volunteer-run bookstore and purchased a pink triangle pin, sticking it to my backpack and feeling immediately on display like the fat lady at a carnival. This tiny pin, I hoped, would be a game changer. Visibility was key, it seemed to me, and I wanted it known what team I was standing out in left field for.

One day a girl approached me after our American History class and asked me about the pin as we were walking out.

"Hi, I'm sorry, I don't want to pry, but I noticed that you have that pink triangle on your bag . . . ?"

"Yeah," I said brightly, not sure that being chatted up by a friendly young lady was really what I'd had in mind when I stuck the pin to my bag.

"Are you single?"

"Yes!" I blurted out, before laughing and then, in a more reserved tone, continuing. "I mean, yes, I am currently single." OH MY GOD I'M SO LONELY PLEASE HELP ME.

"Well, I was just thinking, I have a gay friend . . ."

To a seasoned gay man, this is one of the most horrifying sentences in the English language. But I didn't know this yet. She went on to tell me that her gay friend was newly single and looking, and she would love to set us up.

"Oh, sure," I said and shrugged, going for nonchalant and not at all desperate. "I'd love to meet him."

So a few days later we just happened to meet him after class on purpose. We walked out of the building, and all of a sudden a young gentleman walked up behind us, tapped the matchmaker on the shoulder, and gave her an enthusiastic hug. He was scruffy yet also pretty, like a choirboy after a bender in Berlin. He wore a raggedy old Madonna T-shirt and cut-off jean shorts, and he had eyes as red as a desert sunset.

"Drex! Hey, girl, what the hell is up, hon?"

"Hey, Joel! This is my friend Tim."

He looked me up and down and shook my hand limply. "Hi," he said, with the fakest smile I'd ever seen in my nineteen years.

"Hi, nice to meet you." I smiled. Then, oops, he had to go.

"Well, let's set up a coffee date," Drex said.

"Yeah, OK," he said, businesslike. We settled on an evening a few days away, and he departed.

On the day of our coffee social, I got a call from Drex in the afternoon.

"Hey, Tim, it's Drex," she said, sounding burdened.

"Hey! We still on for tonight?"

"Well, actually, Joel just called, and he said he's not feeling well, so he's cancelled."

"Oh. Oh, OK," I said. This sickness of Joel's was not a total surprise—he'd seemed to fall ill immediately upon meeting me, though I chose not to dwell on that. But denial, as they say, is more than a famous movie theater in Mesa, Arizona, so . . .

"So we'll just reschedule," I said.

"Yeah," she said, meaning the exact opposite. "I'll see if he wants to do that." Bless her, she was trying.

I finally got the picture, and spent the next few hours bitch-slapping myself for not getting the picture sooner.

So this was the "I have a gay friend" matchmaking game. More fun than Chinese water torture, less fun than dancing with a mop.

———

"I'm gonna pierce my tongue," Jennifer said one night as we sat in the living room taking bong hits and listening to Liz Phair.

"You're what?" I said as I drove an ultra-fine insulin syringe into the head of a stuffed bunny, one of a collection of stuffed animals Jennifer had housed on top of the entertainment center when we moved in. I'd always been lazy about properly disposing of my syringes after they were too dull to use, and one night after doing a few beer bongs at our neighbor's house I'd come home to smoke some weed and eat a late-night dinner. Bleary-eyed and world-weary, I'd taken my insulin shot, noticed a fluffy stuffed panda looking at me all haughtily, and a new trend was born. Maybe it was me or the weed or the copious amount of alcohol, but I just thought the little critter actually looked cuter with a syringe coming out of its head. I didn't plan to continue loading up the happy-faced bundles of fluff week after week, but I had really underestimated how satisfying it was to jab a syringe into something besides my own leg or stomach. Soon enough it became a hard habit to break. And it did make for a nice edgy and post-modern art installation for visitors to enjoy between bong hits. Plus, I wanted to see how long it would take for Jennifer to notice. Tonight was the night.

"I wish you'd stop doing that," she said as she exhaled a cloud of skank. "It's creepy. Like, voodoo or something."

"You know what I wish?" I said, placing the stuffed bunny back on the entertainment center. "That Liz Phair would just shut the fuck up about dudes being disappointing. I mean, at least she's getting laid. Like, all the time. Is there anything she does in her day-to-day life that involves *not* getting laid?"

"So I think I'll just do it myself, the piercing," Jennifer said.

"Or, oh, you know who really bugs me? En Vogue. Dancing around all sexy while pointing to some poor schmuck and singing he's never gonna get it, in four-part harmony. It's just cruel."

"Well, maybe next time he'll give his woman a little respect," Jennifer sighed. "Anyway, I figured I could just use one of your syringes."

"Oh, and Mick Jagger, cry me a river about not getting no satisfaction. It's insulting to those of us who are really suffering."

"I'll just inject some Anbesol into my tongue to numb it, and then once I can't feel anything I'll just jab a hole straight through."

"Ugh, and don't get me started on fucking Patsy Cline." I was not inclined to cut any pop, rock, or country star any slack whatsoever. I looked over at Jennifer for an amen of some sort. She stared at me blankly.

"Wait," I said, "did you just say Anbesol?"

"I think that should work, don't you?"

"Piercing your own tongue? With one of my syringes and some Anbesol?"

"Yeah."

I thought about someone else's issue as hard as I was able to for a few seconds.

"Hmm. I'd also have some whisky handy."

———

"I think you have kind of a sour expression on your face when you're just standing around," Drex told me one night when we were having dinner at her and her husband's house in Carrboro. "It might make guys reluctant to approach you?" Drex had made me a little project of hers—she wanted to find me a man who would love me and accept me for the awkward, brittle, gangly little space monster I felt myself to be. "Like when you first got here, you looked like your cat had just shit on your favorite CD."

"But this is just my normal expression."

"You should try to make an effort to brighten your face up. You know, smile and raise your eyebrows or something. You have a tendency to look a little dismissive and judgmental. You know, to some people."

Perhaps she was right. I could be putting guys off with my unwitting scowling. I definitely needed some sort of coaching, because my experience at gay bars could best be described as "lacking any promise of sex whatsoever." I had a hard time approaching anyone, and apparently everyone at the bar had been told by the door guy on their way in to just ignore the guy in the thrift-store shirt that smelled of mothballs because he's got crabs.

"Anyway," Drex went on, "I've got a new guy for you. His name is Matt, and he's just come out of the closet, so he's a fellow newbie."

Matt was a friend of a friend of an old roommate of Drex's. I showed up on a Sunday night at Drex's friend's old roommate's house, where the matchmaking was to happen. The plan was for Matt and me to meet, then go out somewhere to hang. I sat around the kitchen table with Drex, her friend Cindy, and her old roommate Dan waiting for Matt to show up. When he arrived, he entered the room like a dervish saying hello to everyone, grinning from ear to ear, his eyes wide and expressive, his teeth polished and gleaming, his perfectly square jawline seemingly drawn by the good people at Marvel Comics. I stood up, and he shook my hand vigorously.

"It's so nice to meet you!" he enthused. *Really?* I thought.

"It's nice to meet you, too." I smiled while I said it, keeping Drex's advice in mind. I kept my smile attached to my face for as long as I could, then downgraded to a pleasant, engaging lip curl, while still keeping my eyebrows at attention.

"So what are you guys gonna do?" Cindy asked him.

I wasn't sure what the answer was, but Matt had some thoughts.

"I don't know, I'd really like to go to the Power Company, what do you think, Tim?"

The Power Company was a large multilevel gay club in downtown Durham, the biggest club in the Triangle.

"Yeah, sure, that sounds fine," I said, still smiling, my voice overflowing with gusto and verve. Matt's enthusiasm was contagious, and as I took in the view of his awkward fashion sense (silky black shirt buttoned up to the top under an angular tuxedo jacket, plus acid-washed jeans) and what my x-ray gay vision could sense was an impressive washboard stomach, I actually wasn't having to force myself to smile. The guy seemed pretty nice.

We decided that I would drive. I pulled out onto Franklin Street headed for Durham, and Matt kept the conversation going.

"I'm so excited about going to the Power Company! I've never been. Have you been?"

"No," I said, pressing the clutch and preparing to switch gears. "Been wanting to. I've heard it's humongous."

"Me too! Hopefully there'll be some cute boys there tonight, even though it's Sunday."

My foot slid off the clutch as I put the car into fourth, and the car shook and screeched. I slammed the clutch back down, and we stabilized. "Sorry about that!" I said. "Not sure what happened there."

"Hey, Tim," Matt said, "I just want you to know that I'm really happy we're doing this, but I wanted to be totally honest and tell you that I'm really not interested in dating you. I hope we can be friends and do things . . . as friends. Know what I mean?"

I did my best to keep my plastic smile in place as I considered the endless string of words that were coming out of his pie hole. Hmm. Don't people usually say they just want to be friends after a date is over? And does doing things as friends include at least some oral?

"Oh, OK, well," I stammered, "I'm glad you made that clear."

"I mean," he interrupted, "is that cool with you? 'Cause I think you're really cool."

"Oh, you know, sure," I said, my head spinning. "It'll just be nice to . . . have someone to go out to gay clubs with." Yes, that would be nice.

"Oh, I'm so glad that's how you feel!" He hadn't changed his tone of voice during the whole exchange—it was happy, enthusiastic, excited, friendly, cloying, and annoying.

Thank God there was no dancing to be done at the club that night, since there was a drag show on. So we went upstairs, ordered some sodas, and sat overlooking the stage. The crowd was sparse and skewed a little older than us. Matt looked around at the talent like a kid in a candy store while I stared longingly at the exit signs. As the performances started, Matt's face lit up even brighter than before, which I didn't think would be possible seeing as he'd been grinning all night as if he were in a Mentos commercial. A queen named Pristine Taint, enveloped in every imaginable shade of green, took the stage and lip-synced a terrifyingly wonderful rendition of "Here Comes the Rain Again." I nodded and said under my breath, "Amen, sister."

"This is great!" Matt enthused, grinning widely and awkwardly sucking down his soda through the tiniest of cocktail straws. I looked at him with an expression that Drex would probably describe as the kind you have "when your cat shits in your mouth."

As the queens cycled through their sets, I sat there stewing, soaking in the exquisite performances that got at the essence of the bitter and frothing hurt, rage, and irritation that I myself was feeling deep down to my very core. I didn't have the makeup budget or taffeta connections to try my hand at acting out onstage myself, so I was living through the queens. Crystal DeCanter, performing a tragic and glorious "I Fall to Pieces," knew my pain. Juan Nightstand was basically lip-syncing "Breakin' in a Brand New Broken Heart" directly to me. And Miss Diagnosed's "What About Love?" ended the way that song should always end—with a single hand clasping a purple wig and holding it triumphantly in the air.

The performances gave me a second wind of sorts. I'd cycled through the stages of rejection—denial, anger, homicidal mania, hating Matt's stupid face, and acceptance. Of course, I wasn't even that into Matt. He was way too nice. But still, it's terrible not to be wanted, especially by someone who, his cheesy grinning notwithstanding, looked like he could do porn. But somehow, the therapy of the drag show had given me the strength to just say fuck it, let's try to have some fun tonight, OK, Tim?

"Hey, you wanna go to Boxers?" I said after the show was over. "It's still early."

"Sure, what's that?" He was still excited. "Is it gay?"

Yes, Boxers was gay. It was a small pub above a muscle gym back toward Chapel Hill, and it was alleged to have some pretty sexy bartenders. This made Matt more excited.

"YEAH, LET'S GO THERE!"

So twenty minutes later we were sitting at a mellow bar, sipping on sodas, and watching the tight-shirted bucks behind the counter do their thing.

"I like *him*!" Matt whispered excitedly, staring at the one with the tattoo of Divine on his shoulder. "How about you?"

"Hmmm." I considered. "You know, that drag queen that did 'I Touch Myself' had *amazing* arms. Those biceps were bigger than a baby's head."

"Huh," he said. "Are you attracted to drag queens?"

"Not sexually."

It was a slow night, and there were only about five or so lonely sad sacks there, but it took only a few minutes for the aging sexual predators among them to gravitate toward my new gay friend Matt and start asking him penetrating questions such as "What you drinking?" or "Are you a model?" or "You here alone?"

None of these dudes really stood a chance, not even with me (probably). While Matt was fending off the advances of someone's crazy uncle, I went to the men's room to either throw up or cry, I'd make that decision when I got there. As soon as I'd gotten to Boxers I'd lost all the mojo I'd built up during the drag show and just kind of wanted to go home and watch a movie. Didn't we still have *Hannah and Her Sisters* out from VisArt?

I returned to my stool next to Matt and saw that he was talking to a good-looking gentleman who must have just walked in and walked directly up to Matt, because he wasn't there before. I sat there for a few minutes trying to get some scraps from their conversation. I heard the words "fun," "exciting," "single," "drag," "just," "friend," and "fun" again.

Ahem.

"Oh, Tim, this is Richard! He lives in Chapel Hill, too!"

I arranged my face into the approximation of a smile and shook Richard's hand. "Nice to meet you, Richard." He nodded. I sat back on my stool, and they continued talking while I watched the bartender make drinks. A few minutes later they both stood up. Matt looked at me with a sheepish grin and said, "Hey, Tim, Richard and I are gonna go, OK?"

"OK, sure," I said, sucking down my Diet Coke.

"I'm so glad we did this!" he said, shaking my hand. I believed him. He looked pretty glad. That we did this. Whatever it was.

I raised my empty glass and said, "I am, too; we'll have to do it again sometime." We must never do this again. "It was nice to meet you, Richard." Richard, go eat a turd.

They left and, after seeing them drive off, I made my own exit, saying good-bye to all of my fans at the bar.

On the drive home I felt the familiar tingle in my fingertips indicating a plummeting blood sugar. *Oh, right,* I remembered. *I haven't eaten all night.* This brought the first real smile to my face for the first time in hours.

I ended the night on the couch. But I was surrounded by friends. It was me, Hannah, her sisters, Mary Jane, and my dear friend Little Debbie.

———

Sometime during spring semester I started to, discreetly, puke my guts up at least once a day. Anxiety and self-loathing levels having reached a crisis point, I found myself in a perpetual state of low-level panic—stomach churning, armpits soaked, heart racing. Vomiting became my body's way of exorcising the demons and calming itself down, however temporarily. The first time it happened it was not discreet, though. I was in my British Drama class and we were discussing *The Duchess of Malfi.* I started feeling a nervous nausea and my gut started wrenching in the middle of our discussion of the theme of unequal marriage, and by the time we got around to examining the play's depiction of the relationship between female sexuality and tragic violence, I had to politely excuse myself, my hand gripped tightly over my mouth as vomit seeped through my fingers, calmly depart the room, quietly pad down the hallway to the men's room, and then noisily hurl my guts into the closest porcelain receptacle, which in this case was a sink so shallow that puke ricocheted back onto my face. I then splashed myself with water, toweled dry, and thankfully rejoined my class in time for the discussion about incest.

But as this upchuck event developed into something that happened at least once a day, I became more deft at hiding from whoever was around me that I was retching—at a party, in class, on the quad, in the library, at Pepper's Pizza—by putting my hand in front of my mouth and pretending I was yawning or clearing my throat. (Because, kids, it's better to make someone think that they're boring you than that you are about to vomit on their face.) Then I would politely excuse myself and visit the nearest restroom to spew in private like a civilized person.

So all spring and summer there was a pretty steady stream of upchuck spurting out my nose and mouth at inopportune moments, but mostly I took it in stride. Mainly because I spent an increasing amount of time at home smoking weed, taking extra insulin so I could eat more Twinkies/Russell Stovers/Rolos, and watching Woody Allen movies that I'd checked out from the Undergraduate Library after cutting out of class early. That way, if I was compelled to purge while Woody and Diane Keaton discussed pantheism or tried to assassinate Napoleon, the bathroom was right there, and I could retch to my heart's content.

The backdrop for this constant tossing of cookies was a revelation I'd had since coming out: that just because you finally step out of those closet doors doesn't mean the world owes you a boyfriend, a fuck buddy, a pity lay, or even a gay pen pal. It just doesn't. Worse, it doesn't even mean you are going to finally feel like you fit in after all these years. I felt as if I was a minority of a minority. Because, let's face it, I was really a terribly unsophisticated gay guy. I hated shopping, hated house music, had no design sense, and lacked the necessary ability that pros like RuPaul, Gore Vidal, and

Oscar Wilde had to deliver an effortless insult while simply exhaling. I did, however, throw the best self-pity parties in town. So that's what I did, constantly. Only occasionally did I venture out to the gay bar with my dismissive, terribly judgmental face, where I would stand on my own, leave on my own, go home, cry, and want to die, just as it was foretold in the book of The Smiths, chapter How Soon Is Now, verse 6.

On July fourth, I went to a keg party and couldn't even bring myself to get excited about bountiful free beer. I left before the fireworks even started, went home, put on *Love and Death* again, and smoked myself into oblivion. Then I went to the bathroom, threw up saliva, and went to bed. Then I got back up, threw back up, and went back to bed. Then I punched the wall, got up, fought off the advances of a terrifyingly large cave cricket in my bed, then went and threw up air and stomach acid, then went back into my room, punched the wall again, and decided I couldn't get back into that bed until that cave cricket was dead. I rolled up an *Alternative Press* magazine and slammed it down on the bed, but the cricket had quick reflexes. Also, whenever it jumped to get out of the way, it jumped straight at me, sending me into paroxysms of sissy terror. One time I almost had it, but then it slipped into the crevice between the bed and the wall.

I looked at the clock; it was four thirty. I went back to the bathroom and was shocked to realize I didn't need to throw up again. *Hey, things are looking up.* Since I was supposed to go see my parents in Raleigh the next day, I decided I'd just go ahead and get on the road, arrive while they were still asleep, and slip into my old bedroom to get some cave-cricket-free shut-eye.

Because I'd thrown up so much in the past few hours, I had nothing left in my stomach, so I ate some breakfast—a bagel with a side of ramen noodles. But it would only be about a half hour before this meal once again saw the light of day.

Flying down I-40, I saw a dead deer on the shoulder, and as I passed it, the head of a vulture popped up out of the trough of the deer's entrails and looked around.

Yeah, I thought. *That seems about right.*

Soon I felt the familiar churning of my guts and pulled off to the side of the road. I got out of the car and hurried over to the other side, then assumed my regular position and started hurling. As I relieved myself of the burden of my breakfast, my eyes watering and my limbs sprouting tight little goose bumps, a police car pulled up behind my car with its lights going round and round.

Yeah, I thought. *That seems about right.*

I stood up from my vomit stance and turned to face the officer walking toward me.

"G'mornin'," he said. He had an excellent '70s moustache. As I wiped spew from my mouth with my arm, I realized that I was now in the least sexy porno ever.

"Hi," I said.

"Having problems?"

"Uh, yeah, just some stomach issues."

"Have you been drinking?"

"Oh, no, officer. Not at all. I'm just not feeling well. I'm actually on my way to my parents' house." I looked at him with the most sincere face I could muster. It was probably also laced with dismissiveness and judgment, because it was me, but it seemed to do the trick.

"OK, well, I had to stop and see—July fourth and all. There's lots of folks out on the road who shouldn't be."

"I understand."

"All right, well, you have a good day." He nodded and returned to his car.

I got back on the road and a few miles later got a flat tire.

Yeah, I thought. *That seems about right.*

———

A few hours later I woke up in my bedroom at my parents' house feeling like I'd been kicked in the gut. My abdominals were sore from all the hurling I'd done in the past twelve hours, and, though I was starving, I was afraid to eat. A knock came at the door.

"Hey, it's me," my sister, Laurie, said. She came in and looked me over. "You look pretty terrible."

"Yeah, I feel pretty terrible."

"Are you taking care of yourself?"

"Sort of."

"How's the diabetes?"

"OK."

"Are you keeping track of your blood sugars?"

"Not really."

"Any boys in the picture?"

This question upset me.

"Of course not." I scowled.

Laurie furrowed her brow. "Anything I can do?"

"Of course not." I scowled again, then started crying like a little girl.

"Tim," she said, coming to give me a hug, "you've got to take care of yourself. You seem to be flailing." She then lowered her voice to a whisper. "Have you thought about maybe telling Mom and Dad?"

"No. I mean . . . I don't know."

"It might be time."

"When does it end?" I asked her.

"When does what end?"

"I don't know. The bullshit."

"The bullshit doesn't end, Tim."

"Gah!" I screamed.

"It doesn't. You have to figure out a way to live through the bullshit. Kick it aside."

"I can't. I'm just . . . weak. And sick of it."

"So you're just going to give up?" She was raising her voice. "Just lie back and take it? Nothing comes of just sitting and whining."

"I'm not . . . I just . . . No . . ."

"You just what?"

"I just want to be thrown a bone once in a while!" Ha, *thrown a bone.* (I was serious about that.)

"Well, maybe you will be," she yelled, "but until then you've got to pull yourself together and not go off the deep end." I dropped my head into my hands. Laurie stood up and went to the door. "I'm here whenever you need me. You know that." I nodded, and she left the room.

Was it really time to tell Mom and Dad? Ugh, really? What on earth would that sound like?

Mom, Dad, I'm totally gay, but don't worry, I'm really unpopular with the boys.

or

Mom, Dad, I'm dying to suck a dick, I just haven't found the right one yet.

I had no idea how to accomplish this task. I'd always thought I wouldn't tell them until there was a really good reason to, like if I was running away to Amsterdam to marry a Dutch cowboy or if I'd been arrested for buying poppers from an unlicensed adult book-shop. And it wasn't as if I felt I'd catch them totally unawares. Mom had hinted a few times over the past few years that she was on to me.

"Are you checking out all the girls?" she had asked me as we took a walk down the beach the previous August. She was fishing.

"Uh, sure," I'd said, as passionless as a Victorian bureaucrat. I was such a coward.

I eventually ventured out of the bedroom and went downstairs. Mom was in the kitchen, and Dad was out in the backyard mow-ing the grass. I sank into the sofa and watched television for a little while, until Mom chimed in with her obligatory "Are you just gonna watch the tube all day? You should go outside." I turned off the TV with a huff and stomped past Mom and out to the back deck with a book. I was bound and determined to let everyone see how miserable I was. Dad still hadn't, but he'd be done with the lawn pretty soon.

"Hey, buddy," Dad said a little later as he walked up the deck stairs, having finished mowing. I was sitting in one of the lawn chairs dry-heaving behind my copy of Virginia Woolf's *The Voyage Out*, which seemed about right. I had heaved so much that my eyes were watering, and that naturally gave way to a headache, and then some mucus.

"Hi, Dad," I said, swallowing the mucus and wiping my eyes.

"How you doing?"

"Oh, you know . . . fine." Eyes bulging, stomach acid coating the inside of my mouth.

"Have a good Fourth?"

"Yeah."

Dad sat down in a lawn chair, took his baseball cap off, and wiped sweat from his brow with his wrist. Mom came out on the deck looking at me with a penetrating, worried expression that told me unequivocally, "I've just talked to Laurie, and there appears to be something going on with you."

"Tim, are you OK?"

I nodded. Then shook my head.

"What's going on?" She sat down next to Dad without taking her eyes off me.

The tear ducts widened, and I started doing that thing where when you inhale you sound like you're having an asthma attack. So this was it. I was going to have to say it. *I really don't want to say it.* But I have to. I'd been dragged kicking and screaming, despite my Hamlet-caliber wishy-washiness, to this moment.

Tell them, Tim, Jesus, just freaking tell them. What are you waiting for? Open your mouth and do it. You'll feel better. You need catharsis. And maybe your mom will make one of her famous Mississippi mud cakes for you by way of consolation! Oh yeah, you're diabetic, sorry, scratch that. Maybe she'll give you a scoop of sugar-free Cool Whip? (I got nothing.)

"I'm gay."

Without missing a beat, Dad reached over, touched me on the knee, and said, "It's OK, buddy. We love you."

"Tim," Mom said, already starting to cry, "you're our son, and it just doesn't matter."

At that moment I became a puddle of tears and mucus, just like so many gay men had before me, like Plato, Herodotus, and Paul Lynde.

There was much hugging and making-sure-I-was-OK over the next few minutes, and when the dust settled, Mom and Dad stood and went back inside. I told them I wanted to just stay outside and be alone for a while. Such a gay thing to say.

———

A few hours later I was back in Chapel Hill a little less twitchy. As I walked down the steps to my basement apartment I could hear stupid Liz Phair singing about how sad her love life is and how great she is at blow jobs.

Ugh, that *bitch again,* I thought.

Inside, Jennifer was flipping through a magazine on the couch.

"Hey," I said.

"Hey."

Her greeting sounded weird. Cloudy and clinky.

"I told Mom and Dad."

"Really? That'th awethome." At least that's what I thought she said. Because it sounded like she was talking with a mouth full of nails. "Conglatulationth."

I looked at her through narrowed eyelids. "What did you do? Wait. Show me your tongue."

She rolled her giant, bloated tongue out of her mouth, and it looked like a giant sea cucumber. It didn't seem possible that that swollen, red, alien tentacle could possibly fit inside her mouth. With her finger she tugged at the giant hoop she had somehow negotiated onto it, no doubt expending buckets of blood and Anbesol in the process.

Yeah, I thought. *That seems about right.*

*What on earth? This is just too tawdry for words. I don't even know how
to narrate what I'm seeing without being arrested for public lewdness.*

*The night had begun harmlessly enough. The young man started
his night out at a nancy dance club in downtown Durham with his
lady friend Jennifer, and they were shaking their tight young asses to
a revolting selection of house music. The only time I stopped rolling my
eyes was when RuPaul's "Supermodel" played, because that song is
fun-ny.*

*The boy occasionally stopped dancing and wandered around the
three-floor gay monstrosity like Augustus Gloop in the Chocolate Room,
checking out the tail on tap. As far as the eye could see, gym bunnies,
muscle Marys, big old Nellie queens, refugees from Fairytown, preppy
sideburn monkeys, fatties, bears, twinks, power bottoms, fatty twinks,
Nellie twinks, butch fairies, butch monkeys, butch bears, butch bottoms, butch bear preps, and Nellie bear fatties laughed and talked and
drank cocktails and insulted each other and occasionally (often)
shrieked.*

*Our hero wanted to talk to a few of them, maybe even many of
them (all of them), but his shyness and complete lack of game prevented
him from sidling up to some Brad or Dave or Brent or other and shooting the shit about* Melrose Place *or* 90210 *or* Howards End *or whatever the gays of 1993 are into.*

*He did the rounds for a little while, casting his longing gaze from
face to face, supple bicep to supple bicep, hard nipple pushing through
tight T-shirt to hard nipple pushing through tight T-shirt, on the hunt
for someone, anyone who would agree to some sort of arrangement of
the sexual variety.*

But no one was really responding much to his judgmental face, and eventually he returned to the dance floor to perform some more lame tricks. A few terrible songs later, over walked Jennifer with a male friend she'd just met.

He had on a tight stretchy green-and-white referee's jersey, a black baseball hat, and tight, tight pants.

"Tim, this is Greg," Jennifer said. Greg took our hero's hand with a solid grip and shook it. Jennifer winked at our hero as if to say, "He thinks you're cute; don't fuck this up."

The men started chatting, and our hero learned all the key details about Greg. He was from Wilmington. He was the manager of a Wendy's. He was in Durham for the weekend with his friend Bob. They were staying at the Heart of Durham hotel across the street. The mating ritual had officially begun.

All the important details having been covered, the two gentlemen headed back to the half-empty dance floor and flailed around for a while before Greg asked our hero if he would be interested in joining him at his hotel room for a sleepover.

So here we are now in a cheap hotel room that smells of beer and the back room of an adult bookstore. The two men are engaged in a marathon round of naked Twister, starting before the door is even slammed shut, moving quickly in front of the teevee, against the teevee, on the bureau, against the mirror, into the bathroom, onto the bathroom sink, moving into the shower, then back to the sink, around the corner in front of the bed where Greg's friend is inconveniently passed out and spread-eagled, and then over to the love seat, where, after a seemingly endless skit on The Sodom and Gomorrah Show, *things reach their . . . climax.*

So how's our hero's blood sugar, now that he's in a deep, exhausted slumber after such an Olympian workout, during which his virgin card was officially punched? Well, he hasn't had anything to eat in more than six hours, so he should be hitching a ride to Twitchville any minute now. Ah, there we go. Twitch, sweat, more twitching, more sweating, lifting of the head, looking around, dropping of the head, twitch, and repeat. After several cycles of this he finally jerks awake, figures out what's happening, gets up, searches for his pants for what seems like an hour, finally finds them twisted in knots under the bed, pulls some coinage out of them, and limps out to the vending machine to buy a candy bar.

Staggering back to the room, he realizes he's locked out. After a few moments of sighing and eye rolling, he figures he'll just wait outside for a while and let them sleep. He steps toward the railing and looks out at glamorous, glamorous downtown Durham.

He's enjoying this Milky Way more than he's ever enjoyed a Milky Way.

CHAPTER 10
STRANGEWAYS, HERE WE COME

I'd spent two years at two different colleges, and as that second year of beer bonging, traditional bonging, spastic dry-heaving, staring into space with dead eyes, paroxysmal blood sugars, and extreme cave-cricket wrestling progressed, the big question was: Where was I going to run away to next?

The question was easily answered once I, a certified Anglophile, discovered UNC had an exchange program with the University of Manchester: It was time to run away to England, where all young American men go to find validation for their inferiority complexes. And what better city for a gloomy boy with a penchant for self-pity and misanthropy to take up residence than the home of the king of all hilarious miserablists, Morrissey? The answer was: no better city.

After years of pent-up sexual frustration and one night of wild, merciless cherry popping, I spent the final months of the summer preparing to leave the country for the first time and embark on a cross-cultural adventure that would hopefully involve innumerable sexual partners of increasing sex appeal. Having moved to a country full of dour, miserable bastards, I would finally be surrounded by a citizenry who weren't put off by my condescending, judgmental face. Perhaps it would even work in my favor.

By the end of my year abroad, my hope was to have secured the affections of some count or baron or footman or other, who would be drawn by my American otherness. Xavier would propose to me at an Indian restaurant in Rusholme, place a glass slipper on my foot as I spooned rice pudding into my mouth, and carry me to his castle in Whalley Range, where we would spend our days eating Cadbury chocolate bars and finishing each other's X-rated crossword puzzles.

———

They say that if you don't like the weather in London then you should just wait ten minutes. What they don't say is that by the end of that ten-minute wait you might possibly, through no fault of your own, be getting a hand job.

I had just landed at London's Gatwick Airport, and I was heading toward the line for the shuttle to Heathrow for my flight north, which would take place a mere nine hours later. Before I got to the line, though, I stopped at a kiosk to check out the amazing new world of chocolate that I would soon be letting into my life during low blood sugar episodes: Boost, Aero, Dairy Milk, Double Decker, Flake, Milk Tray, Wispa, Star Bar, Twirl—and those were just the swishy-sounding ones.

"Don't care how, I want it now," my inner Veruca Salt proclaimed.

Which one should I choose? I had no idea, so I closed my eyes, reached my hand out, and grabbed. I popped my eyes open and gazed upon the chosen two: Wispa Gold and Star Bar. Now that I had them in my hand, though, I couldn't wait for a low blood sugar opportunity—I had to taste at least one of them now, screw the consequences. In the next few minutes it would set a high bar.

I moved on to get my ticket for the shuttle, and I was standing in line sinking my teeth and gums into the soft, chocolate-enveloped caramel mouth explosion that was the Wispa bar when a weary man behind me sighed.

"This shuttle is so drearily long."

I looked back at him. He was an older gentleman of perhaps fifty, and he had the stiff bearing and aristocratic air of a man who should be wearing a cravat. Where was his cravat?

"Is it?" I said.

"Oh, yes, it's terrible. Have you not taken it before?"

"No, never. This is actually my first time in England."

"Oh, really?" He was ever so excited. "Where are you from?"

I considered his accent. At first I thought he was some sort of British, but hearing him speak further, I had my doubts. He either sounded like a Briton who had spent way too much time in America or an American who'd spent way too much time in Britain and whose American friends no doubt constantly wanted to slap him when he talked.

"I'm from North Carolina."

"Ahhh, North Carolina, I know it well. Mainly Wilmington. I'm well acquainted with the Mickey Ratz bar." He looked at me as if to say, "Are *you* well acquainted with the Mickey Ratz bar?"

As it happened, I was mildly acquainted with the Mickey Ratz bar, but only because there had been a gay-bashing incident outside the bar the previous year that had been in the news.

"Oh, yes, I know that place. A guy got beat up outside last year."

"Oh, really? That's just terrible." He then gestured that I should step forward to the counter, where the nice lady was waiting to sell me a ticket. I got my ticket, then went outside to wait for the shuttle to arrive. The man soon joined me on the curb and decided the topic of Mickey Ratz had not been adequately addressed.

"Yes, whenever I'm in Wilmington, I make it a point to go— such a great place."

At this point I should say that I was twenty years old, I was undersexed, I had a knack for never capturing the attention of any male human in my vicinity, and I was flattered just to be considered. I'd never been wooed this forcefully while out in public minding my own business. Was it England that was the missing ingredient? Or just this new really tight T-shirt I was wearing against my nubile young flesh? A combination? In any case, I decided to take this man's obvious interest and run with it. I put my half-eaten Wispa Gold and the Star Bar in my shoulder bag.

"I've never been," I said. "But I've been meaning to." At this point I was probably batting my eyelashes at him. He nodded as the shuttle approached.

We boarded, and I moved toward the back to a seat by the window. The cravat-less gentleman slid in next to me and, as the shuttle began its forty-five-minute trek to Heathrow, he started getting all grabby, taking liberties with my crotch. Liberties, I say. Sure, I didn't stop him, and my crotch certainly didn't put up a fight. And sure, I just sat there and let him have his way without any complaint at all, but still. Liberties.

He continued his handsy appreciation of my lap off and on all the way to Heathrow. I didn't really know what to do besides sit there and enjoy the new charm of riding in a vehicle on the wrong side of the road (in the literal and the metaphorical sense), occasionally scanning the bus for any witnesses to our utterly wicked fantasia. Once we arrived at the airport, we got out, and I assumed our whirlwind romance was over and done with because, really, what kind of future did we have together? I expected nothing from him beyond this one crotch massage.

But the Man Without a Cravat was not ready to part.

"Wait right here," he said after we'd entered Heathrow, as if he owned me or something. I waited right there, and he went to make a phone call.

He came back a few minutes later with a very determined face.

"I'm trying to get out of this meeting. Would love to pop over to the hotel for a bit."

"Oh," I said, wondering if the hotel would have a heated pool, a heated poolboy, and complimentary Cadbury bars. After a few awkward moments of waiting for him to decide what he was doing, I figured it was as good a time as any to say good-bye.

"Well, I'm just going to go check in and head to my gate, I think."

"Hang on a minute," he said, scanning the concourse. "Let's go this way."

We went that way and soon were rounding a corner and walking down a narrower hallway with wall-sized windows looking out onto the runways.

"Ah, here we are," he said, then walked straight ahead and darted into a door on the left. I stood where I was, patiently waiting for him to see to his bladder needs. A few moments later he popped his head out the door and looked at me. "Come on," he said.

Oooooooh, I thought. That's what this is. He's not going to take me for a drink at the VIP lounge, then smuggle me over to a hotel room that cost more money than my monthly diabetes bill, then give me another crotch-over, then order some room service, then give me a couple hundred dollars for my troubles before paying for a cab back to Heathrow in time for my flight to Manchester this afternoon. No, he just wanted to get his rocks off real quick in that single-person restroom using me as his muse. I wanted to tell him I was not that kind of boy, that I've got a certain sense of decorum and etiquette, that I was raised better than that. No way, no how. *You exceed my age requirement for such behavior.* But then I figured, oh, OK, whatever, just this once.

A few minutes later he darted out of the bathroom, running late for his meeting. I emerged soon after, pulling my Wispa Gold out of my bag and gently reintroducing it into my mouth. As I hobbled around looking for my airline to check in for my flight, a posh female voice on the public address system cooed words that really resonated: "Welcome to Heathrow International Airport."

Manchester is England's second-largest city, behind London, and it has even better weather, and by "better" I mean "much worse." While the nickname of Chapel Hill was "The Southern Part of Heaven," Manchester was known as "The Rainy City," which didn't really do it justice. Better would be "You Think You're Sad? I'll Show You Sad." Because, yeah, it rained in Manchester. It rained a lot. It rained so much, so hard, and so cold that some days you forgot there was a thing called the sun in the sky and emotions to be felt like "happiness," "ebullience," and "not suicidal."

It was the first big city I'd ever been to, much less lived in, and I spent my first few weeks strolling down Oxford Road past the Holy Name Church, home of The Smiths' famous "Vicar in a Tutu"; walking along the canal and into the city center to browse around and maybe find out what a cheese-and-onion pasty was; riding in the front row on the second level of double-decker buses and taking in the majestic industrial gloom of the city; and sitting in pubs just letting those velvety Mancunian accents wash over me. I was typically American in my love of any English accent, no matter how preposterous, and it didn't take long for me to really start to lament my own way of speaking—my nasally American twang, my inability to convey a sneer or an eye roll over the phone, my pronunciation of Edinburgh. Buying a music magazine at a street kiosk soon after arriving, I decided I didn't want to betray my identity as an American interloper to the grizzled gentleman manning the counter, so I tried my hand at some sort of native accent that I stitched together from memory based upon Buzzcocks records, Rodgers and Hammerstein's *Oliver!*, and reruns of *The Young Ones* on MTV.

"'Ave you gotta a *Melody Maykah,* mate?" I asked with a straight face as the man stared at me in disbelief. "*Melody Maykah?*" I repeated. He looked down at the rows of magazines and pointed to the latest issue of *Melody Maker,* which he was pretty sure I'd asked for.

"Cheers," I said, rhyming it with "jizz," just like the Queen does. "'Ow much is that, then?" I said as I fished some coins out of my pocket.

"Fifty p," he said, and I naturally handed him a five-pence coin. He gave me that confused look again, and I started placing more coins in his palm, one by one, until the look and the palm went away.

I was not alone in my Anglophilia. There was also Scott from UNC, who lived in my same block of flats and was already using the word "pissed" to mean "drunk," "knackered" to mean "exhausted," and "silly cow" to mean "dumb bitch." Another American exchange student, Tracy from Buffalo, had dyed-auburn hair and a bad case of trichotillomania—in her case, a compulsion to pull out her eyelashes. Perhaps as a result, she also had an ever-present ring of thick black mascara around her eyes. She was also absolutely obsessed with The Smiths and, in fact, had come to Manchester for the sole purpose of tracking Morrissey down at his home on . . . I don't know, Meat Is Murder Avenue? How Soon Is Now Circle? Paint a Vulgar Picture Parkway?

"He's gone!" she lamented, slumping down at the table I was perched at in the pub at the student union. (That's right: a pub at the student union. Not to be confused with the bar at my residence hall.) "To London!"

"Who's gone to London?"

"Morrissey!" Her lips quivered as she spoke His name.

"So . . . do you think he made the right decision this time?" I asked with a gleam in my eye, referencing an apt Smiths lyric even though it was probably not a good time for that. "I mean, how do you know this?"

"That guy Dave told me. He's a big Smiths fan, and he said Morrissey lives in London now. Ugh, this is a disaster!"

"I bet he still comes back to see family," I said, trying to offer her some comfort. "You know, like his mum and his gran and aunties, and his bits and bobs, and his uncle down at the chip shop or something."

She was not consoled. "But . . . this means I won't see him out."

"Out where?"

"Just out! I don't know. The Salford Lads Club?"

Aha. I know that place. Morrissey and the gang were standing in front of that building on the album sleeve for *The Queen Is Dead*. But did she have no plan for meeting up with Morrissey besides walking the streets, scouting around pubs and bookstores, and maybe going downtown and holding up a sign saying "Morrissey, I've Been Collecting My Eyelashes for You" in front of the Arndale Centre? A stalker's gotta have a more solid plan of action than that, come on.

"Hmm. I'm not sure that place actually exists," I said. "I read somewhere that it's just a disused building now." I then quietly patted myself on the back for successfully using the British word *disused* in a sentence.

I felt for her. Sure, she was a little unstable, and it had probably not been wise to make the stalking of a singer your number-one goal for your year abroad. Still, the girl had been thwarted, and being thwarted is no fun, as I knew all too well. She'd now have to come up with a new reason for being here. Or she'd have to transfer to the London School of Economics. That got me thinking: What was *my* reason for being here? To get the hell out of my country, to live in a big city, to savor the flavor of soggy chips with salt and vinegar. All true. But why else? Maybe something about surrounding myself with hot pasty dudes that talk like sarcastic Prince Charmings, all of whom seem gay? Maybe. Also:

Around 1988, Manchester was ground zero for a music scene whose purveyors were white dudes in baggy clothing dancing around with neon toys and singing drugged-out party anthems about waterfalls, doing drugs, being lazy, having sex, and going to Ibiza to look at waterfalls, do drugs, be lazy, and have sex. The "Madchester" scene lasted into the early nineties, when the drugs ran out or the sex stopped working or the laziness turned into cancer. By 1993, the comedown had settled on the city, just in time for my arrival. But one result of the Madchester scene was that it boosted the city's nightlife cache, and one fortunate byproduct of this was the formation of a section of town called the Gay Village, where Lycra shirts could roam free. Formerly a run-down area by Rochdale Canal that secret gays would use at night for, in the words of Greater Manchester's former chief constable (such an adorable word), "swirling around in a cesspool of their own making," it was now a burgeoning gay neighborhood where both secret and unsecret gays could gather to drink, socialize, boogie, and decide which cesspool to go to next.

So my new favorite thing became going out in the Gay Village. Sure, I'd never really felt at home out on the gay scene, but I'd never had an entire village of options, either. And besides, I'd already learned from my inaugural visit to Heathrow that romance—or at least a quick and frenzied five-minute affair with a gentleman old enough to be your father's boss—can happen where you least expect it. And, let's see, what would happen if amphetamines are added to the mix?

I found out exactly that when I went to Flesh for the first time. Flesh was the monthly gay extravaganza at The Haçienda, a club owned by Factory Records and the band New Order that became world famous during the Madchester days and that was apparently swimming in substance abuse. This club had everything: a coat check, alcohol drinks, split-level dance floors, swirling neon lights, a smoke machine, probably a glow stick closet, and lots of patrons wearing not much more than, say, an Indian headdress. It was what American gays would call "fierce" or "fabulous" or "sick" and what British nancies might call "quite good, actually."

Tracy and I went one night after I begged her to go with me by laying it on thickly with The Smiths references.

"Can't you feel the soil falling over our heads?" I sang-moaned forlornly, adapting the lyrics to "I Know It's Over" for my own selfish ends. She wasn't biting. If we had been in a Smiths musical I would have sung this to her while backing her into a wall, playfully gyrating my hips with my shoulders pressed forward and my butt tight enough to bounce a pound coin off. But she was busy sitting on the floor putting more eyeliner on, so I just sat on her bed and made my case.

"But everyone there is going to be gay," she said. "What's in it for me?"

"Probably some drugs—that place is apparently crawling with them."

"OK, let's go, hurry up."

"Plus," I continued as I put on my faux leather jacket that I'd bought at a shop in the Corn Exchange, "I've heard it's a popular club night for breeders, because of all the drugs and nudity." We hopped a double-decker bus and powered down Oxford Road through the rain.

Flesh that night was fierce and quite good, actually. We arrived and while we were in the queue for the coat check we met some guy dressed as a tranny flapper harlequin and he had pills in his cloche hat that he was ready to negotiate away, so very early on we were set for the night. (Negotiating with a harlequin is pretty straightforward, surprisingly.) We sauntered around the edges of the main floor, going up the stairs where revelers were clustered here and there appreciating/critiquing each other's scanty wardrobes and braiding each other's nipple tassels. I felt the first jittery surge of the magic pill I'd taken just as we made it to the other side of the long balcony, where a grand staircase beckoned us back down to the main bar on the ground floor. And who was standing there at the bar sipping on a drink? That's right: Bernard Sumner, the lead singer of New Order. Was he staring at me from the bar with a come-hither glance and holding a cocktail out toward me so as to coax me down the stairs? No, he was not doing that. But there was a space right next to him at the bar that someone had just vacated, and that space would be mine. And, soon, just maybe, so would Bernard, because I was now officially hopped up on speed, and everything was suddenly possible.

I stepped down the stairs like a jittery pageant contestant, and as I did, some jerk—his head of hair so thick and wide and full of body that it had to be fake—slid into that empty space next to Bernard and started flapping his gums at him. Dammit. And my Bernard was talking back and laughing. They appeared to know each other—what a disaster. Then, as I alighted on the ground floor, I realized that the moppet with the hair was no ordinary gentleman. It was the lead singer of Simply Red—the "Holding Back the Years" guy. As if to rub this realization in my face, at that same moment Mr. Red tilted his head back, laughed, and whipped his luscious locks out of his face in slow motion. That hair was real.

"Tim!" I turned around, and there was Tracy. She was pointing out toward the corner of the main floor. "I think that's one of the Pet Shop Boys!" I looked where she was pointing but couldn't make out who she was talking about. All I saw were swirling lights bouncing off a tumble of gyrating bodies and a couple of boy toys with matching thongs and sailor hats doing the Hustle.

"Which one?" I asked.

"I don't know, the singer maybe?" *Oh, Tracy*, I thought. *Don't you know your Pet Shop Boys? They're very different people!*

"I don't see him!" I screamed sadly over the propulsive house beats thudding against my brain. She pointed again, and I followed her finger, stepping onward to the edge of the dance floor. I turned around to check to see if I was in the right general area she was pointing at, but her finger was now wandering into the hallway, pointing farther and farther away from where I was standing. I tried to follow her fingertip, bounding into excitable punters gulping down their bottled waters and slamming against various striped poles that were scattered around the dance floor. I wandered around mesmerized, the red and blue and green and purple lights cascading all around as I searched and searched for my lost Pet Shop Boy.

I wandered down a hallway and into a wonderland of writhing bodies. I looked and saw a face smiling at me, and that face was connected to a torso being clung to by a dripping wet tank top and undulating like a palm tree in a hurricane. All of a sudden my face and his face were stuck together at the mouths, and we noshed on each other's lips and chins and cheeks for a few glorious minutes until we felt like we were done, then as poetically as we were brought together, we were torn asunder by a new surge of humanity making its bulbous way like a big love blob into the hallway, and we parted forever. I moved onward, jostled this way and that, and suddenly remembered I was still on the hunt for a Pet Shop Boy of some sort. I looked around at all the smeared and glistening faces, seeing no Boy among them. My adrenaline peaking, I determined it was time to dance, and dashed back to the dance floor and gravitated toward the back wall where I could get a better view of all the slippery hunks of flesh jerking and grinding against each other.

I sidestepped toward one grouping of evidently available gentlemen and offered myself up for some grabbing and groping, jumping whole hog into a series of short-lived love affairs with blokes probably named Ian or Nigel or Arthur or Fergus, and they were all really nice. Then I did something I'd never done before ever in public unless forced to by society norms: I took my shirt off. And when I did I heard sirens wailing and the crowd hollering their approval. Were they hollering for me? No, they were yelping at a drag queen who had just taken over one of the cube platforms and was gyrating up a storm. Suddenly I felt a hand against my wet back and turned around, expecting to find another British face offering to clean my molars with his tongue. To my surprise there stood Tracy, fully dressed and bouncing like a pinball among the cluster of dancers surrounding us.

"Hey, I'm gonna go," she said, wiping her hand on her plaid skirt. "I'm tired."

"Really? But we haven't found our Pet Shop Boy yet!"

But she was not in it to win it, as I was. Can't say that I blamed her: There were very few men here that she could win it with, unless she somehow found Bernard again, because though he seemed gay, I was pretty sure he was just English. Or the Simply Red fellow, but that's a lot of hair to have to put up with. Tracy left, and I returned to the comforting womb of the dance.

It felt like only a few minutes later that the lights came up and the night was over.

What? I thought, looking down at my watch. *It's only five in the morning!* I was crestfallen as everyone around me stopped bumping and grinding and started gathering their things and heading for the doors. I couldn't stop, though. My body and, more specifically, the amphetamines raging within it, wouldn't allow me to stop. I jerked myself over to the coat check and joined the queue, but I was unable to stop moving. You don't tell amphetamines when you're done, apparently—they tell you. And my speed-addled body demanded more dancing. In the line I heard talk of an after-party at a club down the road, so I got my coat and followed the trail of Haçienda refugees to the next cesspool.

I danced and danced and danced—the word "dance," of course, being broadly defined as both rhythmic and arrhythmic movement of the body to whatever beat is available at any given moment. Boys filled the floor, loving up on each other in a most unconventional fashion. I had a few more sloppy and short-lived love affairs with an array of dehydrated dudes with kaleidoscope eyes, first in this corner and then in that corner and then in front of the bathroom mirror on the sink and then at the bar, intermittently dancing and grinding my teeth, before I had finally, finally run my body out. At eight a.m. I stumbled out onto the street, where folks were hustling through the drizzle to their offices, like responsible English adults. The majestic/soggy Manchester morning had already fully unfurled, and, now, having left the upper stratosphere of Planet Dance and safely landed back on Earth, I was finding it difficult to move my body in a simple forward motion without the guidance of The Beat. I staggered down Oxford Road, trying mightily not to jerk my arms around constantly and shake my hips and head around like a drunk marionette. I was partially successful, but I wouldn't really be able to say which part.

I knew that my comedown was going to be epic. Those who disco and suck face in zero gravity fall the hardest, or whatever the proverb says; I could barely see straight, give me a break. I would go back to my flat now, fall flat on my tiny prison bed, then wake up in a few hours alone, sad, and paranoid about what I'd done out in public in full view of Bernard Sumner and one of the Pet Shop Boys.

I didn't care what the lead singer of Simply Red thought, to be honest.

"I think she is!" Tracy whispered excitedly. "Oh my God, I think she is!"

Tracy and I were sitting in the university cafeteria training our American eagle eyes at a doddering old lady clearing tables, placing used dishes and cups into her rolling cart, and giving the tables a wipe with her dark rag. There was a rumor going around that this woman was none other than Morrissey's grandmother. Thus far my glimpses of her had been fleeting, usually captured just before she left the dining area and disappeared into the back. But right now we had an excellent, sustained view of her as she did her work a few tables over: We saw her from all sides, and it was amazing how much she favored Morrissey. The pallid potato face, the massive, sloping nose ridged in the middle, the coif. OK, not the coif. But oh, the potato face. It was as if, right before our eyes, doing menial work like some commoner, and wearing an oversized apron, a paper hat, and a fat suit, was the man who once had a girlfriend who was in a coma (it was serious). The very one!

"Wow, she really does look like him," I agreed. I noted the barest hint of a smile curl itself on her lips. She knew she was being watched. Whether she was Morrissey's grandmother or not, she was enjoying the attention this famous young fop was garnering her.

"I want to bleach my hair, I think," I said. It seemed to be a thing that gay guys were doing, and I'd always been a sucker for Billy Idol. Maybe if I'd gone white-hot-blond back home it would have distracted guys from my thoroughly judgmental face.

"Oh, you should! It will electrify your whole head!"

"But what should I use?"

"Oh, any old hair bleach will do the trick."

"But won't some of them peel my scalp off?"

"Only temporarily."

"Hmmm." I wondered if I should be taking advice like this from a girl who pulls out her eyelashes. Perhaps I should get a professional to handle it.

"You going out tonight?" I asked her.

"It's Wednesday."

"Oh," I said, not understanding her point. Then I got it. My social inclinations had totally changed since setting foot in

Manchester. I was living in a flat full of "freshers"—first-year students who, because of the exigencies of the British university degree system, didn't ever have to do a damn thing because all of their coursework for the entire year would add up to only two or three percent of their entire degree. So they spent days on end in the front room playing video games, smoking Olympian amounts of hash, and having the most hilariously articulate conversations I'd ever heard about the space-time continuum, the coming communications revolution, and the Israeli-Palestinian conflict. But they never ever went to class. Ever. And their lack of any scholastic ambition whatsoever was rubbing off on me. I was shedding my "responsible student" shtick, and, as the sun began setting at 3:45 in the afternoon, all I could think of was where I was going to go out and get bladdered. Sometimes I would go with friends; sometimes I would go by myself. Sometimes I would pass out on the floor of a pub and have to be carried home or rely on the kindness of strangers to put me in a cab and not rob me. These things happen. But I always bounced back the next night and was ready to rumble.

I couldn't interest Tracy or anyone else in going out with me that Wednesday, so I set out on my own, down Oxford Road on the 147 bus to Charles Street, where a short hop, skip, and jump later I was entering the hallowed walls of the Paradise Factory, a giant gay club downtown. It was surprisingly hopping for a Wednesday night, so I got a drink and made my way up to the second floor to check out the proceedings.

A few drinks later I was sitting on a bench along the periphery of the third-floor dance floor, nodding along to the music and sucking down a glass of Woodpecker Cider that was profoundly diabetic-unfriendly.

"Are you out on your own?" a female voice beside me shouted into my ear. I looked over at the curly-haired young lady sitting next to me.

"Yeah," I shouted back at her. "You know, it's Wednesday." I shrugged my shoulders in an exaggerated fashion.

"Are you American?" she said excitedly.

I nodded.

"What on earth are you doing in Manchester?"

"Going to school."

This didn't seem to make sense to her, but she nodded anyway.

"I'm Janet, and, oh, this is my friend Stephen." She gestured to the handsome young man on her other side tugging on a cigarette. He extended his hand and shook mine, leaning over his friend to shout "Nice to meet you!" Janet excused herself and took off for the bar, and Stephen scooted over.

"You're American?"

"Yeah, sorry," I said.

"Oh, you shouldn't be sorry. I love Truman Capote." *Ca-PO-tay*, he pronounced it.

I'd never read Truman Capote, and knew nothing of his work. I now knew, though, that he was American, like me, and I knew that I *should* know him, so . . .

"Oh, I do, too!"

"He's my favorite author full stop," he slurred into my ear. This boy was already sloshed. He was way ahead of me. Thankfully, Janet came back from the bar with four drinks, two of which she handed to me.

"Here you go, doll," she said. "You need to catch up."

"What are these?" I asked, looking at the plastic cups of clear liquid over ice.

"Vodka," she said. "Americans like vodka, right?"

She sat on the other side of Stephen, and he kept leaning over and slurring things into my ear that I couldn't really understand, except for the word "CaPOtay." This boy really liked our Truman.

"*Breafasssst at Tifffany'ssss* is loike moi favorite book of all toim, reeeaally."

I sucked down the two vodka drinks, and soon enough I was giving back to Stephen as good as I got, slurring like a champ.

"It'ssss funny that Capote issss your favorite author, becausssssse myyyyyy favorite author isssss Charlessssss Dickenssssss!"

He nodded, then looked puzzled.

"Why isssss that funny, then?"

"Becaussssssse," I started, forgetting why it was funny (it wasn't funny), then remembering, "Capote issssss American and Dickensss iss English." He stared out at the boys and girls hopping around on the dance floor to The Stone Roses, nodding, then tilting his head quizzically.

"You know," I pressed, "Capote isssss American but you're Englishhhh and Dickenssss iss English but I'm Amer[hiccup]ican."

"Oooooh," he said, nodding. "I guess that'ssss kinda funny, maybe." (It wasn't funny.)

With the amount of time we were spending leaning into each other's ears to slur-shout nonsense about Capote and Dickens, we were bound to knock heads at some point. We did this. We were also bound to find ourselves at the optimal angle to start sucking face. We also did this. We did this a lot. For minute upon minute. Did Janet even exist anymore?

After a while, Stephen excused himself to go to the men's room. I asked him for a cigarette before he left, and he tossed one my way. Janet was nowhere to be found, so I just sat there looking around with my glazed eyes. A group of guys were on the other side of the room sitting around a table. The dance floor traffic was sparse. I put the cigarette in my mouth and realized I had no way to light it, so I stood up and strolled over to the table of guys, some of whom were smoking.

"Hey, can I bum a light?" I asked. The guys looked at each other uncomfortably before one of them finally wordlessly pushed a lighter across the table. I scooped it up and lit my cigarette, then placed it back on the table. The guys looked at it, but no one touched it.

"Thanks," I said. They all looked away, apparently not interested in any further discussion.

This is weird, I thought drunkenly. As I returned to my spot on the opposite side of the room I looked down to see if my junk was hanging out of my pants or something. No, it was not. I got to the bench and, before sitting back down, I looked at the flyer that was stuck to the wall above my head.

WEDNESDAYS ARE STRAIGHT NIGHT AT PARADISE FACTORY!

Oooooooooooh. OK. That over there was a pack of straight dudes who'd just had a front-row seat for Stephen's and my furious face-meld that just went on forever and ever, and it made them feel weird. Looking around I suddenly realized that I was simply surrounded by straight people. Surrounded. They were everywhere. On the dance floor. Against the wall. At the bar. On the stairs. Swinging from the rafters, cackling. This was not how I'd planned to spend my Wednesday night, surrounded by . . . *these* types.

Stephen came back from the men's room, and I excitedly gave him the news.

"Didjjjyoo know that it'ssssssss ssssssssstraight night tonight?"

"Oh yeah, they alwaysssssss have that on Wenssssdayssss."

"You knew?! Then why are you here?"

"Janet'ssss idea."

"Oh. Where'ssss Janet?"

"Buggered off somewhere . . ."

"Dammit, Jannnet . . ."

We decided to leave the breeder den before things got any weirder, and he generously invited me over to his flat just down the road. We stumbled over there, made out for a little while, and passed out in his bed.

I snored myself awake the next morning, and there I was, in Stephen's bed. And there was Stephen, still sleeping peacefully, which surprised me because, owing to my superhuman snoring ability, usually folks can't sleep in the same *room* with me, much less on the same *mattress*. I realized for the first time that he was a redhead. His red lashes were long and languorously rested on his soft eyebed. I gracefully rolled off the mattress and onto the floor. I then picked myself up, stepped into the sitting room, sat on the floor next to his small entertainment center, and did what came naturally: started going through his record collection.

Wow. It was a children's treasury of collectibles from British indie pop's last decade. There were items I'd only read about in the pricey British music magazines I'd torn through voraciously in high school but never had proof actually existed: a 45 by The Primitives that came with a little packet of bubble bath; The Sundays' first single from 1989 containing a B-side I'd never heard; The Human League's *Dare* on stunning pink marbled vinyl—*WHAT?* Sleeves from Stephen's collection danced before my eyes: Siouxsie and the Banshees live in Japan, the Co-Stars' single "Kiss and Make Up" in a gatefold sleeve; Public Image Ltd's album *Metal Box* in an actual metal box!

"See something you like, then?"

I whipped my head over guiltily and saw that Stephen had emerged from the bedroom in his robe. "Oh, just all of it," I said, lifting up an Echo and the Bunnymen 45 and gingerly widening the sleeve opening to see if the record inside was on scratch-n-sniff strawberry shortcake vinyl.

"So you like the Bunnymen?"

"Almost more than I like Wispa Gold bars."

Stephen tilted his head to take that last comment in, then pushed his lips into a pout and nodded to convey his acceptance of its rationality.

"Oh, I forgot I had that," he said, pointing to the Shop Assistants album I was holding. "That's Ian's."

"Oh, who's Ian?"

"Oh, you know, ex-boyfriend. Still a friend. He's got more records than I do." He smiled and looked down. I nodded and self-consciously started stacking the albums I'd scattered in a semi-circle around me to clear a path for him to get to the sofa.

"Anyway, cup of tea?" he said with a chipper grin.

We spent all day drinking tea and going through his collection, then making out, then putting on a Joy Division record, then more tea and sucking face, then snacks, then some Altered Images, then getting naked, then staying naked, then some Bronski Beat. We were two kids in a candy store, satisfying our seemingly inexhaustible cravings for chocolate, caramel, nougat, and lap-diving. Also the first Chameleons album and that Sarah Records compilation.

"You should feel free to pop by anytime and copy these," Stephen told me. I took him up on his offer, and started going by once a week with blank cassettes, clean underwear, and a dream.

The next few weeks were colored by an agitated bliss I'd never experienced before. I was nervous yet ecstatic hanging out with Stephen, going drinking, getting coffee and cake at the Cornerhouse Café, going out in the Gay Village—I felt like a real boy with a real boyfriend, like Pinocchio and that guy he dated. We hung out every weekend, and he could be relied upon to call every few days. Whenever I wasn't with him I was thinking about him, obsessing over whether he was thinking about me, wondering if he was talking about his embarrassing American boyfriend to his friends, and waiting for the phone in the hallway of my flat to ring and someone to knock on the door and say, "Tim, phone for you," at which point I could start breathing again.

One weeknight we sat at a table on the second floor of a bar called Manto, where his friend was doing a drag show. Our hands were playfully entwined on the table, and whenever Stephen would pull his hand away to scratch an eyebrow or reach in his pocket or accompany him to the bathroom, I was breathless with longing as I counted down the seconds to when that hand would be back safely clasping mine and I could relax.

Stephen's friend Peter's drag alter ego was Icelandic femme fatale Anyir Lidldógtu, and she was a mess. Her skin-tight evening dress, a bonanza of shimmering gold sequins, was embossed on the butt with the face of Björk, her ex-best friend and nemesis. Her black bob wig was placed on her head ever so lopsidedly, and her eyes were caked with dark brown eye shadow. She stumbled around in busted-up high heels wielding a clutch purse that, halfway into her show, I realized was plastered all over with condom wrappers.

"Wow, she's really hideous," I said as I gawked.

"Oh, you should tell her afterward," Stephen said, leaning in to me. "She's always afraid she looks too presentable."

Anyir Lidldógtu entertained us for the next half hour singing (badly) Björk songs like "Human Behaviour" and "Big Time Sensuality" and lamenting at length her own regrettable lack of dwarfishness, which was what she claimed made Björk a star. It was a compelling story of revenge and betrayal, even before Ms. L started cracking eggs on her face while wailing in her native tongue what I'm assuming is Icelandic for "That elf bitch stole my diamonds!"

After the show and, I imagine, a thorough scrubdown, Peter sauntered up to our table after a brief visit to the bar. Stephen stood and embraced him, kissing him on both cheeks, then turned and introduced us. Peter was tall and thin, with a shaved head and an amazingly kind face for someone who'd just been cursing Björk to hell.

"He's American," Stephen said with a wry grin, as if he and Peter had an inside joke about Americans that they were silently agreeing not to say in my presence. Peter then whispered something to Stephen, and Stephen shook his head.

"Oh, you're American, that's so exciting!" Peter said, shaking my hand with his soft, delicate fingers. "So, how is life in the colonies?"

I was starstruck and couldn't think of anything to say, so I just squeaked, "It's fun!" while smiling stupidly.

"He actually lives here—he's a bloody student," Stephen said. Pronounced "shtyoodint."

"In Manchester?" He looked at me incredulously. "Was the University of Fucking Nowhere all filled up?"

"Ha ha!" I laughed, still stupidly. "Yeah."

Peter lit a cigarette and continued. "Well, I think it's just terrible. You should never go to school, Tim, it leads to nothing but misery. You should quit immediately and just pose for a living." He tugged on his smoke, then looked at my face for an uncomfortably long time. "You have an enormous nose, might as well use it."

"Good advice," I said. "Do you know anyone who would pay me for that?"

"Oh, I know folks who will pay for all sorts of things, especially if you're a Yank!" He winked and tipped his head at me, lightning fast. He and Stephen exchanged grins. "But seriously, why are you here?"

"Uh," I said, not sure how to answer. "Stephen brought me here."

"No, honey, I mean why are you in *England*? You come from the land of opportunity and Jesus, right? What do you need with us?"

I pursed my lips to signify that I was thinking about it. "Hmm. I don't know, really. Jaffa Cakes?"

"Oh, Tim, you should never eat anything but lettuce and never drink anything but vodka. There's no future in fat cells."

"Oh, I only eat them while I'm doing sit-ups."

Peter smiled at my lame attempt to compete with him for Best Witty Comeback.

"Well, just keep it under control, this bar has a strict No Fatties policy. Stephen was once barred for a whole month after the Christmas holiday, weren't you, Stephen?"

"No," he said.

"Sure you were, we just didn't tell you. Anyway, loves, gotta go. Turrah!"

Peter got up to continue his post-show rounds, and Stephen and I sat there silently, as "Relight My Fire," a particularly hideous song by local boy band Take That, burst from the speakers. All of a sudden I realized that Stephen and I weren't holding hands anymore. He was pensively staring into space, one hand under his chin and the other drumming the table.

"I really hate this song," I said, then gave his hand a squeeze.

"Yeah, it's pretty stupid." He looked out the large window behind us.

I nodded and racked my brain for something else, anything else, I could say to keep the conversation going. Because it seemed like he was . . .

"Drink up? It's nearly half ten." He was ready to go.

———

After another few weeks, it was obvious that Stephen was disengaging. First, the phone calls started coming less frequently. Naturally, my calls to him got more frequent and desperate, and on the other end he sounded more distant. One week, the days crept by without a word from him. A boy obsessed, I couldn't look at any object in my room without dwelling on its relevance to my relationship with Stephen, which in my head I'd ballooned into a love affair of the ages. The cassettes, the Capote books I'd picked up and thumbed through, the flyers and promotional postcards for Paradise Factory club nights and drag shows scattered across my floor, the can of Woodpecker Cider in my hand, the many empty Woodpecker cans on the floor. I started staying up all night listening to the music I'd recorded from his collection. Because listening to every Chameleons album back to back would surely provide me with a breakthrough.

Soon I began to fixate over a particular Capote quote I'd come across:

"Life is a moderately good play with a badly written third act."

Clever. And . . . relevant? *Oh my God*, I thought, not having slept for several days. *We're in our final act.* We've had two acts of fun, and now one of us is going to die, because that's how all gay movies end. In tears. Or with a violent beating. And though I might only die figuratively, dying figuratively was bad enough.

I had to see him, to prove to myself that he was just a busy law student with lots of reading to do and his lack of communication was just a function of his being overwhelmed with work and not because he didn't adore me body and soul from my head to my toe, from back to front, inside and out, from Tehran to Timbuktu. Right, Stephen? *Right, Stephen?*

By Wednesday I was a wreck. After a super-indulgent few weeks of candy, I was now being denied it, and you do *not* deny a hungry hypoglycemic his candy. I ditched class and went into town to go record shopping. At Piccadilly Records I found a twelve-inch of *The Thorn* EP by Siouxsie and the Banshees, which offered me the perfect opportunity to drop by Stephen's place with a blank tape. I'd arrive, he'd see the goods I'd brought, and then he'd ask me to marry him and all of his collectible gatefold sleeves.

I knocked on the door, and it took a minute for him to answer. He opened the door a crack and stuck his head out.

"Oh! Hi, Tim, you all right? How's it going?"

"Great! Look what I got!" I produced the album from the paper bag, and he nodded approvingly.

"Oh, good find."

"So I was wondering if I could record it on your system. You know, 'cause I don't have a record player."

"Uh," he said, looking back into his apartment. "Sure, come on in."

I came on in and quickly realized I was crashing a party. A two-person party, the kind that starts on the couch and probably moves into the bedroom eventually.

"Tim, this is Ian," Stephen said as we walked into the sitting room. Ian the Ex-Boyfriend. Or rather, judging by his messed-up hair, the chub in his pants, and the fact that his shirt was pushed slightly above his waistline, Ian the Recently Rediscovered.

"Hi," I said, going to sit down on the floor near the turntable and fumbling to get the record out of its sleeve so I could hurry up and copy it and get the hell out of that flat so I could scream and then jump off a double-decker bus onto a black cab. As I recorded, Stephen sat down on the sofa next to Ian, and they proceeded to cuddle the way ex-boyfriends shouldn't be cuddling. We engaged in small talk about travel and the weather.

"If I ever go to America," Stephen waxed, "I'm going to wear the classic English uniform: a bowler hat, a gray pinstripe suit, and I'll be carrying a cane." He and Ian had a good laugh over that image as I sat there forcing my eyes not to roll.

"Careful with the excessive Englishness," I cautioned. "They shoot folks for that in Texas."

"Duly noted," Stephen nodded, looking lovingly over at Ian as if to say, "Honey, let's not ever go to Texas, let's just stay here and be English! Oh, I love you!" "I love you *more*!" "No, *I* love *you* more!"

I silently thanked the Father, the Son, and the Holy Ghost that Siouxsie and her Banshees had only recorded four songs for this particular record, because I was done copying it in less than twenty minutes. As soon as I was done, I snatched the record from the turntable, slid it into its sleeve, and stood to go.

"Well, it was nice to meet you, Ian," I said. "Thanks for letting me record, Stephen."

"Oh, sure, you know, no problem." He stood to give me a kiss on both cheeks. "Take care, yeah?"

"Sure, you too. Bye."

I walked a deflated and despondent walk to the stairs and down to the grounds of the council estate he lived on, once the poetically dingy setting of my short-lived romance, now just an ugly, depressing building with no redeeming qualities whatsoever. So that was it: His boyfriend was back, and I was going to be shit out of luck, as The Angels might have put it. This little recording session was our good-bye.

I went directly to the Cornerhouse Café, where I proceeded to drown my sorrows in chocolate cake with whipped cream and a giant hot chocolate with whipped cream, and also a side of extra whipped cream, because fuck it, I didn't care, diabetes be damned. Afterward I walked to the drugstore to get some hair bleach, then hurried back to my flat at Whitworth Park, tossed my record on the bed, visited the restroom, and threw up everything in my stomach. I heaved and heaved and heaved, my body convulsing with anger and hurt and sugar and chocolate and whipped cream and lovesickness. When I was finally done I lifted myself up off the floor of the stall, wiped my mouth, and calmly returned to my room.

I spent the next few hours blasting a mixtape of songs copied from Stephen's fantastic record collection while alternately scribbling nonsense in my journal, organizing my recordings, and bleaching my hair white because, hey, let's have a music montage. After forty-five minutes, the purple goop I'd combed through my hair had rendered it, to my massive excitement, as white as a dove. Oh yes, my mane was Billy Idol white. Rent-boy white. I'm-here-I'm-queer-I-have-no-visible-roots white. I then showered, put on my River Phoenix T-shirt, laced up my blue Doc Martens, and headed back into town, down Oxford Road, past the Holy Name Church where a vicar in a tutu twirled on the front steps, past the student union building where Morrissey's grandmother was probably scrubbing toilets while listening to *Ziggy Stardust* on her headphones, down to Whitworth Street where I hung a right and stomped all the way to the Paradise Factory, where my stupid love affair started, and where I planned on starting a brand-new one, by God.

Plenty more fish in the sea, I told myself. *Plenty more. You just need to let them know you're here. And you* are *here, now, Tim. You are here. Here at the door of the Paradise Factory, where there are three floors of nothing but men. Some of whom might like you. Two of whom*

*might love you. One of whom might give you crabs. It is Wednesday
night and time to . . . Wait. Wednesday night?*

It was then that I saw the flyer on the door outside. Wednesday.
Straight Night.

Damn breeders.

After smoking a cigarette and thinking it over, I left the club
and headed farther into the Gay Village. There had to be a drag
bingo going on somewhere.

Our favorite dingbat diabetic is really getting cocky. Just strolling around town with his dumb new hairstyle, feeding his face with all sorts of nonsense he knows he shouldn't be eating, then feeling guilty and taking extra insulin to try to stabilize himself, which is just a bad idea that we all know will only lead one day to hyperinsulinism. And who is paying for that extra insulin that he is so cavalierly squeezing into his dermis like so much smack? The British public, that's who. Yes, over the months our boy has gotten used to the joys of socialized medicine, and he's taking it for everything it's worth.

So he stuffed a Double Decker down his throat and then guiltily ducked into a restroom, whipped out a needle, and stabbed himself with more insulin to atone for the grievous sin. Alas, he overdosed himself, so it was only a matter of time before his blood sugar plummeted and he turned into the Sweaty Twitch Monster once again.

And now here he is, a couple of hours later, at Piccadilly Records in Manchester's city center, sweating up a storm, thumbing through the CDs, and holding on to a Jesus and Mary Chain LP like his life depended on it. Sweat gathers on his face, and he attempts to wipe it away with his clammy hand, a useless gesture if there ever was one.

"Excuse me," some young buck with a moptop covering his eyes says to our hero's face in slow motion as he tries to slide past and join the queue of fanboys at the back of the shop snaking past the registers and stretching almost to the door. All the fanboys are holding copies of an album called Pablo Honey *like brainwashed toddlers, and for what? To meet the assemblage of revoltingly skinny and pale young men who made that album and who are currently sitting at a table offering their signatures, that's what. So whysoever does our hero have no idea this*

is going on around him? Probably because his floundering synapses are too busy trying to communicate to his brain that he doesn't have enough money to purchase more than one album because, though Britain is a place of socialized medicine, it is not yet a place of socialized New Wave post-punk synth-washed indie guitar pop.

So who are these malnourished gremlins who are offering up to the frozen youths of today their over-coveted autographs, then? "Radiohead in-store appearance," the sign says. Radiohead, huh? Doesn't ring a bell. Oh, look at that, though. Our young hero appears to have a thought in his head: "Wait, I know Radiohead," his sebaceous face appears to be saying. "They sing that song 'Creep.' I hate that song."

So he hates this band's most famous song. Is that why he's joined the queue? Must be. They're famous and skinny, so they're obviously worth meeting, even when it would make much more sense for him to go down to the corner shop and get some orange juice or something before he falls over. The line moves quickly, and our boy struggles to find something he can get the band members' bony British twig fingers to sign. He's got nothing, and he's not about to buy their album because, again, he hates that song. Finally, he realizes he's got his literature notebook in his backpack. Amazing that his brain was even able to remember he owned a backpack, much less that he had it on his back.

He pulls out the red notebook as he approaches the table. The first man in black is a smiley bloke named Colin. He moves his mouth and says something pleasant-seeming, but our hero doesn't understand a word. He proffers his notebook, uttering the only two words he can currently assemble—"literature notebook"—and Colin offers his signature, then passes the notebook along. The next degenerate at the table has Mick Jagger lips and cheeks so hollow you could serve oatmeal in them. He curls his massive lips into a smile, unfurls his Gollum-like fingers to take possession of the notebook, and scrawls onto it his name *in his unreadable chicken scratch. He then passes along the notebook to the next guy, and all the while King Clammy Hands just drifts down the table watching as his notebook is manhandled (the word "man" being employed here in the broadest possible sense) in turn by the bald one, and then the dreamy one.*

Finally, finally, the notebook arrives into the hands of the lead singer, whose hair is doing the best '70s Rod Stewart impression we have ever seen. He smiles (the word "smile" being employed here in the broadest possible sense) and flashes a mouthful of teeth, all of which are seemingly staking out a claim to the same patch of gum. This smile appears to frighten our hero, who isn't sure how to process such a traditionally pleasant but, in this case, threatening-seeming facial gesture. The singer takes his Magic Marker in hand and executes his signature with an artistic flourish, then our hero thanks all the Radioheads with a completely nonsensical series of words that only his maker, if he is listening and not too busy rolling his eyes, could possibly understand.

And with that, the sweathog staggers out of the store, tumbles into a corner shop, grabs two handfuls of chocolate delights, piles more than enough pound coins onto the counter to pay for them, and flops out onto the pavement to sit down, forcing pedestrians to go around him as he slowly and determinedly dines on his Starbar, Crunchie, and Cadbury Fruit and Nut one by one by one.

He looks down at his notebook, so recently in the possession of the underfed Radioheads. The artistic scribble produced by the Rod Stewart wig with the teeth is smack in the middle. In addition to providing his priceless signature, "Thom" has provided these words of sparkling wisdom:

"Literature rots the brain."

Our hero disagrees with this assessment, for he feels he's encountered many books that have enriched his life immeasurably. For the life of him, though, as he chomp-chomp-chomps on his late lunch/early dinner, he can't come up with the name of a single one.

He closes his eyes, smiles, and triumphantly whispers to himself the title of the first unarguably life-enriching book to pop into his head.

"Green Eggs and Ham!"

CHAPTER 11

THIS CHARMING MAN

"Hey, yeah, I think maybe you should go."

"I'm sorry, what?" I asked the adorable guy who stood naked in front of me, his firm, partially toweled torso blocking the two turntables against the wall where he'd so recently given me an impromptu, weed-inspired DJ lesson. We were taking a break and cleaning ourselves up after a hot and heavy nude wrestling match that we'd finally, finally fallen into after a nice dinner, a few drinks, a drive to his apartment, a few hits on his pipe, a debate over the quality of mid-period Wire compared to early Wire, a heart-to-heart about a recent bad breakup he went through, and the afore-mentioned DJ session. He'd just walked back into the room after a visit to the bathroom, and I'd assumed we would maybe have a few bong hits, a couple of shots, and then a serious nap before waking up for round two.

"Yeah," he continued, "I'm really sorry, I just—I'm a little messed up from this breakup, and I think I jumped back in too soon."

Wait a minute, I thought. You spent a great evening and part of the night with a semi-handsome devil (that's me), an hour or so of which you spent naked and moaning, and now that the horsy ride is over you are regretting letting such a decent-looking specimen (again, me) get so close to you, because *emotions?* Or is it because you've nutted and now you're done, so get out? Ugh, change the record, this song is *terrible.*

"Oh," I said, nodding and suddenly feeling figuratively as well as actually naked. "OK. Uh . . ."

"It's me, I'm really sorry. I just think I need to be alone." His cute face displayed the same soft, bright-eyed, welcoming expression it had shown all night—to gaze into those eyes you would have thought he was asking me how I like my eggs rather than telling me to get the hell out.

I got up and started putting my clothes back on, my entire lily-white body flushing with embarrassment. I silently got my stuff together, and we got into his cherry-red Mustang for the excruciating ride home to Raleigh from his apartment in Cary.

I looked out at the endless string of strip malls and cookie-cutter houses we passed on our way and thought, "Well, at least I won't have to come to Cary all the time."

Bow Wow Wow was playing on the '80s radio show, which was fitting because I felt like a hound dog. Our trip back to my apartment had so far been completely wordless, but I couldn't stop myself from trying to find out what happened.

"Was it something I did?" I asked as we pulled onto Cary Parkway. "Was I too forward? Too loud? I was too loud, wasn't I?"

"Oh, no. Please, it's not anything like that."

"It was the sweating . . ."

"No, no. I just . . ."

You just . . .

"I just . . . you know, I just moved here from LA, I'm getting my bearings, I just . . . put myself out there too soon."

The operative words being "put" and "out." I nodded, and decided to just try to accept that this little chapter in the Harlequin

285

romance novel of my life was, for whatever reason, a regrettably short one. Too bad, because this was the sexiest car I'd ever been inside.

We pulled up to Mordecai Manor, my apartment building, and my tote bag and I got out of the car.

"Well," I began, leaning down to say my good-byes, "thanks for the . . . you know, for the . . ."

"Yeah, no, you know, I'm sorry, I just . . ."

You just . . .

"I'm an idiot, and I dragged you into my stupid world when I shouldn't have." He looked into my eyes as he said this, and he seemed to mean it. The idiot part. "I'll see you around," he said, shifting his Mustang into gear.

"Sure."

And then he was off, and I was there with only my stupid tote bag for company. I stood there once again channeling Molly Ringwald and her eighties pout and eye roll. This only made me feel worse, though, because it was now the mid-nineties, Simple Minds were long gone, and I was getting too old for this shit.

It had been a fruitless few years in the love department. I'd left England and returned to Chapel Hill to finish school, during which time I had a brief affair with a hunky older man I met in the public library, chased after a poet narcissist for months and months with nothing to show for it at the end except a nervous breakdown, and had a series of drunken, no-strings booty shakings that never led to anything beyond the requisite limp of shame the next morning. Then I went to London to sow more wild British oats before returning home once again to Raleigh and moving in with Dani at Mordecai Manor.

No longer a teat-sucking college student, I'd also lost my health insurance and couldn't for the life of me get a decent health insurance policy. This was because the leaders of our great nation couldn't see the difference between (1) developing a health care system where all citizens have access to what they need to stay alive and (2) communism. There's no difference! Freedom ain't free! HillaryCare! But thanks to the good folks at Blue Cross Blue Shield of North Carolina, I was able to get catastrophic coverage for the low low price of $695 a month with no coverage for anything diabetes-related.

So, in order to stay alive and experience my ennui to the fullest, I was spending all the money I was making at my job waiting tables (really should have chosen a better major than English) on the things I needed to keep my body functioning and upright on a day-to-day basis: daytime insulin, nighttime insulin, glucose test strips, lancets, syringes, and the occasional doctor visit. When money was especially tight, which was almost always, I scrimped on the test strips—the most expensive supplies to keep stocked—and so stopped regularly testing my levels.

At any given moment, I had no idea what my blood sugar level was as I was wandering around used-record shopping, driving to Chapel Hill for a show, swimming laps at the aquatic center, or working at the restaurant. Was it two hundred? Could be. One twenty-two? Maybe. Eighty-nine? Don't know. The only time I knew the general levels of sugar in my blood was either when it was way too high—in which case I would get dehydrated and my bladder would start whining—or when it was way too low—in which case, if I were at work, I might forget to take your order, bring you potato salad when you asked for a cosmo, never give you your bill, keep asking you over and over if you'd like anything else when the answer has clearly been "no" for the past half hour, or sit on a box of wine in the wait station laughing maniacally before falling facefirst onto the floor and having to be carried out by the EMS.

Basically I was growing into an exceedingly sloppy post-collegiate adult diabetic who hadn't even made it through his graduation ceremony without almost passing out. Even worse, I was an exceedingly sloppy post-collegiate adult diabetic without any dating prospects. Never a big fan of the bar scene in Raleigh—"bar scene" being a generous term meaning "two bars on Hargett Street downtown"—I'd recently ventured into the personal ads section of the *Independent Weekly*, with varying results.

> GWM, 24, tall, medium build, big music fan, into Woody Allen movies, very short walks on the beach, and the sound of synthesizers, seeks GM for whatever happens.

I'm thinking I should have been more specific. I got a few responses, only a fraction of which came from people who seemed to have actually read and processed the ad. I called one guy back, and the conversation could best be described as utterly pointless.

"Hi, Gary?"

"Yeah."

"Hi, this is Tim. You answered my ad in the *Independent*?"

"Yeah."

"So . . . what are you up to?"

"Just watching the game."

"The game?" Hmm, he watches games?

"Yeah. Then gonna go for a run."

"So . . . did you want to set up a time to meet?"

"Well, I gotta go for my run."

"Uh-huh. Do you want to maybe call me back then?"

"Yeah. I'm not sure how long I'm gonna be."

[Long pause filled by commotion from the game.]

"OK," I said, unsure of how to proceed.

"OK, see you."

Click.

Couldn't believe this nice man had to resort to the personals to meet people.

Soon after I happened into a physical affair with a guy in his thirties who worked at the thrift store. He had the appearance of a man who'd lived a hard life—a sickle-shaped scar on his face, teeth like fallen dominos, a long and thick burn mark on his arm, and a tight, sinewy little body that he probably, when he was younger, used to sell for cash. He was also very forward. I first met him when I was shopping for some cheap threads—I was getting low on ugly corduroy pants to cut into shorts—and he checked me out, in every sense of that phrase.

"Hey, so," he said, putting my pants into a plastic bag, "give me your digits."

"My digits?"

"Yeah, I'll give you a call and . . ."—he looked at me straight in the eyes to convey his seriousness—"maybe come over later."

I gave him my digits immediately. I then went home, showered, cut my new corduroy pants into a dazzling new pair of shorts, and waited for his call. His call arrived, followed by his pickup truck. I put on some music, cracked a beer open, and in he walked in a wifebeater, a backward baseball hat, and Bermuda shorts. We sat down on the little couch in my bedroom, sparked up a doobie, then, almost before the weed had reached our brain cells, started devouring each other like bacon cheeseburgers.

"All right, cool," he said after we were done and he'd already started putting his minimal amount of clothes back on. "See you later, yeah?"

Fun and very simple. We met up whenever the mood struck us, cracked open a few beers, and had a nice bacon cheeseburger for dinner. When we were not playing nude safari we had nothing to offer each other. I had no idea what he was up to five minutes before he arrived or five minutes after he left. Was he at work bagging up ancient fashions for his store's broke clientele? Huffing paint at the bus station? Babysitting? Who knew? And he had the same amount of knowledge about me and my paint huffing.

In spite of our unstated don't ask/don't tell policy about life details, I did finally find out one thing about him after a few weeks. I booty-called him one day, and who should answer his phone but his boyfriend, who I'd never been told about.

"Hi, is Craig there?"

"No, he's not."

"Oh, OK, can I just leave a message with you?"

"Who is this?"

"Uh . . . , just his friend Tim."

"Tim? Tim? I don't know any Tim! How does he know you?"

"Oh yeah, OK," I stammered, my eyes widening with panic. "Yeah, I don't know, maybe just *tellhimIcalled*." Slam.

Shit, I thought. *I'm a home wrecker. A jezebel. I am . . . the other woman. Like desperate Angelica Huston in* Crimes and Misdemeanors *or that awful woman in* Muriel's Wedding. I felt dirty and gross. You know what made me feel grosser a few hours later?

Beep.

"Hey, Tim, this is Craig. Listen, I'm not sure what you said to my boyfriend on the phone, but I don't really appreciate it. So, yeah, that's about it. You don't have to return this call."

Click.

I stood against the wall, speechless. After a few moments I had collected myself enough to continue the argument to a Craig who wasn't there.

"Well, Craig, you little asshole," I said haughtily to the answering machine, "I wouldn't have said *anything* to your boyfriend if I'd *known he existed*!" I will cuss out an answering machine.

The phone rang again, and I jumped.

"Hey, Tim, it's Karen." Phew.

"And Kelly!"

Karen and Kelly were my coworkers at the Black Dog Café, and thanks to the futuristic technology of the nineties, we were able to talk to each other on the phone all at the same time through the magic of three-way calling. More importantly, they weren't Craig or his boyfriend calling to give me the once-over twice.

"Hey, y'all, what's up?"

"Weeeeelll," Karen started, "weeeee wanna set you up."

Oh God. Not that game again. As all gay folks know, the road to gay hell is paved with the good intentions of straight people. Never before in my short number of years living as a gay man had that phrase—"we wanna set you up"—been a preview to a really good movie.

"Uh-huh," I said.

"It's my boyfriend's friend," Kelly asserted.

"Uh-huh."

"Aaaaaaaand," Karen assisted, "he's apparently a really cool guy, and he thinks you're cute."

"Uh-huh."

"Soooooooo let's all go for drinks!"

"Mmmm, I don't know."

"Oh, yes you do," Karen insisted.

"No, I really don't."

"You do."

"Don't."

"Do."

"Yes!" Kelly jumped ahead. "So this week sometime?"

I reluctantly agreed to go out and humor my friends. I also was, I must admit, a little fascinated to see how hilariously incompatible this "really cool guy" and I were. He'd probably show up carrying a baton and wearing a leotard, a tuxedo shirt, and an eye patch. He would probably also refer to himself as "the barrister" and be ninety years old.

We met at the Stingray, a hipster bar near downtown. I didn't have any expectations whatsoever as I sat down with Kelly and Karen at a booth, with a beer in my hand and a chip on my shoulder.

"There they are," Kelly said. Two guys walked in, one a black gentleman in an Oxford shirt and cut-off shorts, the other a white young man in beige shorts and the most hideously, aggressively ugly Hawaiian shirt I'd ever been nearly blinded by.

Kelly introduced me to Sean, her black friend, who then introduced me to Jimmy, his white friend in the hideous shirt. Jimmy and I shook hands.

"It's nice to meet you," he said with a smile and a businesslike handshake as he sat down.

"Nice to meet you and your shirt," I said.

"It's pretty loud, huh?" Jimmy said.

"Yeah, where did you get it?"

"On the island of Oahu."

"Really?"

"No. Thrift store."

Hmm. I wondered if Craig had bagged it up for him.

Jimmy's head was perfectly, adorably round. I'd never seen a rounder head in my life. In addition to tacky taste in shirts, he had a slight receding hairline and big balloon-like gummyworm lips. Lips like sugar. So far so good.

Sean brought over drinks for him and Jimmy, and we all clinked glasses. Sean and Kelly then started talking about how hot it was outside, trying to come up with the most apt description as Jimmy stared off into space.

"Hot enough to fry an egg on my thigh," Kelly suggested.

"Hotter than a popcorn fart," Sean said.

"Useless as tits on a bullfrog," Jimmy said absently. Sean and Kelly looked at him askance. "We're doing similes, right?" he asked. I liked him. He kept up with things.

I saw Dani walk in with her boyfriend, and strolled over to the bar to talk to them for a minute, keeping an eye on Jimmy and his shirt.

"I'm being set up with a rogue Hawaiian," I told her.

"Wow, that shirt is awesome," she said. "And by *awesome* I mean *revolting*. Is he nice?"

"Yeah, he's kind of funny."

"Funny's good. Better than dumb as a brick. He's not dumb as a brick, is he?"

"Oh, no. He knows the word *simile*."

"Sounds perfect for you."

After a while I went back over to the table. Jimmy, squished into the booth and against the wall by Sean and another of Sean's friends, was still talking to Sean and Kelly. I looked at Karen, who was sitting there talking to no one, and doing it beautifully.

"Karen, you wanna play Ms. Pac-Man?"

"Sure, why not?"

"I gotta warn you," I said. "I'm really good."

I escorted her to the machine over at the end of the bar, put two quarters in, and gestured for her to play first, because of chivalry.

She started moving her little ladies in a herky-jerky fashion across the screen, and boy, did she suck. *Karen*, I thought. *Have you never used a joystick before? It shouldn't look that fraught.*

Her first player got killed off quickly, and soon it was my turn. She stood aside, and I slid in front of the screen.

"Let the game begin," I said, overconfidently. I began my round and lost my first player within a few seconds because I fumbled the joystick like a chump.

"Majestic," Karen said, displacing me from the player position. "Like a kid in a Burger King hat."

Karen's next round was better, and it seemed to go on for days. I found myself openly cheering for the multicolored ghosts.

"Come on, Pinky, step it up! Jesus, Blinky, what's your problem?"

Finally, *finally* Inky ate Karen's next player, and I got to slide back over and set about redeeming myself. I gripped the joystick and prepared for battle.

"Da na na na na na nana nana na na nana nana nana nana na na na!" said the computer music, as the next round began. I improved my performance this time, swallowing power pellets and energizers and transmogrified ghosts and fruit bonuses like a master of the universe. Then I choked and died, and Karen stepped to the helm once again. When her last player finally succumbed to Inky in Level 3, it was clear that victory was within my grasp. I could win this. I really should win this.

I furiously steered my ravenous Mses hither and yon through the labyrinth because I was *not* going to lose this video game featuring a strong female lead to a freaking *girl*. Oh, shit, there was Pinky, closing in on me. Gotta turn the corner quick and slip into the passageway to the other side of the screen. Here it comes! Here it comes!

"Hey, what are you doing?" a soft voice said to me back in the real, noncomputerized world. I looked over, and it was Jimmy in his terrible shirt, leaning against the machine and smiling widely with his head tilted.

"Uh, playing Ms. Pac-Man?" I said, jerking the joystick so as to smack dead into Blinky and die like a little bitch. "Dammit!"

Karen was the victor. And boy, did she know how to gloat. "I'll be expecting a nice expensive drink from the bar to find its way to me sometime very soon," she said with a twinkle in her eye as she waltzed away a sore winner, leaving Jimmy and me alone.

Still reeling from my fatal encounter with Blinky, I suggested we get some drinks. We squeezed our way through throngs of hipster breeders to get the bartender's attention. After she finished yelling at some Germans who didn't tip her, she presented us with our requested beverages. I dropped off a cosmo at the table where Karen was sitting, and Jimmy and I went to another table alone. He got out a cigarette and lit it up.

"So are you from Raleigh?" I probed.

"I was born here, but I grew up all over. Army brat."

We soon discovered that we were born in the same hospital one month apart, that we had been at the same Sugarcubes concert back in '89, and that it's possible we were unwittingly dancing to the same hilariously bleak Nine Inch Nails ditties at the Fallout Shelter back in the day. He started talking at length about his love of Philip Glass and Michael Nyman, which made me wonder if I was highfalutin enough for this conversation. *Minimalist composers, huh? OK, I'll see your artsy film-scoring types and raise you a Nova Scotia fiddler.*

"You know who I'm really into right now? I just got an album by a Canadian fiddle player named Ashley MacIsaac. He's wily and gay!"

Jimmy nodded vaguely.

"He was just on Conan O'Brien and he performed in a kilt and he did a high kick at the end and he wasn't wearing any underwear. It was fantastic!"

"Yeah," Jimmy said, taking a long tug on his cigarette as he seriously considered the most diplomatic way possible to verbalize what he was thinking. "I really hate him."

"You . . . hate him? Wait. You know who he is? And you hate him?"

"Yeah," Jimmy said, exhaling two lungs full of smoke. "I read an article where he was saying he was just gay for now."

"Nooooo."

"Yeah, he said when he gets married he won't be doing any more gay shit."

"That sounds wrong."

"No, I read it."

In the next few years I would learn that every single assertion Jimmy has made about a third party should be subject to the strictest of scrutiny. He has a tendency to jump to the most unflattering conclusions about everyone based upon the slightest of circumstantial evidence or thirdhand knowledge. But my natural tendency had always been to assume everyone else was better informed than I was, so I accepted Jimmy's story at face value and changed the subject.

"Hmm," I said, "OK, well, how about Madonna?"

We agreed that Madonna was like a sometimes awesome, often embarrassing older sister. Though I'd cooled on her when she started talking smack about my secret stepsister Sinéad O'Connor, you just can't stay mad at Madonna.

"So," I said, "should we go out or something?"

Jimmy looked down at the table and replied with an adamant "Yeah, sure, I guess so."

The next night I picked him up at Eckerd Pharmacy on Hillsborough Street, where he was the photo lab manager. He asked if I could follow him in his car, named Chantel, to his apartment just down the road so he could drop her off in the parking lot. I trailed behind him down to the Wilmont Apartments building. "I'm One, Too," a sticker on Chantel's rear end proclaimed. I smiled at his taste in bumper verbiage.

We went to dinner at The Rockford downtown, and I taught him how not to piss off a waitress by grossly undertipping, asking for separate checks, or requesting something that's not on the menu. He taught me how to talk about something you are obviously passionate about—the films of Peter Greenaway, for example, or the music of Momus (who?)—while exhibiting the look of someone who couldn't care less about what he's currently talking about. His normal expression was a long (yet perfectly round) slack face, complete with big sad puppy-dog eyes and lips that seemed to inflate when he was just sitting and thinking. His mopey expression, coupled with his completely monotone, sleepy-robot delivery, made him hard to read. If he said something like, say, "Log Cabin Republicans make me want to jump off a bridge," you'd be hard pressed to tell whether or not he was kidding. He just sounded sad. But then, in the same tone of voice, he'd say something like "That Grace Jones album cover reminds me of my mother because Mom also has five mouths," and you'd realize he's probably fine.

We moved on from the restaurant to the record store, because we all know there's no better way to get to know a boy than to see what albums he picks out and considers purchasing.

In Jimmy's case, these albums were the soundtrack to *A Clockwork Orange* and something by some Eurotrash singer named

Mylène Farmer. I nodded approvingly at these choices, even though I had no idea who this Ms. Farmer character was.

"She's basically the French Mariah Carey," he said. I didn't like that answer. "I mean, she's *popular* like Mariah Carey," he clarified. "Her music is more like tacky Eurovision goth. She does concerts with huge mechanical tarantulas."

Acceptable!

After the record store I felt I should propose something romantic, since we were on a date. So off to the Rose Garden we went. It was on the grounds of Raleigh Little Theatre, where my mom had portrayed Mary Poppins years before, and where I'd played everyone from a Munchkin in *The Wizard of Oz* to the baby brother Michael who always dragged his teddy bear around with him in *Peter Pan*. It was also where we all used to go drink and smoke weed when we were in high school, so, all in all, it had a happy history.

We sat down at a picnic table in the darkness and gazed out at the dramatic labyrinthine hedges.

"So where's your family?" I asked.

"My sister's here in Raleigh. Dad's in Iowa with my stepmom. Brother's in Florida, I think?"

"And your mom?"

"Oh, I don't know where she is. Last I heard she was on her fourth husband and living in Asheville."

Ooooh, we've got a story here. Time to ask some tough questions.

"When's the last time you talked to her?"

"'Bout five years ago. I was desperate for money and had to beg her for some."

In the next few minutes I mined a mother lode of inside info on this terrible woman. Among other things, she'd sent him to a mental hospital after he came out of the closet at fifteen, and then forced him, when he returned home, to use separate cutlery, plates, and glasses so that he didn't give her AIDS.

"Wow," I said, suddenly newly re-impressed with how sane and loving my own mother was. "Your momma sounds like a gorgon."

"Yeah," he mumbled. "She is."

A silence engulfed the Rose Garden as all the romance was sucked out of the atmosphere by my insistence on talking about Jimmy's mother. Even the rosebushes seemed to be twisting up their faces at me in the darkness as if to say, "Jesus, can you just talk about trip hop or something?"

Jimmy sighed and looked at the sky. "You want to come back to my place and listen to the CDs I bou—"

"Sure, let's go!"

We set off back to the fourth floor of the Wilmont Apartments, where Jimmy, after quietly urging his roommate Bill to please stay in his room, proceeded to get me high and ply me with beer. His game of seduction was simple: He put on the Mylène Farmer album, sat on the couch next to me, and brought out a vulgar art book done by artist Jeff Koons that had been tucked away under the coffee table. It had Mr. Koons on the cover holding a baby piglet, flanked by a full-grown pig. Inside, the artist was photographed getting up to all sorts of nude mischief with his loose blonde wife. It was quite disgusting/titillating, and so very pink. Then he brought out a prized possession from the same stack under the coffee table, and my head nearly exploded: the French edition of Madonna's *Sex* book.

Although there was a regrettably large number of photos featuring lesbian muff diving, one thing we'd both already agreed on about Madonna was that she knew how to surround herself with good-looking men, and, if this book was anything to go on, she often found herself naked and splayed with a bunch of them at once. Best of all, the text was all in French, so there were no pesky readable words getting in the way of all the smut. After getting through the section where Vanilla Ice and a platinum-blonde Madonna get down to it, I closed the book. The Mylène Farmer album was still on the stereo, the singer cooing out a bunch of breathless, wispy, and tuneless French because she obviously couldn't sing for shit.

"This album is terrible," I said.

"Yeah," Jimmy agreed. We kissed, rolled around on the floor, fumbled for each other's belts, and eventually took it into the bedroom, where we shed our clothes and enacted scenes from our favorite Fassbinder films as images of the past hour—of Jeff Koons's junk, of Vanilla Ice's butt, of Madonna hitchhiking while naked and smoking—danced in our heads.

———

Oh, lookee here, he's lost control again. He and his longtime male companion of three days, the mysterious, pillow-lipped James, were sleeping peacefully in James's wooden, poorly constructed bed, when all of a sudden the twitching started. James's head popped up, and now he's looking through the darkness and seeing our boy's profile doing a frenetic jig on the pillow. Ooh, and there goes his shoulder jerking up and sending his arm flapping. James hops out of the bed and goes around to turn on the light. His eyes widen. Then they narrow. Then they register remembrance that the wet, rather desperate-looking naked man jiggling on the bed is a diabetic.

Oh, shit, *he thinks, realizing that he never actually asked his diabetic sex partner what to do in the event of some sort of after-hours diabetic emergency, like, for example, whatever is happening now.*

Then he remembers that his roommate Bill's boyfriend has the same dreaded disease.

"Bill!" James whisper-screams as he opens Bill's door and flips on the light. "Bill!"

"How may I help you?" Bill, the consummate customer service professional, says in response, his eyes still closed, his head still resting on his soft, silky pillow.

"I think Tim's having a diabetic . . . thing. He's shaking and sweating and jerking around."

"He needs sugar," Bill says sagely, eyes still closed, head still resting. "Get him sugar. Pour it into his mouth."

Of course, how is James to know that Bill means the word "sugar" in the broad sense—i.e., something with sugar in it, such as orange juice or honey or ice cream or Duncan Hines buttercream frosting? James, naïf that he is, takes Bill's instruction at face value, so he bee-lines it to the kitchen, pulls out a big bag of Imperial Sugar, and rushes it back to the bedroom, where His Twitchiness is holding court.

"Tim. Tim!" he says. "Eat this." He opens the bag, forms a spout with the edge, holds his head still with one hand, and starts pouring. Just stone cold pouring sugar into the poor boy's gaping maw.

We all know what happens next. The bed turns into an elegant Xanadu of glittery sugar crystals as our hero becomes agitated at being held down and asserts his independence from the sugar monster trying to rape his mouth. He flails his hands around, sending the white stuff flying all over the bed, the floor, his hair, his eyes, and, most unforgivably, all over his cat Stella, who was watching the proceedings at the edge of the bed and now looks royally pissed as she hops off the bed and goes into the other room to get away from this bullshit.

James is undeterred. "I am not," he says to himself, "letting another naked man die in my bed." He then laughs because that was a funny *joke, and he's always laughing when he should be concentrating on the shit-show in front of him. He again holds down the alien boy from planet Spasm and pours more sugar into his mouth, setting off another glitter storm when the hands once again, this time in slow motion, Matrix-style, send sugar flying. James keeps a solid grip on the bag and waits for the flailing to temporarily abate, then forces the spout back into the young man's face. The boy moves his head away and locks his jaw shut. Nothing, it appears, is getting into that mouth anytime soon. Poor James.*

The boy continues to shake his moneymaker on the bed as James leans against the wall wondering what to do next. Releasing an epic sigh, he heads into the living room and picks up the phone.

"Hi, yeah, I need an ambulance at the Wilmont Apartments on Hillsborough Street. Diabetes attack. Yeah. He's in the bed, shaking. I gave him some sugar, but he's not letting me give him any more, for some reason. 3200. A8. Thanks."

He walks back into the bedroom. The naked hobgoblin has sugar all over his face and torso. James looks around for clothing that he can negotiate onto the boy's body before the EMS folk arrive. He sees a pair of Andy Warhol Campbell's Soup shorts on the floor and begins threading the boy's feet through them.

"What'sgoingon?" The hobgoblin speaks!

"You were freaking out," James says calmly. "Shaking and jerking. And you're completely wet. How do you feel?"

"M'sorry." Like clockwork, the crippling guilt is setting in.

"I called an ambulance."

"Cancel."

"Cancel?"

"Cancel. Don't need."

James walks out of the room and gets back on the phone.

Our hero looks down at his feet, then all around him. He wipes sweat from his brow and looks at his fingers. They're glistening. And they taste great. Num num num.

"Mm-mm good. Mm-mm good," he hums as he sucks every last crystal of sugar off every last finger.

"Meow," says Stella. He looks over at her. She's sitting on the hardwood floor staring directly at him with her giant orb eyes.

What a condescending, judgmental face.

———

"This quiche is pretty good," Jimmy announced in his emotionless, deadpan way, as we sat on the balcony of Mordecai Manor with Dani eating brunch. "It's almost as good as mine."

He was really making quite an impression on this dear friend of mine he was hanging out with for the first time. Dani, who had made the quiche, smiled and, ever the diplomat, thanked him for his paper-thin praise.

"Wow," she said. "Thanks, Jimmy. I'm glad you like it. I haven't been so flattered since the time my dad called me a slut in high school." Dani understood that Jimmy meant no harm. I'd warned her about his says-what-he-means-even-if-it's-mean tendencies. And to be honest, his comment about the quiche was one of the most robust endorsements he'd given in a while. After all, he was very proud of his quiche-making abilities.

"Jimmy, we're going to need to work on your complimenting skills when we get home," I said. We'd only been together for a few weeks when I moved into the Wilmont. Over the past few months I'd been doing my best to make him understand that folks don't live inside his own head like he does, so when he's in a social situation and he wants to express himself verbally he needs to think not only about what he wants to say to someone but also about how the person would probably like to receive that information. Like saying "Nice haircut!" instead of "What happened to your hair?"

"Yeah," Jimmy said, not missing a beat, "and right after that we'll work on your not-having-sugar-attacks-in-the-middle-of-the-night skills."

Dani looked at me and knew he'd won that particular exchange.

"Touché, Tim," she said. "I'm afraid he's got you there. Jimmy, I could write a book on it. I think it'd be called *Tim's Top Twenty Insulin Reactions of the '90s*. It will feature nudity."

"I'll write part two," he said, and Dani laughed. It's such fun when folks enjoy themselves at your expense.

"Seriously, though," Jimmy said, looking straight at me. "You need to get your shit together. Because this . . ." He stopped.

"This . . . ?"

"You just need to get your shit together."

Bam. I tried to laugh off this comment, but I saw that Jimmy's normally unreadable face was locked and loaded in the stink-eye position, pointed directly at me.

"Yeah, well, *you* need to . . ." I stammered. Jimmy looked at me with an "uh-huh, I need to *what*?" face. Now it occurs to me I should have recognized that face. Dress Jimmy in nursing scrubs, put a thermometer in his hand, and fit him with a brown, stringy, greasy head of hair and voilà! Nurse Kimberly! After all these years, she'd found me. And I was dating her. And she was a man named Jimmy.

"*You* need to . . . ," I continued stammering as I stuffed my mouth full of quiche, "mcfuhcghmsflmp."

"Yeah," Jimmy said, "I'll be sure to do that."

There was nothing else to say—I *had* been having more than

my fair share of low blood sugar attacks lately. Trying to control your diabetes when you're not checking your glucose levels and when you're not visiting a doctor and when you're just blindly dosing out your insulin on a wing and a prayer is . . . a challenge.

"But every time I check my blood sugar it costs a dollar!" I lamented.

"Work it out," Jimmy said. "Just work it out."

Ouch.

"Besides, you've got lots of dollars, you wait tables."

Well, lots of dollars, phsh. I didn't have those; he was exaggerating. I was, as my dear friend Claire the bartender once put it, "the worst waiter in the world." Still, I did make *some* dollars, and surely some of them could be put toward making sure I didn't constantly almost slip into a coma at night. So I commandeered Jimmy's empty piggy bank and started depositing into it any extraneous bills and coins I'd managed to accumulate on a given day. Once a month I started visiting the pharmacy and grudgingly plunking down all my barely earned cash to pay for some test strips to go with my insulin. The first month I brought them home, tossed the pharmacy bag on the couch, and asked Jimmy accusingly, "Are you happy now?"

"Uh-huh," he said before asking me if I was planning on replacing the piggy bank I'd broken because I couldn't manage to remove the rubber stopper on the bottom and ended up shattering the poor pig on the floor because *Give me my money, pig!*

I slumped down on the couch, and tested my blood sugar for what seemed like the first time in years. Jimmy leaned over to witness the verdict: 130.

"Wow, it's totally normal," I said. "I could have saved that dollar."

Jimmy looked at me with his serious face. "Yeah, well, one of these days you'll check it and it'll be, like, forty or something and you'll save yourself and me a shit-ton of trouble by going ahead to the cabinet and getting a damn cookie."

I couldn't really disagree with his logic. I put away my glucometer.

"We should go to the Asian market," he said. "Get another pig."

I checked my wallet. "I don't got a lot of dollars."

"I'll split it with you," Jimmy said.

"Well," I said, "as long as we're doing it we should get one that's sparkly and has Japanese letters on the side. Do it up right."

"Agreed."

We both stood and headed to the door.

"Oh," I said, "you know what else, we might as well go by Bojangles and get some Cajun chicken biscuits."

"Mmm-hmm." Jimmy nodded, opening the door. "And some unsweet tea. Don't forget your insulin."

———

Me again. Yeah, it's four o'clock in the morning, and the chivalrous James is busy chasing our batty hero around the apartment trying to get him to eat ice cream. It's a real hoot.

The diabetic wunderkind has just run into the living room and is "hiding" in the corner. The thing is, though, it's not really hiding if you're just crouched in the corner with your eyes scrunched shut next to the big potted plant. You can still be seen! This is called object permanence, and it's something humans learn when they are quite young. But apparently diabetics forget about it when their blood sugar is, say, twenty-one.

Of course, our boy has always been seriously grumpy when he's in this particular situation. His love of piles of sugary sweet treats being offered to him during normal waking hours notwithstanding, for some mysterious reason he doesn't like being bullied into downing ice cream or Nutella or whatever when he's about to pass out from sugarlessness. "Leave me be!" he insists. "Allow me to convulse violently and then slip into a coma in peace!"

Somehow or other James finds him in his secret hiding place there in the corner next to the plant in the fully lit living room and forces delicious, fatty ice cream into his mouth while berating him thusly:

"Eat it!" he demands. "Eat this shit! You need to eat it! Put it in your mouth! That's right, put it in your mouth! Open your mouth, you asshole! Goddamn it, when you come to, I'm going to fucking smack the shit out of you!"

Wow—didn't know James had it in him. Rowr. Work it out, girl. Work it out.

Our hero relents and allows the cookies 'n' cream into his drooling mouth. He slowly gets his groove on and starts to enjoy the taste, swiping the container away from James and stumbling over to the couch to sit down, because even in the state he's in he knows full well that you have to be sitting down to fully enjoy dessert.

"M'sorry," he says.

"Great!" James snaps. "So, guess how you're making it up to me?"

The boy answers by wiping ice cream from his face with a couch pillow and looking wanly at James.

"We're going to your doctor! Yes! Get on that phone in the morning! Can't wait to meet him!"

Our hero scrapes the bottom of the container with the spoon.

"We got any more?"

Jimmy and I sat in the examination room waiting for Dr. Cook to return with a sample of a brand-new type of insulin that I would be switching to.

"Is this a good thing, do you think?" Jimmy asked.

"Sounds like it. If it's a shorter-acting insulin that means I can take it just minutes before I eat, and then it leaves my body quicker. So there's not an excess amount of insulin in my system constantly."

Jimmy's expression conveyed great confusion. He appeared to be trying to solve for x without being able to write anything down.

"Basically, it means fewer insulin reactions in the middle of the night," I clarified.

"Oh, good."

Dr. Cook walked back into the room with a small rectangular box, which held the new device, called an "insulin pen," that I would be using to inject myself. That's right: The days of syringes were over, at least until I decided to become a junkie. Dr. Cook pulled it out, and I got a look: The pen was about the size of a Magic Marker. Into it I would insert a 300-milliliter cartridge of Humalog insulin, twist the knob on the bottom to the desired dosage, and then just plunge the pen into my flesh like normal and, a few minutes later, I could be happily eating some of Jimmy's quiche or whatever.

After Dr. Cook had given me my little Humalog pen tutorial, we turned to another topic closer to Jimmy's heart.

"So you've been having lots of low blood sugars at night?"

"Yeah, way too often," Jimmy said. "And always between three and four o'clock."

"Well, this Humalog will definitely be of some help with that," Dr. Cook assured us, "though you've really got to make sure you're testing right before bed—ideally twice before bed, about two hours apart, so you can see if it's headed in a particular direction. Obviously I'm limited in the advice I can give you because you didn't write down your levels in your sugar diary for me." A little guilt-tripping was par for the course by now with Dr. Cook.

"OK," Jimmy said, looking at me sternly, "he'll do that."

"So, Jimmy," Dr. Cook began, standing up and going over to the small fridge in the corner, "it's time for your initiation into the wonderful world of glucagon."

The dreaded glucagon—the hormone secreted by the pancreas to fight low blood sugar levels, basically acting as the anti-insulin. It came in individually wrapped, prefilled syringes with big fat needles and could be used in emergencies to stabilize a low level. I was introduced to it upon my diagnosis in Baltimore, when the nurses explained to Mom how to administer it during extreme low blood sugars before placing it in my mom's fearful hand. Once we got home to Raleigh, the glucagon never moved from the fridge because neither Mom nor Dad could bring themselves to use it when I was flailing about like a rag doll in a blender. When the glucagon expired, it was thrown out, and we never thought about it again, satisfied to rely on orange juice, cake icing, and the grace of God.

But Jimmy had somehow found out about the existence of glucagon—though God knows how because the Internet was still in its GeoCities phase—and he wanted to learn how to use it for/against me.

Dr. Cook directed me to sit on the examination table, and as I slid onto it and got uncomfortable, he filled an empty glucagon syringe with a saline solution so that Jimmy could not only practice stabbing me with it but could also practice pushing the liquid in. Sure, I'd been giving myself shots for years now, and I never even thought twice about pulling out a syringe and jabbing myself any old time, whether I was perched on the couch, sitting at a restaurant, or driving. But, again, this was a big. Fat. Needle. Much fatter than my sleek, slender syringes. And it was going to be plunged into me by a rank amateur.

"OK, you ready?" Dr. Cook asked Jimmy. Jimmy looked more scared than I was. He himself had never given me a shot, not even for kicks, and it appeared now that he was getting cold feet.

Dr. Cook lifted up my short sleeve and wiped an alcohol swab over a patch of my upper arm, getting it ready to receive.

"Now, squeeze the flesh with your fingers like this"—Dr. Cook grabbed a chunk of my tricep and held it tightly—"and just go for it."

Jimmy did as he was told. He took the patch of arm between his fingers and thumb and, in typical Jimmy fashion, squeezed it extremely weakly.

"Jimmy, you can grab it harder than that," I said. "I don't want you to hit bone."

Jimmy sighed and gripped the skin harder. He then plunged the big fat needle into my arm, and I quietly received it, biting my lip and closing my eyes. Then he pushed in the medicine, and I screamed.

The pain was real and sustained. I squirmed and struggled to stay still on the examination table as Jimmy slowly pushed the solution in, trying to hold the needle steady and looking like he was on the verge of panicking and accidentally breaking it off inside my arm. It took ten long years for him to finish. When those ten years were finally over, he pulled out the needle, and I gasped, eyes bulging. I looked up at the doctor, and he was smiling playfully.

"Oh my God, that hurt like hell!" I said, breathing heavily. "Did you know it was going to hurt like that?"

"Oh, no," Dr. Cook said unconvincingly. "But you're tough; look at you. You can take it."

The doctor had a point: I *was* tough. Like a male gymnast or a ballroom dancer. And though I was still reeling from the assault, why not just let the doctor's empty flattery work on me? I looked at Jimmy, who had the appearance of someone who'd just seen a ghost and stabbed it with a big fat syringe.

"Jimmy, you OK?" I asked.

He stood there with the needle still in his hand, looking at it as if it were a murder weapon.

"Jimmy, you can put it down now."

He placed it on the counter and wiped his brow.

"Jimmy, come on, I'm fine! I mean, it hurt, but I'm fine."

As we walked out to the car, Jimmy was silent.

"You OK?" I asked as I unlocked his door.

"I just . . . ," he mumbled. "Didn't enjoy that nearly as much I wanted to."

It was the nicest thing he'd said to me in weeks. My heart melted. As he slumped into his car seat, looking like a wounded animal, it hit me: That injection he gave me hurt *him*. My stupid diabetes and I had been regularly irritating the hell out of him for months, but now we'd really done it—we'd hurt *him*. How dare we?!

"I'm really sorry, Jimmy," I said. "We should have started small—like, you know, with the finger pricker."

Jimmy nodded and then shuddered.

"We should do that tonight—sit down and teach you how to get a blood sample for checking my sugar. OK?"

Jimmy was silent for a moment. "Yeah. Guess I should learn."

"Then once you're comfortable with that we can graduate to injections. It'll be fun."

Jimmy nodded, then shuddered again.

———

"Have you ever astral projected yourself?"

I looked at Jimmy's friend Nicole, confused, wondering if I'd heard her correctly. It was a few months later, and we were at the apartment, where a party for my twenty-sixth birthday was in full swing. Prince was on the stereo, and folks were yammering a bunch of nonsense.

"Have I ever what?"

"Astral projected yourself?"

"Oh, definitely not," I said, trying to give the most honest answer I could. "Well, not on purpose." Didn't even know what it was.

"Really? Oh, wow, you should really try it, it's eye-opening."

"But," I said, picking up our malnourished new cat, Finley, and plonking her on the couch, "how do you do it?"

"Oh, well, first you've got to let go of your fear," she said, as if that's even possible. "Then you have to go into your room, and lie on your bed, because you have to relax, both physically and mentally."

"What if one of your fears is silence?" I wondered aloud, looking over at grumpy, gray little Finley. She was a stray who'd shown up at our apartment building the previous month looking desperately underfed. After a few weeks of seeing her roam around the gravel parking lot by the fire escape stairs looking more haggard and forlorn every day, we finally relented and brought her inside, much to the chagrin of Stella, whose first reaction was to corner me in the bathroom and say, "Who *that* bitch?" Within a week we realized that Finley, in addition to being malnourished, balding, and misshapen, was also pregnant.

"Oh, you can do it," Nicole assured me. "Trust me, you can. *I'm* a basket case, and I can do it."

Finley jumped off the couch and walked out of the living room.

"Tim, let's go ahead and cut that damn cake," Mandy said, stumbling up to me and holding a glass of wine. "I wanna eat it."

"Yeah, I wanna put it in my mouth," Dani said, sidling up beside her.

"OK," I said, "but hold on a sec, I have to be a good diabetic first." I went and got my diabetes case, pulled out the glucometer—a new one that only took a minute to give results rather than two—and sat back down.

"Wait, I'll do it," Jimmy said, coming into the living room from the kitchen and sitting down on the couch. I handed the case to him. He pulled out all the tools excruciatingly slowly, and I offered him my left index finger, my most reliable blood-giving digit. He only winced a little bit as he placed the lancing device up to the finger and pressed the button. I didn't feel a thing, mainly because the pricker didn't even make contact. He squeezed my finger to milk it for blood, but, of course, none came.

"Jimmy, you need to really press it against the finger," I instructed. "I don't think the lancet is actually hitting the skin."

He once again pressed the device against my finger but was again being too cautious. With my other hand I pressed it more tightly so we wouldn't be here all night. *Click*. This time he managed to squeeze out the tiniest of blood droplets, but it was enough to feed the test strip. He looked at me for confirmation that he'd done good.

"That'll do, pig," I said, smiling. "That'll do."

Jimmy nodded and gazed at the glucometer screen, waiting for the results. A minute later the meter told me my blood sugar was 123, an admirable level. I then took out my Humalog pen, dialed the doser to four units, and slammed the needle into my stomach. It was my birthday, dammit. Gimme cake.

Jimmy brought out the cake—a Mississippi mud monstrosity that I'd asked Mom to make. It was the first dessert I remember eating as a child, and once every few years I put in a request to her to please re-create that childhood magic for me. She'd baked it in a Pyrex dish and included all the trimmings: coconut, chocolate drizzle, marshmallow cream, and nuts. Jimmy placed it on the coffee table, and I grabbed our fancy plastic knife to start cutting.

Suddenly the Prince album finished, and the room was bereft of the funk. Under the din of naked human voices chattering I heard a new sound, a strange sound, an adorable new, strange sound. It was squeaky and heart-meltingly tiny. I looked over at the linen closet, the direction from whence the sound came, and there stood Finley outside the cracked closet door, looking tired as ever, but somehow different. The squeaking continued behind her. There was something in the closet. And I had a hunch it would be cute.

I rushed over to the door and swung it open. On the floor inside, resting on a now bloodied sleeping bag, was a tiny little critter, a baby Finley, mewing blindly. Finley meowed at me with irritation, so I pushed the door until it was once again only cracked, and Finley went back inside. A few minutes later she came out again and sauntered to the opposite corner to take a break. I reopened the door, and, sure enough, there was another little newborn. In a little bit Finley went in one more time for a third delivery, and then she was done.

"I'm going for a cigarette," she said upon exiting for the final time, walking over to the corner to give herself a bath. She then slunk into the living room, where she and Stella proceeded to get into a fierce staring contest. ("Bitch, you better look away." "No, bitch, *you* better look away.")

Excited by the newborns, I asked Jimmy to put on another CD and returned to the cake. In a few minutes we were all enjoying the taste of dark, wet, gooey Mississippi mud to the strains of Prince's "Pussy Control."

"So how does it feel to be a granddaddy at such a young age?" Dani asked as she, Mandy, Jimmy, and I all sat on the sofa and licked our plastic plates of any remaining chocolate goo.

"Mmmm," I said. "It's delicious."

It's been a while since we've checked in with our hero, so let's just pop in and say hi and see how things are going because it's sure to be hilarious. Wow, has it really been ten years? Good God, time flies when you're a type 1 diabetic.

The two young men are still together, which is just unheard of. Gay years, of course, are counted differently, so ten years for the gays equals to about 117.8 years for breeders. So well done, boys!

They have moved up to New York City, where all homosexuals end up eventually. And right now they're on a Metro-North train that will take them to Connecticut, where they're visiting friends for the weekend. They picked up a cute bottle of Mexican rum as a gift for their hosts. It's shaped like a Mexican man, and the bottle cap is a huge sombrero. Classy, and not at all racist.

Anyway, we wouldn't be here if something wasn't about to go horribly wrong, so let's get this party started. Thing is, our hero looks completely fine. He's not twitching, he's not sweating, he's not running to hide in the corner of the train compartment and refusing all offers of ice cream. He does look worried, though.

Looks like he's getting out his glucometer to test his blood sugar. He's got health insurance again, so he no longer has to put aside loose change to save up to buy test strips. And, let's see, what is his blood sugar? Oh dear, it appears to be creeping downward: forty-nine. Yikes. Well, he's still good and conscious, so all he has to do is dip into his bag for a quick fix, and he'll have his level back to normal in no time.

"Hey, Jimmy," he whispers, tossing his case back into his Adidas bag. "Do you have any candy?"

James looks at him through narrow, irritated eyelids.

"Noooo, did you not get anything on the way? What's your blood sugar?"

Before answering, our hero experiences a twinge of guilt: He knows he was supposed to put some Little Debbie snack cakes in his bag before they left for the station, but as they rushed out the door he forgot, so he told himself he'd just buy a few candy bars at Grand Central but then they had to rush to get on their train and now he's ended up bug-eyed and candyless. It is a few hours to their stop, and there's no snack bar on the train.

"Sixty-nine," he lies.

"Do you not have anything?"

He doesn't want to answer because it will incur the wrath of James. James's wrath is a quiet, somber wrath that weighs on a person's shoulders like a Kevlar vest.

"I'm going to just check and see . . . ," he says as he stands up. He walks the length of the train to see if there is a snack machine or a secret passageway that leads to Candyland. (There is not.) Meanwhile James embarks on a fruitless search for something, anything in his bag that will do the trick. Bike lube? No. Colored pencils? They're sugar free. Then he looks down at the gift bag containing the Mexican rum.

Mr. "Sixty-nine" returns to his seat and slumps down, looking out the window. Poor thing, he's actually facing his biggest nightmare: being stuck somewhere with a plummeting blood sugar and no Cocoa Puffs to save the day. He gazes out the window at the blur of foliage flying by and wonders how long he has until his brain becomes a big bowl of gravy.

"Could just open this," James says, proffering the rum bottle. "It's got sugar, doesn't it?"

The boy looks at the bottle. It's just terrible that he would have to take such drastic measures, but he knows he's rapidly entering the Land of Make-Believe and needs something now. So, with a good amount *of guilt and shame—who shows up with a gift of rum that's already been opened and drunk from?—he takes the bottle, pops off the sombrero, and downs a mouthful. Yuck. Not something you want to taste first thing in the morning. He takes another swig, then gives the bottle back. There's got to be another way. He's going to be wasted by the time they reach Connecticut.*

Soon the train glides into Southeast Station, in Brewster, where they have to transfer to another train going to Wassaic. Maybe there'll be a vending machine. Or a Waffle House. (There are not.) It is simply a platform where people stand and wait for the train to arrive.

The young men board the train when it comes and sit down. They claim seats in a nearly empty compartment, and James goes back to his National Geographic.

Nearby, three train employees are sitting in the front of the cabin eating their packed lunches. Sandwiches, chips, bananas, Cokes. Any one of these items could make a real difference in a young man's life. Particularly the young man with a dead pancreas a few rows behind them.

"Jimmy," he says, "sorry, I lied, my blood sugar's lower than sixty-nine, it's forty-nine, probably lower now, so I'm going to have to go ask those guys for some of their food."

James puts his magazine down. He shakes his head. He sighs.

"Do what you gotta do."

Our hero stands up and clambers over to the working stiffs enjoying their midday meal.

"Excuse me," he says, "I'm really sorry to ask this and sorry to interrupt your lunch, but I'm diabetic, and my blood sugar is really low right now. It's kind of an emergency. Would you be able to let me have any of your food?"

The men look at each other to see which of them will be having to deal with this hobo standing before them.

It feels like several years of waiting for the young man, but one of the men actually gives him his banana admirably quickly, though grudgingly.

"Thank you so much," he says, bowing to the men like they're Japanese royalty. "And I'm sorry. Thank you. I'm sorry. Thank you. And I'm sorry. And thank you. So sorry."

He goes back to his seat and slides in next to James. He peels the banana and sheepishly puts chunks of it in his mouth. Thrown a life raft, he relaxes a little and allows himself to enjoy the banana, even though it wasn't dunked in chocolate. He puts his headphones on and eases back into Kraftwerk's Autobahn.

James rolls his eyes, shakes his head again, and gazes at his companion with the Look of Judgment. He then holds out toward him a National Geographic *spread featuring an array of giant droopy African boobs, and they both smile as the train glides along the tracks toward the Wassaic wilderness.*

ACKNOWLEDGMENTS

I must first of all thank Amazon superhero Terry Goodman for his enthusiastic support for this book. If you see a man flying around Seattle in a red cape with a big G on his chest, you should say hi, 'cause that's Terry. Many thanks also to David Downing for his outstanding editing work on the manuscript and for being a kick to work with. As far as I know, David isn't partial to capes.

Many *danka*s to my early readers for their feedback on and help with the manuscript—and for letting me write about them: my sister, Laurie, who introduced me to the magic of mixtapes; and Dani, Mandy, and Jennifer, all of whom for years endured my ungainly tape collection at stupid high volumes.

Much love to my aunt Sue and Nana, who treated me like a prince when I was a child and taught me in their elegant way not only the simple bliss of a chocolate malt but also the dangers of sticking your hands outside of a moving car while you're on the interstate and the importance of regular bowel movements.

Many *merci*s to Mom, for her love and support and Mississippi mud cake.

Muchos arigatos to my husband, Jimmy—for helping keep me alive over the past seventeen years, yes, but also for being hilarious, usually when he's not even trying. And, most importantly, for his macaroni-and-cheese casserole.

A profound ありがとうございました to Harvey Fierstein, creator of *Torch Song Trilogy*. Harvey once said, in a documentary about closeted Hollywood, that he believed in "visibility at all costs." Thanks, Harvey, for being unapologetically, spectacularly visible.

And, of course, a special спасибо to The Smiths, Echo and the Bunnymen, Siouxsie and the Banshees, Sinéad O'Connor, Love and Rockets, The Primitives, Depeche Mode, Lush, Wire, Ride, Dead Can Dance, New Order, Joy Division, Close Lobsters, and The Cocteau Twins, among tons of other hilariously named weirdos, for giving me incredible music to listen to during all of my youthful cravings.

 Tim Anderson is the author of *Tune in Tokyo: The Gaijin Diaries*, which *Publishers Weekly* called "laugh-out-loud funny," *Shelf Awareness* called "so much fun," and Michiko Kakutani of the *New York Times* completely ignored. He lives in Brooklyn with his husband, Jimmy; his cat, Stella; and his yoga balance ball, Sheila. Tim also writes young adult historical fiction under the name T. Neill Anderson and blogs at seetimblog.blogspot.com. His favorite Little Debbie snack cake is the Fudge Round.